MW00955867

Train at Home to Work at Home

Train at Home to Work at Home

How to Get Certified, Earn a Degree,
or Take a Class From Home to Begin a
Work-at-Home Career

Michelle McGarry

iUniverse, Inc.
New York Lincoln Shanghai

Train at Home to Work at Home
How to Get Certified, Earn a Degree,
or Take a Class From Home to Begin a Work-at-Home Career

All Rights Reserved © 2003 by Michelle McGarry

No part of this book may be reproduced or transmitted in any form or by any means, graphic, electronic, or mechanical, including photocopying, recording, taping, or by any information storage retrieval system, without the written permission of the publisher.

iUniverse, Inc.

For information address:
iUniverse
2021 Pine Lake Road, Suite 100
Lincoln, NE 68512
www.iuniverse.com

The author does not specifically endorse or recommend any particular training program. Note that tuition and fees are subject to change.

ISBN: 0-595-28450-7 (Pbk)
ISBN: 0-595-65802-4 (Cloth)

Printed in the United States of America

To my mom,
who always encourages me to follow my dreams and to do what I love

ACKNOWLEDGEMENTS

I have many thanks to give to the incredible authors out there who have written fabulous books that I cannot do without.

To Faith Popcorn, author of *Clicking, EVEolution,* and the *Dictionary of the Future,* whose words constantly remind me to think out-of-the-box.

To Marilyn and Tom Ross, authors of *Jump Start Your Book Sales,* who reminded me about everything I forgot I learned in grad school, and helped me build a better book.

To *Victoria* magazine, for its devotion and help to entrepreneurs, and especially for the entrepreneur workshop they offered in Boston a few years ago that gave me such great ideas about home business. (It's also a great magazine. Check out their book, *Turn Your Passion Into Profits,* on page 139).

And to moms:

- Cheryl Demas (www.wahm.com, and author of *The Work-at-Home Mom's Guide to Home Business* and *It's a Jungle Out There, a Zoo in Here*)

- Liz Folger (www.bizymoms.com, author of *The Stay-at-Home Mom's Guide to Making Money from Home*)

- Lisa Roberts (www.en-parent.com, author of *The Entrepreneurial Parent*),

- Maria T. Bailey (www.bluesuitmom.com, author of *The Women's Home-Based Business Book of Answers*)

- Ellen Parlapiano and Patricia Cobe (www.mompreneurs.com, authors of *Mompreneurs* and *Mompreneurs Online*) and

- Lesley Spencer (www.hbwm.com, creator of the *Mom's Work-at-Home Kit*)

for creating such great Web sites and books for work-at-home moms and wannabes.

Last, but not least, many thanks to my family and friends, especially my husband Eddie and our children for having patience while I obsessed over this book!

P.S. And a million thanks to whoever thought up the Internet and subsequently enabled me to work from home, or from Tahiti.

CONTENTS

Why train at home for a work-at-home career? 1
Train-at-Home-to-Work-at-Home Programs 12
  Association Management Service 12
    ASAE School of Association Management Online..............................13
    George Mason University 13
    Union Institute and University 14
  Bed and Breakfast Owner 15
    Sage Blossom Consulting 15
    Oates & Bredfeldt 16
    Professional Association of Innkeepers International (PAII)..................16
  Bookkeeping Service................................18
    American Institute of Professional Bookkeepers.....................18
    USDA Graduate School Correspondence Program 18
    Allied Business Schools 19
    Professional Career Development Institute (PCDI) 19
    Distance-Learning College Programs in Accounting 19
  Catering Service 22
    National Association of Catering Executives (NACE) 22
    University of Houston Online................................23
    Professional Career Development Institute (PCDI) 23
    Education Direct................................24
  Childbirth Educator 25
    Lamaze International................................25
    International Childbirth Education Association (ICEA) 26
    American Academy of Husband-Coached Childbirth®................27
    Association of Labor Assistants and Childbirth Educators (ALACE) 27
    Childbirth & Postpartum Professional Association (CAPPA) 28
  Child Day Care Provider 29
    Northampton County Area Community College 30
    St. Mary-of-the-Woods College................................30

Professional Career Development Institute (PCDI) 31

Education Direct..31

BizyMoms..32

Desktop Publisher 33

Rochester Community & Technical College 34

Minot State University 35

Rochester Institute of Technology 35

Education Direct..35

Allied Business Schools 36

New Horizons...36

Video Professor 36

Self-Training: Quark and Adobe 37

Doula 38

Doulas of North America (DONA)..39

Association of Labor Assistants and Childbirth Educators (ALACE) 40

International Childbirth Education Association (ICEA) 41

Childbirth & Postpartum Professional Association (CAPPA) 41

Editorial Services 42

Pace University 43

St. Mary-of-the-Woods College..43

Northern Arizona University 44

University of Central Florida..44

Washington State University 44

University of California, Los Angeles (UCLA)......................45

Northampton County Area Community College 45

USDA Graduate School Correspondence Program 45

Education Direct..46

Professional Career Development Institute (PCDI) 46

Barnes & Noble Online University 46

BizyMoms..47

Financial Planner 48

Golden Gate University..49

City University 50

University of California, Los Angeles (UCLA)......................50

University of Alabama 51

College for Financial Planning...51

Florida State University Online 52
Great Plains Interactive Distance Education Alliance (GPIDEA) 52
Kaplan College 53
Metropolitan Community College 53
Professional Career Development Institute (PCDI) 53
Gift Basket Business 55
The Basket Connection, Inc. 55
The Gift Basket Mentor, Inc. 56
Gift Baskets 101 56
Newport Media BasketBusiness 56
Sweet Florals 57
Gift Basket Review magazine 57
Le Gourmet Gift Basket, Inc. 57
Sweet Survival 58
BizyMoms 58
Graphic Designer 60
The Art Institute International Online 60
Academy of Art College 61
University of California, Los Angeles (UCLA) 61
Home Inspector 62
Carson Dunlop 63
HomePro Systems, Inc. 64
Inspection Training Associates (ITA) 64
HE School of Building Inspection 64
Accu-Spect Home Inspector Institute 65
Building Specs Inc. Inspection Systems 65
National Institute of Building Inspectors 65
Allied Business Schools 66
Education Direct 66
Professional Career Development Institute (PCDI) 66
Image Consultant 68
The Image Maker, Inc. 68
Color Profiles Ltd./Lindquist Associates 69
Image Resource Group 70
Indexer 71
Book Indexing Postal Tutorials (BIPT) 72

USDA Graduate School Correspondence Program 72

Broccoli Information Management 73

Holbert Indexing Services 73

Society of Indexers...74

Information Broker 75

University of Maine-Augusta 76

MarketingBase Mentor 76

Interior Designer/Decorator 77

The Art Institute International Online 78

Academy of Art College..79

University of California, Los Angeles (UCLA)...............................79

Sheffield School of Interior Design 80

Professional Career Development Institute (PCDI) 80

Education Direct..80

Medical Billing and Coding 82

Santa Barbara City College 82

Southwest Wisconsin Technical College 83

Pitt Community College 83

Weber State University 83

Rochester Community & Technical College 84

Association of Registered Medical Professionals (ARMP)...................84

American Academy of Professional Coders (AAPC)...........................84

American Medical Billers Association (AMBA) 85

Medical Association of Billers (MAB) 85

National Electronic Billers Alliance (NEBA) 86

Electronic Medical Billing Network (EMBN) 86

Andrews School..86

Claims Transit 87

Meditec..87

Professional Career Development Institute (PCDI) 87

Allied Business Schools 88

Claims Security of America 88

Medical Transcription 90

Patrick Henry Community College 91

California College of Health Sciences 91

Northwest Technical College..92

Southwest Wisconsin Technical College 92
Rochester Community & Technical College 92
Health Professions Institute 93
Andrews School...93
Career Step 94
Medical Transcription Education Center (M-TEC) 94
Meditec...95
MedTrans 95
Global Medical Transcription, Inc. 96
Laird's School of Medical Transcription 96
Professional Career Development Institute (PCDI) 97
BizyMoms..97
Paralegal Service 98
University of California, Los Angeles (UCLA).....................................99
Ashworth College 99
The Paralegal Institute, Inc..100
St. Mary-of-the-Woods College 100
Tompkins Cortland Community College 100
University of Great Falls 101
Western Piedmont Community College 101
The Washington Online Learning Institute..101
American Paralegal Institute (API)...102
Kaplan College 102
USDA Graduate School Correspondence Program 102
Allied Business Schools 103
Professional Career Development Institute (PCDI) 103
Education Direct...103
Personal/Life Coach 104
Abundant Practice..105
Academy for Coach Training 105
ADD Coaching Academy 106
Advantage Coaching 106
Career Coach Institute 106
Ciris Alliance..106
Coach for Life 106
Coach University (CoachU) 106

The Coaches Training Institute (CTI) 106
Coaching from Spirit..106
Coachville 107
College of Executive Coaching 107
Comprehensive Coaching U 107
Corporate Coach University International...................................107
EDUCOACH...107
Executive Coach Academy...107
Fill Your Coaching Practice 107
International Coach Academy 107
Institute for Life Coach Training..107
Kadmon Academy of Human Potential 108
Life on Purpose Institute 108
Life Purpose Institute 108
Live Your Dream by Joyce Chapman 108
MentorCoach 108
Optimal Functioning Institute 108
Parent as Coach Academy 108
Relationship Coaching Institute 108
Results Life Coaching 109
Personal Trainer 110
United States Sports Academy 111
University of California, Los Angeles (UCLA)...........................111
American Council on Exercise..111
International Fitness Professionals Association (IFPA) 112
National Association for Fitness Certification (NAFC) 112
International Sports Sciences Association (ISSA) 113
National Endurance Sports Trainers Association (NESTA) 113
St. Augustine School of Medical Assistants and Health Sciences 114
NDEITA..114
Education Direct...114
Professional Career Development Institute (PCDI) 115
Public Relations Specialist..116
Rochester Institute of Technology 117
University of California, Los Angeles (UCLA)...........................117
St. Mary-of-the-Woods College..118

Scopist 119
   Internet Scoping School 120
   BeST Scoping Techniques 120
Virtual Assistant/Secretarial Services 121
   Virtual Assistance U 122
   University of Northwestern Ohio 122
   Madison Area Technical College/International Association of
   Administrative Professionals (IAAP) 122
   Allied Business Schools 123
Web Site Designer/Webmaster 124
   Minot State University 125
   The Art Institute International Online 125
   Wytheville Community College 126
   Pennsylvania State University 126
   Bellevue Community College 126
   Regis University... 127
   College of Southern Maryland... 127
   National American University 127
   Northwestern Michigan College 128
   Webster University 128
   Champlain College 128
   East Carolina University 129
   Rochester Community & Technical College 129
   Professional Career Development Institute (PCDI) 129
   Education Direct.. 130
   Barnes & Noble University 130
   BizyMoms.. 130
Wedding Planner 131
   Weddings Beautiful Worldwide 132
   June Wedding, Inc.® 132
   Wedding Careers Institute, Inc. 133
   Association of Certified Professional
   Wedding Consultants (ACPWC) 133
   Association of Bridal Consultants (ABC)............................. 133
   Education Direct.. 134
   Professional Career Development Institute (PCDI) 134

Out-of-the-Box Work-at-Home Careers 137
Michelle's Bookshelf and Bookmarks:Recommended Books and Web Sites ..139
Bibliography 143
About the Author..155
Index 157

WHY TRAIN AT HOME FOR A WORK-AT-HOME CAREER?

I know what you're thinking: "Egads, not *another* home business book!" (Well, maybe not "egads," that's just me, but you get the idea.) But, wait! I really do have a unique take on the topic, and it may just get you started—for real this time— in that home career you've always wondered how to begin. I've got something that no one else has: information about *home training* for *work-at-home careers*. But if you already have a home biz—don't close the book. There's some great stuff in here for you as well.

First of All: Is a Work-at-Home Career for You?

I might as well let you know that I don't care for the phrase "home business." It seems like the phrase has gained an unsightly blemish. Because of all the unfortunate home biz scams out there, any legitimate service or information associated with "home business" has to work twice as hard to prove itself. (If you're not familiar with home business scams, here's one example: Don't ever give money to anyone who says they will pay *you* to stuff envelopes. It's a scam.) But the phrase "home business" also covers a wide range of careers, from direct sales reps (Avon calling) to freelance writers (like me) to home daycare providers to gift basket retailers to Web site owners to a plethora of others. There's an awful lot of variation is what each of these home businesses need. There is also a wide variance in the kind of skills and experience you need to *start* each of these endeavors. "Home business" is often associated with (and promoted as) something you can start very easily, make money quickly, without very much training. The reality is, the opposite is usually true.

I like the phrase, "work-at-home career." Instead of focusing on how "easy" it is to start, choosing a work-at-home-*career* seems much more like a *commitment*—and it should be. Choosing a new career is a big deal. It's unfair that we get sucked into "Start today, earn tomorrow!" promotions, when what we really should be doing is getting a fair assessment of what our drive, talents, skills, and experience can lead us to do—from home. When you're choosing a career,

1

not a home business, you need training and education. The need for information about training and education for home careers is what led me to write this book.

**"Go confidently in the direction of your dreams.
Live the life you imagined."—Henry David Thoreau**

Is working at home for you? Only you can answer that question. Can you work independently with little supervision? Do you have the drive to market and promote yourself and your business? Do you mind working alone, or you do need the flutter of feet around you (besides your kids)? Do you have skills that you can apply to a work-at-home career (or are you willing to learn them)?

There are a number of great home business books that can help you determine if working at home is for you. Rather than duplicating their efforts, I prefer to refer—See "Michelle's Bookshelf and Bookmarks," (p. 139) for books that have really helped me. But let's move on to the focus of *this* book.

What is Distance Learning?

Distance Learning: How to take classes from home. Huh? How do you take a class without physically *going* to school? Well, many schools and organizations offer education to students without any on-campus or in-person requirements. For many years, only a handful of accredited schools offered distance learning, mostly through the mail. Students would receive readings and assignments in the form of books and worksheets, do the assignments, and mail them back to the instructors for review. At the successful completion of the program, students would either receive a high school diploma, an Associate degree, or a certificate in their field of choice.

Why did I write a book on home training for work-at-home careers? Well, distance learning isn't what it used to be. It's no longer just a program-by-mail option, and in addition to the long-standing education companies, now accredited colleges and universities are jumping on the bandwagon. Why? In one word: Internet. Since the birth of the World Wide Web, distance-learning programs have *exploded*. I knew someone a few years back who was getting a college degree through a paper-based distance-learning program, and my friends were making fun of her! I think the misunderstanding about distance learning was that it wasn't a *real* education. But she was completing the same assignments that other students were completing, and doing it with the instructor's tutelage and support just the same. But with the birth of the Internet, distance learning is no longer the realm of the postal service. Now there are a wide variety of mediums to communicate what needs to be taught.

The Internet is an interactive medium. You can communicate quickly—via e-mail—or even instantly, with instant messaging and chat rooms. You can view video, even a live lecture taught halfway across the world. You can listen to music or other students or instruction. Computers can play CD-ROMs with large amounts of information contained in an interactive lesson. Now, you can even play a DVD on your computer. Colleges and universities have recognized the importance of these facts, and identified a huge market of students—students who don't have the time to take a traditional class, but need continuing education for their current job, or for a new career. Colleges now offer courses online, or via other mediums, such as paper-based programs, teleclasses (on the phone), on audiotape, on videotape, and on CD-ROM. Many universities recognize online courses as a service to their on-campus students, as well. Why take Biology 101 at 8:00 a.m., when you can take it online? Plus, degree options have grown, as well. Now you can earn a Bachelor degree, a Master degree, or even a Ph.D. via distance learning. These updates in distance learning have opened up education for lot of people.

> "Training is everything. The peach was once
> a bitter almond; cauliflower is nothing but
> cabbage with a college education."—Mark Twain

Distance learning is so popular now that new programs are popping up almost every day. And colleges aren't the only ones formulating them, either. Small companies have gotten into it, with tutorials about their line of work, as well as large companies like Adobe and Microsoft that offer training in their software and products. You will find a wide range of companies in this book that offer training. Some are accredited schools, some are companies, some are national associations, and still others are individuals and entrepreneurs marketing their intellectual property.

Before You Spend a Dime...

Not all distance-learning programs operate the same. Some are *self-paced*, which means you can complete the assignments when you can. These programs usually have open start dates (you can begin anytime). Other programs are *instructor-led*, which means they have a specific start times and students must complete assignments on a regular basis (with due dates). Instructor-led courses usually follow the academic calendar. Both kinds of programs allow for interactive communication with the instructor, and sometimes with other students. In addition, some programs are self-paced but give a *time limit* to complete the entire curriculum (like 2 years, for example), while others allow an unlimited amount of time.

Education, and paying for it, is no small feat. You want to invest your dollars into a program that is going to teach you what you want to learn and help you begin a work-at-home career. Is the school accredited? With whom? What have other students gone on to do? If it's not a college, but an individual, what are his or her qualifications for offering this course? Never hand over money until you're sure that this is the program for you. Also, be aware that application fees for colleges are nonrefundable, and don't necessarily guarantee your acceptance into the program.

Always verify that what you're learning is satisfactory to the industry standards. Check with national associations if this program will satisfy their certification requirements. Ask industry leaders if you need a Bachelor degree, or if a certificate will suffice. Do you need in-office experience in this field before breaking out on your own?

Don't choose a career only because it can be done from home. Try to match your skills and interests to a traditional work-at-home career, or find a way to *do what you love* from home. Highly recommended: *Finding Your Perfect Work: The New Career Guide to Making a Living, Creating a Life*, by Paul and Sarah Edwards (J.P. Tarcher, 2003). I love this book, as it helps you explore all the ways your talents, skills, and experience can fit into the world of work. Do some personality searching as well. Talk with a career coach, or figure out what your personality type is with *Do What You Are: Discover the Perfect Career for You Through the Secrets of Personality Type*, by Paul D. Tieger and Barbara Barron-Tieger (Little, Brown & Co., 2001). This book has great tips on the kinds of work that fit different personality types. Both books have lots of worksheets to brainstorm.

You also need to determine your budget: What are you willing to spend? Some classes are as low as $100; others are a couple of thousand dollars. Choose wisely! You want your tuition to be an investment in your future career, not a loss in something that didn't work out for you. Investigate free mini-courses offered, and trial periods as well. Or, take an introductory course before you take the whole program. Don't be afraid of high-priced courses, at first. Even though $3,000 is *a lot* of money, say for a financial planning certification program (for example), it pales in comparison to the $5,000 you might spend over the next two years on home business scams, direct sales starter kits, pyramid schemes, home business ideas you have no experience in, and other start-up failures. It's just something I've learned in hindsight—planning is worth a lot more than money.

Distance-Learning Tips

Is distance learning for you? Distance learning, just like working at home, is not for everyone. It takes a certain amount of discipline to complete the assignments and to finish what you start. It also takes an ability to work independently, and you need good reading and comprehension skills.

I've found through my research that no two distance-learning programs are alike. Make sure you understand the requirements of each program. Do you need to be accepted into the program, for example? Is there an application fee? For CD-ROM and online courses, many schools require you have a specific type of computer with a specific amount memory and speed, and a particular Internet connection. For technologically advanced careers, such as graphic design or Web design, you will need a great computer as well. Here are some other tips:

- Note that, especially at universities, the availability of classes varies *greatly*. Especially if there is just one class you are interested in, always check if it's only offered once a year or something!

- Sometimes shipping and handling is included, and other times it's added on to the cost of the package. Shipping and handling fees of course materials can be *substantial*, depending on what is delivered (books are much heavier than CD-ROMs, for example.).

- Make sure you know whether you need to buy the software required, or if they will furnish you a copy.

- Make sure you know which software you're going to be learning. (If a course only teaches PageMaker, but your work projects will be on QuarkXpress, find another course.)

- The tuition stated (for most programs) is per-credit. You need to tabulate the cost of the program by multiplying tuition-per-credit by total number of credits. (I did it this way in case some students chose to take only a few classes within a program.)

- Most colleges have application fees just to apply to the program ($25-$250), and lab fees, textbooks, and other extraneous fees are often tacked on to the price of the program, unless stated otherwise.

- When considering an Associate or Bachelor degree, keep in mind that a lot of the credits required are general education courses (e.g. English,

Math, Science, etc.). If you already have a college degree, you probably don't need liberal arts courses. You might want to look into a certificate program that only includes the courses you need to take.

- Sometimes there are different phone numbers and Web sites listed for programs within the same school. The reason? I tried to list the departmental phone number, when available, so you can talk to the program coordinator instead of reaching the school's main number. Also, some schools, like Education Direct, have sub-Web sites of each individual program they offer.

- Some programs teach you the basics of getting started as an entrepreneur in that career; others don't. Make sure you have the resources to support you in putting your newfound knowledge to work in your career.

Questions to Ask the Program Coordinator:

1. Are courses self-paced, or are they instructor-led?
2. Is there a time limit to complete the program once I begin?
3. Aside from tuition, are there additional fees? What are they?
4. What are the technical requirements I must meet—what kind of computer must I have; software; etc?
5. Are all courses in the program available via distance learning?
6. Is the program online, paper-based, CD-ROM, e-mail, teleclass, audio/video, or a combination?
7. Does this program certify me, or does it qualify me to sit for national certification exams?
8. Is your school accredited, and by whom?
9. What have some of your graduates gone on to do?
10. Is there a trial period or free mini-course to try?
11. Once I purchase the program, is it refundable in any way? (Most are not, by the way. Once you have their intellectual material in your possession, they assume you have read it, and therefore, cannot return it.)
12. Is there financial aid available? (Some programs are eligible for standard college financial aid programs; others are not.) Is there a payment plan available?

13. For individual teachers, not necessarily colleges: How long have you been in business? What are your qualifications for teaching this course/program?

14. What is a passing grade? (Usually "C" is passing, but for graduate programs it is usually "B.")

15. Are there any prerequisites I need to have or tests I have to pass to be accepted into the program? Can you help me fulfill the prerequisites?

16. Can I take individual classes as a continuing education student, instead enrolling in the entire program?

17. How long does it take to complete the course, on average?

FAQs About *Train at Home to Work at Home*

Why did you write this book?

I wrote this book primarily because I have a love for the information. I have been interested in the fascinating variety of college majors and careers out there ever since I graduated college. (I plan to write a book about fascinating college majors in the future.) When I got married and had a baby, I became interested in home business because I wanted leave my office job as an editor to stay at home with my daughter. The two topics have meshed in a great way, because I have found that many people—at-home parents like myself, for example—still wonder how to begin a work-at-home career. How do we get the training we need, when we are already at home with the kids? We have no time to go back to school, right?

When I discovered the distance-learning renaissance that was taking place, I realized that it *was* possible to train for a work-at-home career. I've read a ton of great home business books over the years, but not many had detailed educational information. I wrote this book as a companion—an essential one—to the home business books out there that have done all the front work (See "Michelle's Bookshelf and Bookmarks," p. 139). I wanted to fill in the blanks.

It also occurred to me that people who already *have* home businesses/careers also don't have time to go back to school to help them grow their current business. If you already have a home career, you might want to browse through a couple of sections. Topics where a class or two might assist your business include: Bookkeeping (p. 18), Desktop Publishing (p. 33), Editorial Services (p. 42), Financial Planning (p. 48), Image Consulting (p. 68), Personal/Life Coaching (p. 104), Virtual Assisting (p. 121), and Web Site Design (p. 124). Because home business owners have to wear many hats, you may be able to brush up on some skills, or perhaps find someone to pick up some of the slack!

Why did you go into so much detail about individual courses for each program? Don't all the programs have basically the same courses?

Well, yes and no. I went to the trouble (and the space) to write out individual courses for each program because sometimes one school has a particular class that another doesn't. It may seem repetitive (and believe me I know because I typed it all in), but sometimes that one class makes a difference. If a school you're interested in because the tuition is right doesn't have the one class you really want to take, it may be worth it to you to explore the more expensive school. Or, you may be able take that one class at the expensive school as a continuing education student. I tried to give you as much information as I could to make comparisons and contrasts possible.

I also tried to highlight when one school had something different from others, such as live discussions with the instructor online, or included some reference or book having to do with entrepreneurial aspects of that career.

Why do you list so many books, Web sites, and organizations?

Because I can! No, really, you deserve to have as much information in front of you as possible. It's hard enough to research multiple home careers—spending time and money on a book—only to have to research more details yourself. Some careers have a lot of professional organizations (Child Day Care, for example), and others have only a few (like Image Consulting). The same is true of books and Web sites. (Often there are only a few Web sites listed because the program Web sites provide more than enough information.)

Why is some information missing, or why is a program missing?

Some programs don't use mailing addresses as contact information (they may be individuals with only a home address). Some prefer not to be contacted via e-mail, or they list departmental e-mails on their Web site. If part of a listing is missing, it's either because they don't furnish that information, or they couldn't respond to my inquiries. But, if there is an *entire program* missing, please feel free to let me know—there is a form in the back of the book where you can tell me what I missed (p. 177), or anything else about the book, for that matter. Or, e-mail me at michelle@michellemedia.com.

I welcome suggestions for the next edition of this book (planned for February 2004) and I will also frequently add programs to my Web site (www.michellemedia.com).

"Opportunity is missed by most people because it's dressed in overalls and looks like work."—Thomas Edison

Why did you self-publish this book?

You may not have known this book was self-published, because it looks just like other books—and it is. Ordinarily I would not broadcast the fact that this book is self-published, because for some, self-publishing *sounds* less credible than the prestige of getting accepted at a major publishing house. But there are many reasons why I self-published:

- **Print-on-Demand (POD) allows self-publishers to manufacture a professional trade quality book one-at-a-time, as orders come in.** This option, available from companies like iUniverse (iuniverse.com) and FirstBooks (1stbooks.com), is a very affordable way of producing a book. Also, it is a relevant topic to this book, because self-publishing is an option for home-based entrepreneurs to market themselves as an expert and expand their business. (If you want information about self-publishing, visit my Web site, www.michellemedia.com/selfpublish.htm.)

- **I am a professional writer and editor with a Master of Arts degree in writing and publishing**—I know how to plan, write, edit, and market a book. I also have been researching home business for 6 years, and college programs for 10 years.

- **Large publishing companies don't necessarily assign a nice budget to promote a book like mine.** Big bucks go to proven best-selling authors. Even if your book gets accepted at a publishing house, you might end up investing your own dollars to promote it.

- **Online bookselling has allowed nonfiction books with the right keywords to get as much exposure as the big boys.** Authors are no longer at the mercy of brick-and-mortar booksellers who won't carry their books. Amazon.com and BarnesandNoble.com make *all* books "browsable." (And, if customers ask, brick-and-mortar booksellers everywhere can order POD books from their wholesaler, as well.)

- **I wanted complete control over the editorial.** One purpose of this book is to provide information others don't—or can't. Traditional publishing houses assign a set page number to a book, and if it goes over, the cutting begins. And publishing houses want more uniformity—only three books, Web sites, and organizations per topic, for example. I wanted to include all the pertinent information, have control over my own page count, and edit as I felt necessary.

- **Self-publishing has a really fast turnaround.** From author-to-market, self-publishing takes about 6 weeks. A traditionally published book, once written, may not appear on the market for 12-18 *months*! By that time, this information would be outdated. I can whip out future editions as often as I like, and I plan to do so to keep the information fresh.

- **POD self-publishing is low-investment, not like self-publishing used to be,** or like it is to produce an independent CD (I've also done this with my husband Eddie, www.eddiemcgarry.com). A few years ago, self-publishing meant hiring book designers and editors, and shelling out thousands of dollars for a printer/bookbinder to print 1,000 books. Now I can have a book on the market, professionally designed, with an ISBN number, and available at any bookstore, for as low as $199.

- **I'm an entrepreneur at heart,** and self-publishing seems to go with this book.

Think Out of the Cubicle and Receive Free Updates

The programs in this book are notorious for changing quickly. Class availability, tuition rates, and even program requirements sometimes change overnight. But I want to keep the information fresh and keep you up-to-date. After all, you spent your hard-earned money to buy the book—why be frustrated with a program that is no longer available, a book that's gone out of print, or a dead Web site link? On the other hand, distance-learning programs are also *growing* so quickly that new programs are popping up constantly too. I want to let you know about these as well. Why wait for the next edition?

To this end, I am offering a free e-mail newsletter—*Think Out of the Cubicle!* (get it?). The aim is to update readers on new programs, old programs no longer available, new tuition rates, new phone numbers—that sort of thing. It is also a forum for readers to network and communicate with each other about their home career searches and education. To subscribe, see p. 175 to drop me a note, or send a blank e-mail to cubicle@michellemedia.com. And don't worry, I will never let anyone get a hold of your e-mail address. I despise SPAM more than anyone.

To Sum Up: My Experience in the Work-at-Home-Career World

Knowing how much money I've spent on home business information, I want yours to be spent wisely. I'm not here to tell you that home business or work-at-home careers are easy. They aren't. They take more time and money to start and keep going than most people are willing to spend. But it's better to know that before you begin, rather than believing it is easy and then fail at several attempts. But trial and error is part of the process as well.

I didn't discover home business and then set out to write a book about it. I wanted to start one. I read the big books, and then over the next six years I tried many things. I contemplated starting both a referral service and a mailing list service by doing *a lot* of groundwork. I tried direct sales, matching my publishing experience to selling children's books at home parties. I freelanced as a book editor. I subcontracted for a large company doing word processing. I even managed to land a full-time telecommuting position as an editor for a magazine. But none of these jobs or businesses really fit me. I didn't stick with them because they didn't mesh with my childrearing schedule (deadlines when you freelance can mean 12+hour days) or they required that I keep strict M-F/9-5 business hours, requiring me to hire childcare (telecommuting job), or it required me to solicit my friends and family (direct sales), or it was too tedious for very little money (word processing company). I eventually came back to what I loved (and what I had education in)—writing—and used what I learned through my experiences to find the gap in the home business information. Here it is. I really hope it helps you discover the perfect work-at-home career for you.

P.S. And please let me know how you do—michelle@michellemedia.com.

TRAIN-AT-HOME-TO-WORK-AT-HOME PROGRAMS

Here you will find the programs that can train you to work at home. Each home-career topic has an overview description of the career. For even more details about that career, including potential earnings, overhead costs, and more, see the books recommended just below each topic in "For More Information," or refer to Paul and Sarah Edward's book, *The Best Home Businesses for the 21st Century* (Putnam, 1999), which covers most of the home careers in this book.

Association Management Service

You name it, it's got its own association—from The American Bed & Breakfast Association (see p. 17) to the Association for Wedding Professionals International (see p. 135). They all need help organizing themselves, often outsourcing their needs to association management services. There is even an association for association management professionals, which is one of the primary places for education—the American Society of Association Executives (ASAE).

Association management services accomplish a wide variety of tasks, depending on what each client needs done. They may keep membership lists, publish the association's newsletter, answer phone calls and send out information, handle incoming mail, collect dues and keep financial records, arrange for membership meetings and events, and even get involved in membership development, fundraising, and marketing. New associations are constantly popping up, so the pool of potential clients is in the thousands and always climbing.

Association managers need to be detail-oriented and possess good people skills. Writing, computer, and secretarial skills are essential. A great place to start is to first volunteer for an association to get a feel for the ins and outs of how one operates. After that, you could find association clients, or even start an own association of your own!

At-Home Training Programs

American Society of Association Executives (ASAE), School of Association Management Online, 1575 I Street NW, Washington, D.C. 20005-1103, Tel: 202-626-2723, Web: www.asaenet.org, E-mail: elearning@asaenet.org

You can discover the fundamentals of association management right from the horse's mouth: the ASAE. All courses are self-paced online courses, which are developed with the assistance of ASAE volunteer experts, who serve as content advisors and course facilitators. To complete the learning experience, an online conference area or discussion board is available and enables participants to communicate with each other and the course facilitators. Participants are not tested or graded, but if you complete all the course requirements, you will receive a course certificate and earn credit toward the Certified Association Executive (CAE) designation. Non-members of the ASAE may enroll in these courses with no extra charge. You will earn 18 hours of CAE credit for completion of any 6-week online course, and 12 hours for completion of any 4-week online course. Courses offered include Managing in an Association, Membership Marketing, Public Relations for Associations, Selling to Associations, Education Program Management for Associations, Finance and Administration for Associations, Legal Issues for Associations, Meetings Management, and Publishing in Associations. Tuition: $299-$399 per class.

Association Management (Graduate certificate), George Mason University, 4400 University Drive, Fairfax, VA 22030-4444, Tel: 703-993-1411, Web: www.gmu.edu/depts/npmp, E-mail: mpa@gmu.edu

George Mason offers a Graduate Certificate in Association Management, which is available online. Required courses include: Association Management; Nonprofit Law, Governance and Ethics; and Financial Management for Public and Nonprofit Organizations. Elective courses available include: Public Policy Process; The Community, Marketing, and Public Relations; Philanthropy and Fund Raising; Human Resource Management in the Public Sector; and Nonprofit Leadership and Change. The certificate is 15 credits (five courses). Tuition: $183.85/credit for Virginia resident graduate students; $561.25/non-residents.

> "Whenever you are asked if you can do the job, tell 'em 'Certainly I can!' Then get busy and find out how to do it."—Theodore Roosevelt

Association Management (Ph.D.), Union Institute & University, 440 E. McMillan Street, Cincinnati, OH 45206, Tel: 800-486-3116 or 513-861-6400, Web: www.tui.edu

The Union Institute and University offers a Ph.D. in Association Management in collaboration with the ASAE. The program combines online study and learning sessions that are coordinated with ASAE regional and national conferences, so that you can complete your Ph.D. on your own time with limited travel. The program offers you a combination of independent study and collaborative learning with colleagues. It is comprised of an entry colloquium (a four-day face-to-face meeting followed by a virtual online component), three seminars, and a virtual community of faculty and learners. The program is 66 credits. Tuition: $580/credit.

For More Information...

<u>Books</u>

Principles of Association Management, by Henry L. Ernstthal and Bob Jones (American Society of Association Executives, 1996).

The Executive's Handbook of Trade and Business Associations, by Charles Mack (Greenwood Publishing Group, 1991).

The Nonprofit Lobbying Guide: Advocating Your Cause—and Getting Results, by Bob Smucker (Jossey-Bass Publishers, 1991).

Professional Practices in Association Management, 2nd ed., by John Cox (American Society of Association Executives, 1998).

The Complete Guide to Nonprofit Management, by Smith Bucklin & Associates (John Wiley & Sons, 2000).

Encyclopedia of Associations (38th edition), edited by Kimberly Hunt (Gale Group, 2002).

<u>Organizations</u>

The American Society of Association Executives (ASAE), 1575 I Street NW, Washington, D.C. 20005-1103, Tel: 202-626-2723, Web: www.asaenet.org.

International Association of Association Management Companies, 414 Plaza Drive, Suite 209, Westmont, IL 60559, Tel: 630-655-1669, Web: www.iaamc. org, E-mail: info@iaamc.org.

<u>Web Sites</u>

www.memberclicks.com—software for association management

www.associationoffice.net—an example of an association management company

www.marketingsource.com—subscription Web site to view their directory of 35,000 associations

Bed and Breakfast Owner

Yes, you can even learn how to purchase, start, and run a bed and breakfast via distance learning. Amazing, isn't it? To be successful as a bed-and-breakfast owner, you need at least a spare bedroom (or an inn), a flair for cooking, an out-going personality, and a love of people. Bed & breakfasts are springing up all over the country—there are more than 15,000 today, compared to only 400 in 1975. The Professional Association of Innkeepers International predicts that the current number of B&Bs will double in the next century.

What do you need to know? Courses taught by experienced B&B owners will teach you how to shop for and acquire the right property, marketing techniques, daily operations, start-up costs, budgeting, and staffing issues, to name a few. In addition to these programs, check out your local community college or adult education program—often these types of seminars are offered right in your neighborhood.

At-Home Training Programs

Sage Blossom Consulting, Online Overview Seminar, P.O. Box 17193, Boulder, CO, 80308-0193, Tel: 303-664-5857, Web: www.thebandblady.com, E-mail: kit@thebandblady.com

Delivered by veteran B&B owner Kit Riley, this online course introduces you to the B&B industry. The course is designed to help students distinguish between the reality of the business and the romanticized lifestyle. The first half of the session covers the money aspects of innkeeping. The second half covers the business and hospitality aspects. Topic titles include: Getting In; How Much Money Can a B&B Make; How Much Money Does it Take to Run a B&B; What is Your Market Niche; Guest Services and Policies; and Avoiding Innkeeper Burnout.

This seminar is also offered face-to-face with Kit in Boulder, Colorado. Kit Riley is a former innkeeper with many years of experience in the hospitality industry and the B&B real estate market. She has offered consulting and seminars to aspiring innkeepers since 1987. Payment for the online seminar is available only via PayPal (www.paypal.com).Course fee: $147.

Oates & Bredfeldt, 40 High Street, P.O. Box 1162, Brattleboro, VT 05302, Toll-free: 866-720-4667, Web: www.oatesbredfeldt.com, E-mail: seminars@ oatesbredfeldt.com

This seminar is not available via distance learning, but it is available in several locations around the country, from New Jersey to California to North Carolina. If you're serious about opening a B&B, it might be worth a weekend trip to Jamaica, Vermont, the home base of seminar leaders William Oates and Heide Bredfeldt. The couple has offered educational, operational, and marketing services to inns and innkeepers throughout the country for more than 20 years. They also own and operate the Three Mountain Inn, where the Vermont seminars are held.

The intensive three-day seminar, "How to Purchase & Operate a Bed & Breakfast or Country Inn," provides attendees with the information needed to determine whether or not you are personally and financially qualified to be an innkeeper, as well as outline the steps involved in taking charge. Topics include: establishing the proper price and terms, the pros and cons of starting/buying an inn, developing a sound business plan, internal operations, and marketing for the smaller inn.

Interested in knowing how seminar graduates have fared? If you attend the seminars in California, New Jersey, or North Carolina, you will stay at the B&B of seminar graduates. The seminar fee includes a 119-page manual and a free focusing conference with the leaders. Oates & Bredfeldt also offers a 30-day structured apprentice program to seminar graduates at the Three Mountain Inn. Seminar fee: $550 per person or $750 per couple.

> ### "This place certainly reeks of hospitality and good cheer, or maybe it's this cheese."—Jean Harlow

Audio Cassettes from past PAII Conferences, Professional Association of Innkeepers International, P.O. Box 90710, Santa Barbara, CA 93190, Tel: 805-569-1853, Web: www.paii.org/library/audio.php

The Professional Association of Innkeepers International (PAII) sells audiotapes from past PAII conferences on topics including direct mail, getting started, focused markets, food, legal/financial issues, operations, service, staffing, and burnout. See "Organizations" below for more information from the PAII. The tapes are available to members and nonmembers ($5-$9 each).

For More Information...

Books

So…You Want to Be an Innkeeper: The Definitive Guide to Operating a Successful Bed-and-Breakfast or Country Inn by Mary E. Davies, Pat Hardy, Jo Ann M. Bell, and Susan Brown (Chronicle Books, 1996).

Innkeeping Unlimited: Practical Low-Cost Ways to Improve Your B&B and Win Repeat Business, by Ellen Ryan (Can-Do Press, 1998).

Organizations

The Professional Association of Innkeepers International (PAII), PO Box 90710, Santa Barbara, CA 93190, Tel: 805-569-1853, Fax: 805-682-1016, Web: www.paii.org.

American Bed & Breakfast Association, 1407 Huguenot Road, Midlothian, VA 23113, Tel: 804-379-2222, Web: www.abba.com

National Bed & Breakfast Association (NBBA), P.O. Box 332, Norwalk, CT 06851, Tel: 203-847-6196, Web: www.nbba.com, E-mail: nbbaoffice@aol.com

Newsletters

Innkeeping by the PAII. Subscription for PAII members: included in membership. Non-members: $95 or $8/issue.

Yellow Brick Road: Innsight for Aspiring Innkeepers, PO Box 1600, Julian, CA 92036, Toll-free: 800-792-2632, Web: www.yellowbrickroadnl.com, E-mail: info@yellowbrickroadnl.com. Subscription: $54.

Web Sites

www.bbchannel.com—Bed & Breakfast channel

www.innstar.com—B&B guidebook reviews

www.ibbp.com—International B&B Pages

www.orbitz.com; www.expedia.com; www.travelocity.com; www.tripadvisor.com —travel sites

Bookkeeping Service

Bookkeeping, accounting, and auditing clerks are an organization's financial record keepers. They update and maintain one or more accounting records, including those that tabulate expenditures, receipts, accounts payable and receivable, and profit and loss. They have a wide range of skills and knowledge, from full-charge bookkeepers, who can maintain an entire company's books, to accounting clerks who handle specific accounts. All of these clerks make numerous computations each day and increasingly must be comfortable using computers to calculate and record data.

Bookkeeping, accounting, and auditing clerks held about 2 million jobs in 2000 (*Occupational Outlook Handbook, 2000*). Although they can be found in all industries and levels of government, a growing number work for personnel supply firms, the result of an increase in outsourcing of this occupation.

At-Home Training Programs

Courses in Bookkeeping, The American Institute of Professional Bookkeepers, 6001 Montrose Road, Suite 500, Rockville, MD 20852, Tel: 800-622-0121, Web: www.aipb.com, E-mail: info@iapb.com

The AIPB offers continuing education self-teaching courses on basic bookkeeping, payroll, adjusting entries, depreciation, inventory, financial-statement analysis, completing the four basic business tax forms, and more. They also offer the AIPB Certification Program. Applicants to the certification program must have at least two years full-time experience or the part-time/freelance equivalent, and they must pass a national examination given at Sylvan test centers nationwide. A free 26-page booklet offers in-depth information. Class fees: $49-$69 each; discounts for members.

Courses in Accounting, USDA Graduate School Correspondence Programs, 14th and Independence S.W., Room 112S, Washington, D.C. 20250, Tel: 888-744-GRAD, Web: grad.usda.gov, E-mail: selfpaced@grad.usda.gov

The USDA Graduate School formerly offered a certificate in accounting, but they have discontinued their certificate programs. However, they still offer the courses in accounting, including Cost Accounting, Federal Government Accounting, Intermediate Accounting, plus eleven more. Some courses are approved for college credit by the ACE College Credit Recommendation Service (www.acenet.edu/cale/corporate). All but one course is paper-based (the last is by CD-ROM), and each consists of 12 lessons. Course fees: $125-$300 each.

Fundamentals of Bookkeeping Course, Allied Business Schools, 22952 Alcalde Drive, Laguna Hills CA 92653, Tel: 888-501-7686, Web: www.alliedschools.com, E-mail: allied@alliedschools.com

Allied Business Schools offers a "Fundamentals of Bookkeeping" course, which has been successfully evaluated for college credits by the American Council on Education's College Credit Recommendation Service. The course contains 17 lessons which provide instruction in: assets, liabilities, journalizing and posting transactions, financial statements, adjusting and closing procedures, the cash journal, costing merchandise inventory, pricing merchandise, payroll, the partnership, the corporation, and more. The course also has students actually processing company financial transactions to complete the accounting and systems requirements for a fictitious small business. The course includes a software tutorial program (Excel 2000), an extensive textbook, a 10-key skill-builder training program (software and workbook), a desk calculator, columnar pads, mechanical pencil, and AICPA information (see "Organizations" below). Course fee: $788. A payment plan is available.

Accounting Course, Professional Career Development Institute (PCDI), 430 Technology Parkway, Norcross, GA 30092-3406, Tel: 800-223-4542 or 770-729-8400, Web: www.pcdi-homestudy.com, E-mail: info@pcdi.com

The accounting course at PCDI consists of 16 lessons. Lessons include: Basic Concepts of Accounting; Analyzing Business Transactions; Using T Accounts; The General Journal and General Ledger; Adjustments and the Worksheet; Closing Entries and the Post-Closing Trial Balance; Sales and Accounts Receivables; Purchases and Accounts Receivables; Cash and Banking; Payroll; Payroll Taxes; Accruals and Deferrals; Financial Statements and Closing; Accounts Receivable and Uncollectable Accounts; Merchandise Inventory; and Property, Plant, and Equipment. Course fee: $889.

> ## "There's no business like show business, but there are several businesses like accounting."—David Letterman

College Programs in Accounting

If you're interested in accounting rather than bookkeeping, there are about gazillion programs in accounting from accredited colleges across the country, and all the following are offered via distance learning.

Key to the degree abbreviations: AA=Associate of Arts; AAS=Associate of Applied Science; AS=Associate of Science; BA=Bachelor of Arts; BS=Bachelor of Science;

Cert.=Undergraduate certificate; Grad. Cert.=Graduate certificate; MBA=Master of Business Administration; Courses=individual courses available

Alaska Pacific University (AA, BA), Anchorage, AK: www.rana.alaskapacific.edu

Ashworth College (AS), Norcross, GA: www.ashworthcollege.com

Athabasca University (Cert.) Athabasca, AB Canada: www.athabascau.ca

Brenau University (Courses) Gainesville, GA: www.online.brenau.edu

Caldwell College (BS) Caldwell, NJ: www.caldwell.edu

Champlain College (AS, Cert.) Burlington, VT: www.champlain.edu

Chippewa Valley Technical College (AA) Eau Claire, WI: www.chippewa.tec.wi.us

City University (BS) Renton, WA: www.cityu.edu

College of Southern Maryland (Cert.) La Plata, MD: www.csmd.edu

Davenport University Online (BS, MBA) Grand Rapids, MI: www.online.davenport.edu

Excelsior College (BS) Albany, NY: www.excelsior.edu

Florida Atlantic University (Courses) Fort Lauderdale, FL: www.mastersoftaxation.edu

Golden Gate University (Grad. Cert., MBA) San Francisco, CA: www.ggu.edu

Graceland University (BA) Lamoni, IA: www.graceland.edu

Indiana Institute of Technology (BS) Fort Wayne, IN: www.indtech.edu

Ivy Tech State College-Wabash (Courses) South Bend, IN: www.ivytech.edu/southbend

Lakeland College (BA) Sheboygan, WI: www.lakeland.edu/online

Northampton County Area Community College (AAS), Bethlehem, PA: www.northampton.edu/distancelearn/

Northwest Missouri State University (BS) www.northwest-online.org

Parkland College (AAS, Cert.) Champaign, IL: www.online.parkland.edu

Piedmont Community College (AAS, Cert.) Roxboro, NC: www.piedmont.cc.nc.us/frames

Robert Morris University (BSBA) Moon Township, PA: www.rmu.edu

St. Mary-of-the-Woods College (Cert., AS, BS) St. Mary-of-the-Woods, IN: www.smwc.edu

Southern New Hampshire College (Cert.) Manchester, NH: www.snhu.edu

Strayer University (AA, BS, Cert., MS, Grad. Cert.) Newington, NH: www.online.strayer.edu

Thomas Edison State College (ASM, BSBA) Trenton, NJ: www.tesc.edu

The University Alliance (BA) Tampa, FL: www.universityalliance.edu

University of California, Los Angeles (Cert.) Los Angeles, CA: www.uclaextension.org

University of Maryland University College (Courses) Adelphi, MD: www.umuc.edu

University of Northwestern Ohio (AAB, BS) Lima, OH: www.unoh.edu

University of Phoenix Online (BS, MBA) Phoenix, AZ: www.uoponline.edu

Upper Iowa University (MS) Fayette, IA: www.uiu.edu

Winthrop University (MBA) Rock Hill, SC: www.winthrop.edu

For More Information...

Books

Bookkeeping & Tax Preparation: Start and Build a Prosperous Bookkeeping, Tax, & Financial Services Business, by Gordon P. Lewis (Acton Circle Publishing Company, 1996).

Bookkeeping on Your Home-Based PC by Linda Stern. Check amazon.com for used copies, because this is out of print.

The Encyclopedia of Journal Entries published by the American Institute of Professional Bookkeepers (see below).

Keeping the Books: Basic Record Keeping and Accounting for the Small Business—2nd edition, by Linda Pinson (Dearborn Trade Publishing, 2001).

Starting and Building Your Own Accounting Business—3rd edition, by Jack Fox (John Wiley & Sons, 2000).

Building a Profitable Online Accounting Practice, by Jack Fox (John Wiley & Sons, 2001).

Organizations

The American Institute of Professional Bookkeepers, 6001 Montrose Rd, Suite 500, Rockville, MD 20852, Tel: 800-622-0121, Web: www.aipb.com, E-mail: info@aipb.com.

American Institute of Certified Public Accountants (AICPA), 1211 Avenue of the Americas, New York, NY 10036, Tel: 212-596-6200, Web: www.aicpa.org.

<u>Newsletters</u>

Journal of Accounting, Taxation, and Finance for Business published by the AIPB (see above).

<u>Web Sites</u>

www.allbookkeepingresource.com—all kinds of resources for bookkeepers

www.virtualbookkeeping.ca—an example of a bookkeeping service online

Catering Service

How do you learn to become a caterer from home? Well, you probably need to know how to cook first—although there are plenty of places to learn that too. Local community colleges and adult education centers are a great place to start for that. If you're really serious about becoming a chef, you can refer to *Peterson's Guide to Culinary Schools* (www.culinaryschools.com) for a program near you. But there are also distance-learning classes you can take that will teach you the ins and outs of the *business* of catering.

Catering is obviously popular with people who love to cook, plan, and work with people. And there are a wide range of possibilities when focusing your target market—will you deliver food to business meetings, or perhaps specialize in baby showers? Or perhaps you specialize in a cooking specialty—are you a clambake wiz? Or is Mexican food your thing? Or perhaps you are the world's best low-carb chef. The possibilities are endless. Here are some places to get your food, I mean foot, in the door.

At-Home Training Programs

Certification Program for Professional Caterers, National Association of Catering Executives (NACE), 5565 Sterrett Place, Suite 328, Columbia, MD 21044, Tel: 410-997-9055, Web: www.nace.net

The National Association of Catering Executives (NACE) offers a certification program, a comprehensive package of continuing education, certification, networking, and career support for professional caterers. Achievement of the Certified Professional Catering Executive (CPCE) designation demonstrates expertise in catering earned by taking a comprehensive exam that covers all aspects of professional catering.

A candidate is considered eligible to sit for the CPCE exam if they have 30 "points," achieved during catering experience and education. (For example, employment in catering earns 5 points, and a degree in hotel/restaurant management earns 10 points.) For a full list of points eligible, download the CPCE brochure (in PDF format) from the Web site.

Upon application approval, candidates will receive an outline of the CPCE Certification Program Content Domain, a suggested reading list, and a glossary of terms to prepare for the exam. You may also purchase a Study Guide from NACE Headquarters. The application fee for the certification packet is $295 for NACE members; $395 for nonmembers.

"You don't have to cook fancy or complicated masterpieces— just good food from fresh ingredients."—Julia Child

Class in Catering Management (HRMA 6326), University of Houston Online, 229 C.N. Hilton Hotel & College, University of Houston, Houston, TX 77204-3028, Tel: 713-743-2457, Web: www.mhmonline.uh.edu, E-mail: mhmhrm@uh.edu

This course is 3 graduate credits, and is offered as an elective as part of the University of Houston's Master of Hospitality Management program. The class is a comprehensive study of the catering industry. Students learn what is involved in catering from an entrepreneurial aspect, as well as from the hotel industry perspective. Tuition: $138/credit for Texas residents; $374/credit for non-residents.

Professional Gourmet Cooking & Catering Program, Professional Career Development Institute (PCDI), 430 Technology Parkway, Norcross, GA 30092-3406, Tel: 800-223-4542 or 770-729-8400, Web: www.pcdi-homestudy.com, E-mail: info@pcdi.com

The Professional Gourmet Cooking & Catering Program at PCDI is comprised of 20 lessons. The lessons include: The Basics of Gourmet Cooking; Nutrition and Recipes; Tools and Equipment; Kitchen Staples and Dairy Products; Starches and Salads; Fruits, Sandwiches, Canapés, and Hors D'Oeuvres; Baking and Breads; Pies, Cookies, and Cakes; The Management Guide; Tricks and Tips; Stocks and Sauces; Soups and Meat Cookery; Beef, Veal, Lamb, and Pork; Poultry and Game; Fish and Eggs; Deep Frying and Vegetable; Banquet Service Fundamentals; Banquet Management and Booking; Managing the Function; The Banquet Function Sheet; Getting Started in Catering; and Success in Catering. Course fee: $589. A payment plan is available.

Catering/Gourmet Cooking, Education Direct, 925 Oak Street, Scranton, PA 18515, Tel: 800-275-4410, Web: www.learncatering.com, E-mail: info@educationdirect.com

The Catering/Gourmet Cooking program from Education Direct consists of 10 modules of instruction. Lessons include: Learning Strategies; Introduction to Catering; Dynamics of Catering, Food Styles of Catering; Alcoholic Beverages; The Gourmet Kitchen; The Culinary Professional; Stocks, Sauces and Soups; Fruits, Vegetables and Herbs; Meat; Poultry and Game; Fish and Shellfish; Grains, Legumes and Pasta: Baking and Pastry; and Breakfast. The program is made up of books, lessons, special supplements, videos, progress reports, and recipe supplements. Student services include toll-free student support. Course fee: $999. A payment plan is available.

For More Information...

Books

How to Start a Home-Based Catering Business, 4th edition, by Denise Vivaldo (Globe Pequot Press, 2002).

How to Become a Caterer: Everything You Need to Know from Finding Clients to the Final Bill by Susan Wright (Citadel Press, 1996).

Start Your Own Catering Business by Kathleen Deming (Prentice-Hall Trade, 1997).

Successful Catering by Bernard Splaver, William N. Reynolds, and Michael Roman (John Wiley & Sons, 1997).

Peterson's Guide to Culinary Schools 2003 (Peterson's, 2003).

Organizations

National Association of Catering Executives (NACE), 5565 Sterrett Place, Suite 328, Columbia, MD 21044, Tel: 410-997-9055, Web: www.nace.net.

Hotel & Catering International Management Association (HCMIA), 191 Trinity Road, London SW 17 HN, United Kingdom. Web: www.hcima.org.uk.

International Association of Culinary Professionals, 304 W. Liberty Street, Suite 201, Louisville, KY 40202, Tel: 502-583-3783, Web: www.iacp-online.org.

Web Sites

www.culinary-careers.org—a directory of culinary classes

www.directcatering.com and www.localcatering.com—online directories of caterers www.catersource.com—catering resources

www.cateringmagazine.com—*Catering Magazine*

Childbirth Educator (*see also* Doula)

Okay, we're all heard of Lamaze, the most recognized brand of childbirth education. But there are actually quite a few organizations out there that can train and certify you as a Childbirth Educator. All of them have a common goal: To teach expectant mothers strategies to use to effectively go through labor without medical interventions. They focus on birth as a natural experience, and aim to give women the confidence and skills to have normal births. Each organization has its own slant to their methods—if childbirth education is for you, do some research into what you feel is the best method. Also, many childbirth educators receive training and certification by multiple organizations.

Childbirth education can also go hand-in-hand with doula services. A birth doula acts as an assistant during labor and delivery, and postpartum doulas help mothers after the birth at home (see Doula, p. 38). Many of the same organizations that teach childbirth education also teach how to become a doula. In addition, breastfeeding education can be an add-on as well.

Most of these programs are completely learn at home, but some have components where you need to attend an in-person workshop. For certification, most require you do some work outside the home witnessing births, attending childbirth classes, etc. Childbirth education can be done at home if you have a space to teach the classes, or you might network with local hospitals, birthing centers, or community centers.

At-Home Training Programs

Lamaze International, 2025 M Street, Suite 800, Washington, D.C. 20036-3309, Toll-free: 800-368-4404 or 202-367-1128, Web: www.lamaze.org, E-mail: info@lamaze.org

Learning the Lamaze technique is largely a self-study, self-assessment program. Candidates in the program traditionally come from a wide variety of educational and experiential backgrounds. As a result, how the study guide is used varies from one person to another. In general, you do the recommended readings, and choose to do the suggested learning activities that you believe will add to your knowledge and assist you in meeting the objectives. Learning activities include: observing births, observing Lamaze classes, attending a Lamaze Childbirth Educator Seminar, designing a curriculum for Lamaze Childbirth classes, and student-teaching Lamaze classes. It is possible to fulfill some requirements with the use of video and interactive computer.

At the completion of the Lamaze Childbirth Educator Program, you are eligible to sit for the Certification Examination. Successfully passing the exam demonstrates you have achieved the Lamaze competencies. Study guide: $200. Lamaze members get a big discount. Also available on the Web site are some *free* mini-study guides in PDF (Adobe Acrobat) format.

International Childbirth Education Association (ICEA), P.O. Box20048, Minneapolis, MN 55420, Tel: 952-854-8660, Toll-free: 800-827-ICEA. Web: www.icea.org, E-mail: info@icea.org

The International Childbirth Education Association (ICEA) supports educators and other health providers who believe in freedom of choice based on knowledge of alternatives in family-centered maternity and newborn care. They provide professional continuing education and training programs, educational resources, and professional certification programs. In addition to Childbirth Educator Certification, they also offer in Postnatal Educator Certification, Perinatal Fitness Educator Certification, and Doula Certification.

ICEA certification programs are independent study programs, with some face-to-face requirements. The self-paced independent study portion of the experience is contained in 10 modules, which cover topics from family-centered maternity care to labor coping skills to teaching skills. In addition, the ICEA requires that candidates obtain contact hours (similar to nursing continuing education units—CEUs), which are awarded to programs offering face-to-face learning. The ICEA offers such in-person training workshops throughout the year at several locations (see Web site for locations and dates). At least half of the required contact hours must come from face-to-face learning. The remaining half may come from alternative means, such as correspondence courses, slide-tape programs, or video programs.

ICEA certification examinations consist of multiple-choice questions taken directly from the learning objectives and content of the modules and readings. The exam is a closed-book proctored exam. Candidates have one year to take the certification exam after they have submitted their application, which includes documentation of completed prerequisites. Note: Maintaining continuous ICEA membership is a requirement of keeping your certification. Program fees: ICEA membership—$50 per year; Application—$80; Contact hours—$125-250; Required readings—$125-$300; Certification exam fee: $200.

"When I was born I was so surprised I
didn't talk for a year and a half."—Gracie Allen

The American Academy of Husband-Coached Childbirth®, Box 5224, Sherman Oaks, CA 91413-5224, Tel: 800-4-A-BIRTH or 818-788-6662, Web: www.bradleybirth.com

The American Academy of Husband-Coached Childbirth® was founded by Robert A. Bradley, M.D. and Marjie & Jay Hathaway for the purpose of making childbirth education information available. The AAHCC teaches The Bradley Method®, created by—who else—Dr. Bradley himself. The method endorses: natural childbirth, active participation of the husband as coach, excellent nutrition, early-birth classes, relaxation and natural breathing, and immediate and continuous contact with your new baby.

Trainings for The Bradley Method are in-person 3-day workshops (12 classes total), but they are available around the country and supported by materials that you take home to study. The twelve classes cover: Introduction to the Bradley Method®; Nutrition in Pregnancy; Pregnancy; The Coach's Role; Introduction to First Stage Labor; Introduction to Second Stage Labor; Planning Your Birth; Variations and Complications/Postpartum Preparation; Advanced First Stage Techniques; Advanced Second Stage Techniques; Being a Great Coach; and Preparing for Your New Family. Included in the workshop are: a teacher's manual; public relations items; a teacher's copy of the student workbook; support and guidance; dues for the workshop year; national affiliation; utilization of their Web site and 800-number for referrals; and certification as a Bradley® instructor. Workshop fee: $995.

Association of Labor Assistants and Childbirth Educators (ALACE), P.O. Box 390436, Cambridge, MA 01239, Tel: 617-441-2500, Web: www.alace.org, E-mail: alacehq@aol.com

The Association of Labor Assistants and Childbirth Educators (ALACE) offers certification as a childbirth educator and teaches you a seven-class curriculum in modular format as a suggested guide for your own class series. Classes you will learn to teach include: Birth Today; Pregnancy—Growth and Decision Making; The Process of Birth; Creating *Your* Birth; When Giving Birth is Difficult; The Newborn, Postpartum & the Family; and Potluck and Community Building. In addition to childbirth education, they also offer certification as a labor assistant (doula).

The complete program includes: the ALACE Teacher's Manual with more than 600 pages of learning modules, background material, and resources; networking and support from their Director of Teacher Training, regional directors,

ALACE affiliates in your area, and an active national office; membership in ALACE ($50 value), and two teaching videos—*Special Delivery* and *Gentle Birth Choices*. Program fee: $725.

Childbirth and Postpartum Professional Association (CAPPA), P.O. Box 491448, Lawrenceville, GA 30049, Tel: 888-548-3672, Web: www.cappa.net, E-mail: info@cappa.net

The Childbirth and Postpartum Professional Association (CAPPA) offers childbirth educator and doula certification. Candidates must be a member of CAPPA and complete their Distance Childbirth Educator Program (with Childbirth Educator Manual, certification packet, and CBE workshop video series). In addition, you must observe a childbirth education class, a breastfeeding class, and a newborn care class—if none are available, CAPPA has video alternatives. You must also observe 2 labors/births totaling 10 hours. Finally, candidates must pass an open-book test, submit 2 letters of recommendation and a video of yourself teaching, plus a class outline and curriculum. Program fee: $590 (includes membership fee, distance-learning packet, and administrative fees).

For More Information...

Books

Childbirth Education: Practice, Research and Theory by Francine Nichols and Sharron Humenick (W.B. Saunders, 2000).

Husband-Coached Childbirth: The Bradley Method of Natural Childbirth, by Robert A. Bradley (Bantam Doubleday Dell Publishing, 1996).

Pursuing the Birth Machine: The Search for Appropriate Birth Technology by Marsden Wagner (ACE Graphics, 1994).

Birthing from Within, by Pam England (Partera Press, 1998).

Childbirth Instructor Magazine's Guide to Careers in Birth: How to Have a Fulfilling Job in Pregnancy, Labor, and Parenting Support without a Medical Degree, by Suzanne Robotti and Margaret Ann Inman (John Wiley & Sons, 1998).

The Birth Book, by William Sears, M.D. and Martha Sears, R.N. (Little, Brown & Co., 1994).

The Thinking Woman's Guide to a Better Birth, by Henci Goer (Perigee Books, 1999).

The Womanly Art of Breastfeeding, published by La Leche League International, ISBN: 0-912500-24-7.

More Organizations

Doulas of North America (DONA), P.O. Box 626, Jasper, IN 45747, Tel: 888-788-DONA, Fax: 812-634-1491, Web: www.dona.org, E-mail: doula@dona.org.

La Leche League International (LLLI), 1400 N. Meacham Road, Schaumburg, IL 60173-4808, Tel: 847-519-7730, Web: www.lalecheleague.org.

International Lactation Consultant Association (ILCA), 1500 Sunday Drive, Suite 102, Raleigh, North Carolina, 27607, Tel: (919) 861-5577, Web: www.ilca.org, E-mail info@ilca.org.

Magazine

Childbirth Instructor Magazine, P.O. Box 15612, North Hollywood, CA 91615, Tel: 818-760-8983, E-mail: thebabymag@aol.com.

Web Sites

www.childbirth.org—pregnancy and childbirth information

www.pregnancyweekly.com—observe your baby's growth week by week

www.babyzone.com—more pregnancy info

www.childbirtheducation.net—childbirth education and support

www.birthprep.com—childbirth education materials in both English and Spanish

www.midwife.org—American College of Nurse Midwives

www.motherfriendly.org—Coalition for Improving Maternity Services

www.childbirthgraphics.com—childbirth education products and materials in both English and Spanish

Child Day Care Provider

So you've thought of opening a day care, but don't know where to start? Investigate these programs, because they can be a great source of information, even if you take only one or two classes. Nothing says you can't take multiple classes at different schools either—that's the beauty of distance learning. You have a whole world of opportunity open to you.

Note that each state has its own guidelines for licensing day care centers, though. These courses and programs do not necessarily license you to operate a day care in your state. They are avenues for education in early childhood professions and childcare—to license your day care, you must go through the proper channels for your state. Also, if you plan to operate your day care in your home, you need to check your city's zoning laws for home-based business.

At-Home Training Programs

Family Child Care (Undergraduate certificate), Northampton County Area Community College, 3835 Green Pond Road, Bethlehem, PA 18020, Tel: 610-861-5300, Web: www.northampton.edu/distancelearn

This program is offered for persons planning to provide home-based childcare or those already providing such childcare. Knowledge of child development, educational activities, and business aspects are covered. The diploma is offered in six 1-credit modules (6 credits total) via the College-at-Home program. Classes included in this specialized diploma include: Observing Children and Guiding Their Behavior; The Home as a Nurturing and Learning Environment; Promoting Learning with Movement, Music, and Visual Arts; Promoting Learning with Language, Math, and Science; Building Relationships with Parents and the Community; and Family Child Care as a Business. All classes are online. These courses also transfer into the college's Associate Degree Program in Early Childhood Education. Tuition: $100/credit.

School Age Child Care (Undergraduate certificate), Northampton County Area Community College, 3835 Green Pond Road, Bethlehem, PA 18020, Tel: 610-861-5300, Web: www.northampton.edu/distancelearn

The School-Age Child Care program provides both new and experienced childcare staff with the skills and knowledge required to plan and implement a high quality school-age program and how to develop as a professional in the field. The program is offered in six 1-credit courses (6 credits total). These courses also transfer into the Associate Degree in Early Childhood Education. The courses include: The School-Age Professional; Developmental Needs of School-Age Children; Commitment to Quality; Developing a Creative Curriculum; Exploring the Arts in School-Age Programs; and Exploring the Sciences in School-Age Programs. All course are online. Tuition: $100/credit.

Not-for-Profit Day Care Management (Bachelor degree), Women's External Degree Program (WED), Saint Mary-of-the-Woods College, St. Mary-of-the-Woods, IN 47876-0068, Tel: 800-926-SMWC or 812-535-5186, Web: www.smwc.edu, E-mail: smwc@smwc.edu

The Not-for-Profit Day Care Management Bachelor degree consists of 125 credits, 41 of which are not-for-profit core courses that include: NFP Fundamentals; Macroeconomics; General Psychology; Principles of Management; Not-for-Profit

Administration; Principles of Marketing; and more. The child care administration courses include: Introduction to Early Childhood; Principles of Teaching Young Children; Educating Diverse Learners; Partnerships with School, Law, and Community; Introduction to Early Childhood Developmental Disabilities; Methods and Diagnostic Procedures for Developmental Disabilities; Early Childhood Program Administration; and NFP Internship. Tuition: $307/credit.

"There's no point in being grown up if you can't be childish sometimes."—Doctor Who

Professional Child Day Care Program, Professional Career Development Institute (PCDI), 430 Technology Parkway, Norcross, GA 30092-3406, Tel: 800-223-4542 or 770-729-8400, Web: www.pcdi-homestudy.com, E-mail: info@pcdi.com

The Professional Child Day Care Program prepares you for the child day care field. As a student in the program, you'll receive several accessories in addition to the program materials, including: *ABC's of Baby Care* slide guide; *First Aid for Children* slide guide; a 12" x 18" marker board and color marker; and a first aid kit. The programs consists of 18 lessons, including: Families and Child Care; Your Role in Child Care; Basic Principles of Development; Understanding Infants and Toddlers; Understanding Preschoolers and School-Agers; Operating an Early Childhood Program; Providing an Appropriate Environment; Keeping Children Safe and Healthy; Handling Schedules and Routines; Food for Young Children; Developing Professional Skills; Language and Dramatic Play; Social Studies and Music Activities; Science, Math, and Active Play; Caring for Infants and Toddlers; and Caring for School-Age and Special Needs Children. Bonus lessons include: Business Skill Supplements—First Aid for Children, CPR for Children; Starting an At-Home Child Care Business; and Developing Your Career in Child Care, Growing as a Professional. Program fee: $589. A payment plan is available.

Child Day Care Management Program, Education Direct, 925 Oak Street, Scranton, PA 18515, Tel: 800-275-4410, Web: www.educationdirect.com, E-mail: info@educationdirect.com

The Child Day Care Management Program teaches all you need to know on accreditation and certification, working with parents, and financing and budgeting a child care center. The program includes all the books, lessons, equipment, and learning aids you need; storybooks, videos, charts, and checklists; toll-free instructional support; and access to student services by phone, mail, and Web site. Subjects covered include: How to Start Your Child-Care Facility; Licensing,

Accreditation, Certification; The Facility; Staff; Program Planning; After-School Programs; Working with Parents; and Financing and Budget. Course fee: $499.

Day Care for Profit, Online Class from BizyMoms.com, Web: www.bizymoms. com, E-mail: Tessii1@mchsi.com

Day Care for Profit from BizyMoms.com will help you discover how to start a profitable and fun day care business in your home. You will learn: how to set up your day care; learn the paperwork of the business and the tax breaks; how to add a preschool class and themes to your day care; working with parents and using the right communication skills to handle problems; and how to find inexpensive advertising. The instructor is Teresa Lyons of Little Angels Daycare. For more information about taking this 4-week online class, you can e-mail her at Tessii1@mchsi.com. Course fee: $60.

For More Information...

Books

How to Start a Home-Based Day Care Business, by Shari Steelsmith (Globe Pequot Press, 2000).

The Daycare Provider's Workbook, by Cyndi Beauchemin (TCB Enterprises, 1999).

Start and Run a Profitable Home Daycare, by Catherine Pruissen (Self Counsel Press, 2002).

Family Child Care Marketing Guide: How to Build Enrollment and Promote Your Business as a Child Professional, by Tom Copeland (Redleaf Press, 1999).

So You Want to Open a Profitable Day Care Center? By Patricia C. Gallagher (Young Sparrow Press, 1995).

Family Child Care Contracts and Policies: How to Be Businesslike in a Caring Profession, by Tom Copeland (Redleaf Press, 1991).

The Home Daycare Complete Recordkeeping System, by Brigette A. Thompson (Datamaster, 2003).

E-book

Bizy's Guide to Starting Your Own Successful Child Care Service, by Karen M. Potter, www.bizymoms.com ($18.95).

Organizations

National Child Care Association (NCCA), 1016 Rosser Street, Conyers, GA 30012, Tel: 800-543-7161, Web: www.nccanet.org.

National Association for Family Child Care (NAFCC), 5202 Pinemont Drive, Salt Lake City, UT 84123, Tel: 801-269-9338, Web: www.nafcc.org, E-mail: nafcc@nafcc.org.

National Association for the Education of Young Children (NAEYC), 1509 16th Street NW, Washington, D.C. 20036-1426, Tel: 800-424-2460, Web: www.naeyc.org, E-mail: naeyc@naeyc.org.

National Child Care Information Center (NCCIC), Administration for Children & Families, 370 L'Enfant Promenade SW, Washington, D.C. 20201, Web: www.nccic.org, E-mail: info@nccic.org.

National Resource Center for Health & Safety in Child Care, UCHSC at Fitzsimmons, Campus Mail Stop F541, P.O. Box 6508, Aurora, CO 80045-0508, Tel: 800-598-KIDS, Web: http://nrc.uchsc.edu, E-mail: natl.child.res.ctr@uchsc.edu.

National Association of Child Care Resource & Referral Agencies (NACCRRA), 1319 F St., Suite 810, Washington, D.C. 20004, Tel: 202-393-5501, Web: www.naccrra.org, E-mail: info@nccrra.org.

Web Site

www.daycareproviders.com—all kinds of resources and links

www.childcareaware.org—resources for finding quality child care

www.icomm.com/daycare/—lots of links!

www.abcsoftware.co.uk—childcare administration software

www.daycarecrafts.com—arts and crafts curriculum for daycare providers

www.tuffware.com—online catalog of nearly 500 daycare related products

www.providerware.com and www.daycaresoftware.com—childcare management software

www.daycaretax.com—professional tax advice for home daycare providers

Desktop Publisher (*see also* Graphic Designer)

Desktop publishing is one of those careers that is sometimes part of other careers, such as writing and publishing, graphic design, and Web site design. Desktop publishers use publishing software to design and print various kinds of documents, from restaurant menus to company newsletters to Web sites to marketing materials. Desktop publishing work can be done from home, but there are quite a few freelance opportunities out in the workforce too. The trick is to gather the

right combination of skills. Desktop publishing being one of my skills and specific knowledge bases, I'll share what I know.

It all depends upon what you want to do. For simple documents like a restaurant menu, for example, you could use a program like Microsoft Publisher, or
even MS Word. But for larger documents with multiple images, such as a
newsletter or a book, you'll want a sophisticated page layout program like Adobe
PageMaker or QuarkXPress. Then, there are photo manipulation software programs (Photoshop) and illustration programs (like Adobe Illustrator) that can be
helpful, depending on the level of designing you're doing. If you're planning to
work for yourself, you can choose the programs you like the best. But if you are
going to contract out to companies or freelance outside the home, you need to be
knowledgeable in a wide range of programs—they usually require you to know
and use *their* computers and software. The problem with this is that there are *a lot*
of desktop publishing programs out there. And in addition to shelling out money
to learn the programs, you will have to purchase a couple as well, which will run
you several hundred dollars each.

Desktop publishing also requires a broad range of skills in addition to software. Some desktop publishers write and edit too. Others have branched out into
Web design. Depending on the kind of work you do, you also might need to
know standard proofreader's marks in order to make corrections to manuscripts.
And in addition to desktop publishing courses or programs, I highly recommend
you take one or two graphic design classes if you need the basics in typography
and page layout (See Graphic Designer, p. 60).

One final note: Many of the software programs you can learn by yourself at
home, with tutorials from the companies that manufacture them. A lot of these
tutorials (as well as demo software) are free, so take a look at "Self-Training"
below.

At-Home Training Programs

**Digital Arts: Computer Graphics (Undergraduate certificate), Rochester
Community and Technical College, 851 30th Ave SE, Rochester, MN 55904-
4999, Tel: 507-285-7210 or 800-247-1296, Web: www.rctc.edu**

Rochester Community and Technical College's certificate program in Computer
Graphics focuses on illustration and animation. The purpose of the program is to
provide students an opportunity to learn to draw on the computer and use it as a
creative tool of expression for illustration, Internet design, and multimedia production. The core requirements total 24 credits: Computer as Creative Tool;
Computer Graphics I; Drawing I; Computer Graphics II; Designing for the

Internet; Animation and 3D Modeling; Introduction to Multimedia; and Intermediate Multimedia. Tuition: $103/credit for Minnesota and North Dakota-approved residents; $192-$232/credit for non-residents.

Web and Desktop Publishing (Undergraduate certificate), Minot State University, 500 University Avenue West, Minot, North Dakota 58707, Tel: 800-777-0750, Web: http://online.minotstate.edu, E-mail: msu@minotstateu.edu.

The Desktop and Web Publishing Certificate Program includes training in basic software programs, as well as specialized training in the design of business documents (letterhead, business cards, certificates) and Web pages. Newly acquired skills are further enhanced with actual application techniques in the E-Commerce Technology course. All courses are available online and can be applied toward the MIS Bachelor of Science degree. Courses include: Information Processing; Internet and World Wide Web; Desktop Publishing and Design; Web Site Design; JavaScript; and E-Commerce Technology (18 total credit hours). Students have 16 weeks in the fall/spring semesters to complete the course, or 8 weeks in the summer. Tuition: $126.83/credit hour.

Graphic Arts Publishing (Master degree), Rochester Institute of Technology, One Lomb Memorial Drive, Rochester, NY 14623-5603, Tel: 585-475-2411, Web: http://distancelearning.rit.edu, E-mail: online@rit.edu

Rochester Institute of Technology's Master's program in Graphic Arts Publishing is designed to prepare individuals for production and management positions in the ever-changing and multifaceted industry of printing and publishing. A main focus is in the production and publication of magazines and books using cross-media digital applications, as well as traditional printing processes. The program is 48 graduate credits. There is one on-campus requirement—a one-week technology practicum that occurs during the summer. Core courses include: Applications of Digital Printing & Publishing; Color Image Processing Systems; Document Processing Languages; Tone and Color Analysis; Database Publishing; Trends in Printing Technology; Markets for Print & Graphic Media; and a Research Project. Specific questions can be directed to Barbara Birkett at babppr@rit.edu. Tuition: $307/credit.

Desktop Publishing & Design Course, Education Direct, 925 Oak Street, Scranton, PA 18515, Tel: 800-275-4410, Web: www.educationdirect.com, E-mail: info@educationdirect.com

Education Direct's Desktop Publishing course teaches Adobe PageMaker software; page layout, elements of design, illustration, and printing; planning and designing single-page or multi-page documents; selecting, sizing, and placing art in documents; and creating an online document. Adobe PageMaker software is included with your program. Subjects covered include: Elements of Design; Illustrations; Planning and Designing Short Documents; Planning and Designing Multipage Documents; Introduction to Windows®; Using Windows®; and Adobe PageMaker Study Guide. Course fee: $799.

Desktop Publishing, Allied Business Schools, 22952 Alcalde Drive, Laguna Hills, CA 9253, Tel: 888-925-2114, Web: www.desktoppublishingclass.com, E-mail: allied@alliedschools.com

With Allied's Desktop Publishing course, you'll gain an understanding of how to incorporate text and graphics effectively into documents. You'll also receive instruction on the use of color, typefaces, and white space to create visually appealing brochures, flyers, newsletters, invitations, and more. Students should have access to a personal computer and a working knowledge of one of the following programs: QuarkXPress, PageMaker, Microsoft Word, or FrameMaker. Materials you will receive include the Allied Student Workbook, *Desktop Publishing Basic Skills* textbook, six diskettes with enrichment exercises, a CD-ROM holder, bookstand, dictionary, and more. Allied will also include a special report on how to start your own home-based business. Course fee: $613-720, depending on payment plan.

> "Computers make it easier to do a lot of things, but most of the things they make it easier to do don't need to be done."—Andy Rooney

Self-Paced Online Anytime Training, New Horizons, New Horizons Computer Learning Centers, Inc., Corporate Headquarters, 1900 S. State College Blvd., Anaheim, CA 92806-6135, Tel: 714-940-8000, Web: www.newhorizons.com.

New Horizons offers Web-based training for practically every desktop publishing software program you would want to know. They also have training centers around the country—check out the Web site to search for your location. What can you learn? QuarkXPress, PageMaker, Illustrator, Photoshop, InDesign, FrameMaker, Acrobat, GoLive, FrontPage, and much more. Fees: Each course differs, but approximately $200-$500 per course.

Video Professor, Tel: 800-525-7763, www.videoprofessor.com, E-mail: cservice@videoprofessor.com

Okay, you've probably seen these on TV. Video Professor is a CD-ROM you insert into your computer and it takes you through each software program step-by-step, like a video. You just follow along. This is a great resource for someone who has had very little computer experience. You can learn Windows, MS

Publisher, MS Works, and MS FrontPage, as well as Word, Excel, Quicken, PowerPoint, Lotus, DOS, WordPerfect, and QuickBooks. You can get a 10-day free trial—afterward you pay $69.95 to keep the whole set.

DESKTOP PUBLISHING SELF-TRAINING

The larger companies, such as Adobe and Quark, offer free training for their software programs. Some even offer a demonstration copy of the software that allows you to learn at no cost! In addition, in some cases you can become certified as an expert, or even as a teacher.

QuarkXPress, www.quark.com, 800-676-4575

QuarkXPress is the premium desktop publishing program on the market. If you're going to be working with publishing houses or magazines, Quark is the program 90% of companies use. They offer free demo software and free online training—QuarkEd. QuarkEd consists of 18 free lessons in 3 modules—Quark Fundamentals, Quark Essentials, and Advanced Techniques. The lessons are in Adobe Acrobat format. To download, go to www.quark.com/service/learning/quarked. Or to order the lessons on CD-ROM with sample files, you can pay $25 + tax and shipping (see phone number above).

Adobe, www.adobe.com/misc/training.html

Adobe owns the majority of the rest of the best desktop publishing programs. They offer classroom-in-a-book, free tutorials, the Adobe Certified Expert program, and Adobe Certified Trainer program. The software they manufacture includes: Adobe Acrobat (very useful program for both desktop and Web publishing); Adobe Photoshop (unmatched photo manipulation program—the standard); Adobe Illustrator (a very good drawing program); Adobe PageMaker (page layout); and Adobe In-Design (their latest page layout program). You can sample a course for free, or pay $49-$129 for each one.

For More Information...

<u>Books</u>

How to Start a Home-Based Desktop Publishing Business, by Louise Kursmark (Globe Pequot Press, 1996).

No Sweat Desktop Publishing, by Steve Morgenstern (Amacom, 1995).

Owning and Managing a Desktop Publishing Business, by Dan Ramsey (Upstart Press, 1995).

The Non-Designer's Design Book, by Robin Williams (Peachpit Press, 1994).

Looking Good in Print, by Roger C. Parker (Paraglyph Press, 2003).

Teach Yourself QuarkXPress, by Christopher Lumgair (McGraw-Hill, 1999).

Teach Yourself Visually Illustrator 10, by Mike Wooldridge and Michael Toot (John Wiley & Sons, 2002).

Teach Yourself Visually Photoshop 6, by Mike Wooldridge (John Wiley & Sons, 2001).

<u>Organizations</u>

The Association of Desktop Publishers, 3401 Adams Ave, Suite A800, San Diego, CA 92116, Tel: 619-563-9714.

National Association of Desktop Publishers (NADTP), Museum Wharf, 462 Boston Street, Topsfield, MA 01983.

Graphic Artists Guild, 90 John Street, Suite 403, New York, NY 10038-3202, Tel: 212-791-3400, Web: www.gag.org.

Society of Publication Designers, 60 East 42nd Street, Suite 721, New York, NY 10165, Tel: 212-983-8585, Web: www.spd.org, E-mail: spdnyc@aol.com.

<u>Web Sites</u>

www.dtpjournal.com—DTP resources and links

www.desktoppublishing.com—lots of DTP resources and links

www.thunderlizard.com—sponsors huge teaching conferences on desktop and Web publishing software

www.creativemoonlighter.com—freelance job site for desktop publishers and other creative types

www.paperdirect.com and www.ideaart.com—great paper supplies and more for desktop publishers

Doula (*see also* Childbirth Educator)

Doula is the Greek word for "mother's helper," and their services are growing in popularity each year, as more and more women are opting for natural childbirth. Doulas help coach expectant mothers through labor and delivery, adding valuable support to the mother and greatly enhancing her birth experience. Birth doulas help the mother to rest and relax, provide support to the woman's partner, assist the mother in using a variety of helpful positions and comfort measures, and help the environment be one in which the mother feels secure and confident.

Research has shown that mothers who had doulas present during their births had much lower rates of cesarean sections and shorter labor times! To be exact, women supported by a doula during labor had a 50% reduction in cesarean rate, 25% shorter labors, and a 60% reduction in epidural requests (www.cappa.net, 2002). The research is so strong that I believe the time is coming when insurance companies will cover doula services, so keep an eye out. Sometimes doulas double as childbirth educators (see p. 25). In addition to birth doula services, some women also offer postpartum doula services, giving help and support to new mothers and babies, from assistance with breastfeeding to help with diapers and even housework.

At-Home Training Programs

Doulas of North America (DONA), P.O. Box 626, Jasper, IN 45747, Tel: 888-788-DONA, Fax: 812-634-1491, Web: www.dona.org, E-mail: doula@dona.org

Doulas of North America (DONA) is an international association of doulas who are trained to provide emotional, physical, and educational support to women and their families during childbirth and postpartum. Membership in DONA includes more than 4,500 birth and postpartum doulas. In addition to training opportunities, they also have an annual conference, discussion boards, and a doula referral service.

Applicants for DONA certification must purchase a DONA Birth Doula Certification Packet ($35) and complete the application, which includes membership in DONA, completion of the required reading of four texts, and completion of a training in childbirth education/midwifery, nurse's training with work experience in labor and deliver, or attendance at a childbirth education series or a DONA-approved doula course. In addition, applicants must attend a DONA-approved birth doula training workshop of sixteen hours or more. Other requirements include good evaluations from at least three clients and an essay on the value and purpose of labor support.

You can find DONA-approved doula workshops on their web site, www.dona.org. DONA does not handle scheduling or anything related to the workshops unless noted as a DONA sponsored training. Trainings are available throughout the country—refer to the Web site for specifics.

Association of Labor Assistants and Childbirth Educators (ALACE), P.O. Box 390436, Cambridge, MA 01239, Tel: 617-441-2500, Web: www.alace.org, E-mail: alacehq@aol.com

The ALACE labor assistant training program is distinguished by its foundation in the practical skills of midwifery and homebirth as the standard for normal birth. This means that the training stresses confidence in a woman's body to birth normally, confidence in the process of birth itself, and recognition of the value of a knowledgeable and supportive woman to help facilitate birth that is free from unnecessary interventions.

Training is offered around the country in the form of a weekend workshop. Complete tuition of $425 paid to ALACE (payment plans are available) includes the ALACE program manual, certification, one-year membership in ALACE, personal attention and support, and the weekend training seminar. After taking the seminar, most applicants will be able to complete all requirements for certification within 12 months, although there is no time limit to completing your certification. To check for training near you, visit www.alace.org/schedule.html.

In the course of the weekend workshop and certification program you will learn how to develop and define the scope of your practice; conduct prenatal and postpartum visits; communicate effectively with mothers, partners, and families; create and preserve a safe birthing environment; work in collaboration with physicians, midwives, nurses, and staff; provide highly effective labor support; and market yourself as a professional Labor Assistant in your community. In addition you will learn about maternal vital signs during pregnancy and birth, palpation of fetal position and presentation, auscultation of fetal heart tones by fetoscope, sterile technique, understanding common tests and techniques, and basic pelvic exam.

To get certified by ALACE you must attend the weekend workshop, complete the required reading list, obtain infant and adult CPR certification, successfully complete the written exam, audit a series of childbirth classes, provide written self-evaluations of six births you have attended, and provide written performance evaluations from three people you have attended or worked with. Course fee: $425.

"Somewhere on this globe, every ten seconds,
there is a woman giving birth to a child.
She must be found and stopped."—Sam Levenson

International Childbirth Education Association (ICEA), P.O. Box20048, Minneapolis, MN 55420, Tel: 952-854-8660, Toll-free: 800-827-ICEA. Web: www.icea.org, E-mail: info@icea.org

ICEA certified doulas are trained professionals who recognize birth as a key life experience. In addition to supporting the physical, emotional, and social needs of women in labor, they offer guidance and referrals to community resources regarding maternal self-care, lactation, and other issues pertinent to healthy parenting through the first six weeks postpartum. They have two options—one for ICEA certified educators (ICCE or ICPE) and a second for non-certified educators. ICCEs and ICPEs who enter the program must complete the required reading, verify attendance at an ICEA Doula and Labor Support Workshop, and submit materials within one year of enrolling in the program. Other candidates must fulfill these requirements also, as well as maintain ICEA membership, audit at least one childbirth education/postpartum series, and verify three labor support experiences. Enrollment fee: $80, plus ICEA membership fee and contact hour requirements.

Childbirth and Postpartum Professional Association (CAPPA), PO Box 491448, Lawrenceville, GA 30049, Tel: 888-548-3672, Web: www.cappa.net, E-mail: info@cappa.net

Certification as a Labor Doula with CAPPA is for people who are not certified by DONA or the ICEA. The distance labor doula certification program was designed for the many women unable to attend a doula training. The program offers training with the use of a professionally produced video series version of a CAPPA labor doula-training workshop. The video series is approximately nine hours in length. Each participant also receives the labor doula training manual and the certification packet. You must be a member of CAPPA in good standing; write a letter explaining why you want to be doula and why the distance program is best for you; read five books from the required reading list; attend a local breastfeeding class; purchase the doula training video series; complete the open book labor doula test; attend three births, and submit good evaluations and two letters of recommendation. Total cost: $395 (includes $40 membership fee, $280 distance labor doula program, and $75 processing fee).

For More Information...

Books

Family Centered Maternity Care, by Celeste Phillips (Mosby, 1996).

The Birth Partner: Everything You Need to Know to Help a Woman Through Childbirth, 2nd edition, by Penny Simkin (Harvard Common Press, 2001).

From Start to Finish...A Practical Guide for Your Labor Support Business, by Barbara Ross Ellis (Pennypress).

The Doula Book: How a Trained Labor Companion Can Help You Have a Shorter, Easier, and Healthier Birth, by Marshall Klaus, M.D., Phyllis Klaus, and John Kennell (Perseus Publishing, 2002).

Special Women: The Role of the Professional Labor Assistant, by Paulina Perez and Cheryl Snedeker (Cutting Edge Press, 1994).

E-book

Fabjob's Guide to Becoming a Doula, by Rachel Gurevich, www.fabjob.com ($29.95).

More Organizations

La Leche League International, 1400 N. Meacham Road, Schaumburg, IL 60173-4808, Tel: 847-519-7730, Web: www.lalecheleague.org

National Association of Postpartum Care Services (NAPCS), 800 Detroit St., Denver, CO 80206, Tel: 800-453-6852), Web: www.napcs.org, E-mail: doulacare@napcs.org.

Web Sites

www.childbirth.org—pregnancy and childbirth info

www.doulaworld.com—doula info and resources

www.birthbalance.com—info about water birth and labor support

www.doulanetwork.com—searchable directory of doulas

Editorial Services

There are many different kinds of at-home jobs possible under the topic "Editorial Services." You may be a proofreader, a copyeditor, an editor, or even a desktop publisher (see p. 33). You may choose one specialty, or you may choose to combine several skills. From books to magazines to Web sites, there are a plethora of places to find work, although competition is also quite fierce. To get your feet wet and build a reputation, you often have to get experience writing for free. The following training programs will help you with the basics of writing and editing, including standard proofreader's marks, copyediting skills, and desktop publishing skills.

You can also go into business for yourself, publishing a newsletter, authoring a Web site, or writing a book. Self-publishing is extraordinarily easy and affordable these days; just check out www.iuniverse.com to publish that manuscript you've had sitting in a drawer for years. (This book was published through iUniverse.com.) You can also visit my Web site for information on self-publishing at www.michellemedia.com/selfpublish.htm.

At-Home Training Programs

Business Aspects of Publishing (Undergraduate certificate), Pace University, 861 Bedford Road, Pleasantville, NY 10570-2799, Tel: 800-874-PACE, Web: www.pace.edu, E-mail: infoctr@pace.edu.

Designed specifically for business professionals who want to extend their knowledge of the publishing field, this certificate features courses in marketing, distribution methods, editorial principles, and magazine circulation, as well as legal aspects of publishing. The certificate is 12 credits (4 courses), which can be selected from: Principles of Publishing; Book Sales and Distribution Methods; Legal Aspects of Publishing; Seminar on Books and Magazines; Editorial Principles and Practices in Publishing; Marketing Principles and Practices in Publishing; Magazine Circulation; and Publishing Business Communication Skills. Tuition: $556/credit.

Professional Writing (Bachelor degree), Women's External Degree Program (WED), Saint Mary-of-the-Woods College, St. Mary-of-the-Woods, IN 47876-0068, Tel: 812-535-5186 or 800-926-SMWC, Web: www.smwc.edu, E-mail: smwc@smwc.edu

The Bachelor degree in Professional Writing at St. Mary-of-the-Woods has two tracks: the creative writing track and the journalism track. Each program is 125 credits. Courses include: general education courses; News Reporting; Introduction to Mass Media; Publication Production; Editing; Advanced Reporting; Layout and Design; Feature Writing and Commentary; Communication Law and Ethics; Creative Writing; Advanced Creative Writing; Nonfiction; Poetry; Women Writers; and more. Tuition: $307/credit.

Professional Writing (Undergraduate certificate), Northern Arizona University, NAU Net, P.O. Box 4117, Flagstaff, AZ 86011-4117, Tel: 800-426-8315, Web: www.distance.nau.edu, E-mail: distance.programs@nau.edu

The Professional Writing Certificate consists of 18 credit hours, and includes classes such as Advanced Technical Editing, Professional Editing, Rhetoric in Professions, Information Design, Project Management & Documentation Design, and Issues in Technical and Professional Writing. Tuition: $274/credit.

Professional Writing (Graduate certificate), University of Central Florida, 12424 Research Parkway, Suite 256, Orlando, FL 32826-3269, Tel: 407-823-6234, Web: http://online.ucf.edu, E-mail: mbowdon@mail.ucf.edu

The Certificate Program in Professional Writing at UCF is open to students with a baccalaureate degree or higher from an accredited university. The 15-hour online program, which can be completed in three semesters, studies the theory and practice of organizational writing. Courses include: Modern Rhetorical Theory; Writing for the Business Professional; Editing Professional Writing; Persuasive Writing; Proposal Writing; Current Topics in Professional Writing; The Writer's Marketplace; Teaching Professional Writing; English Grammar and Usage; Writing/Consulting Theory and Practice; Methods of Bibliography and Research; Proposal Writing; Project Management in Technical Writing; Production and Publication Methods; and Document Usability. Tuition: $147.34/credit hour for Florida residents; $465.33/credit hour for nonresidents.

> ## "You have to know how to accept rejection and reject acceptance."—Ray Bradbury

Professional Writing (Undergraduate certificate), Washington State University, Distance Degree Programs, 104 Van Doren Hall, P.O. Box 645220, Pullman, WA 99164-5220, Tel: 800-222-4978, Web: www.distance.wsu.edu, E-mail: distance@wsu.edu

The Washington State University Professional Writing Certificate allows students to develop a base of skills and knowledge of effective communication (including editorial and electronic skills and the broader skills of analysis and synthesis) useful to the professional worlds they want to enter. It consists of 15 credits. Courses include: Speech, Thought and Culture; Writing and Rhetorical Communication; Multimedia Authoring: Exploring New Rhetoric; Technical and Professional Writing; and an internship. The courses are offered in varying formats, including print, videotape, and Internet. Semester-based courses are offered only during semesters, and enrollment may be limited. Flexible enrollment courses can be taken at any time as long as the course is still available. Tuition: Semester-based courses: $226/credit for Washington residents; $339/credit for nonresidents. Flexible enrollment courses: $165/credit for all students.

Journalism with specialization in Print Journalism (Undergraduate certificate), University of California, Los Angeles (UCLA), 10995 Le Conte Avenue, Los Angeles, CA 90024-2883, Tel: 310-825-0641, Web: www.uclaextension.org, E-mail: bbortnic@uclaextension.edu

The certificate in print journalism from UCLA consists of 29 credits. Courses include: Fundamentals of Reporting; Legal and Ethical Issues in Journalism; Advancing Your Skills in News Writing; Writing and Marketing the Magazine Article; Copy Editing; Investigative Reporting Techniques; Proofreading; Cutting-Edge Photojournalism; Basic Reporting and News Writing Skills for Spanish Language Media; Opinion Writing; Newsletters—Writing, Editing, and Preparation; Travel Writing; and Writing About Food. Tuition: $300-$500/course.

Journalism Courses, Northampton County Area Community College, 3835 Green Pond Road, Bethlehem, PA 18020, Tel: 610-861-5300, Web: www.northampton.edu/distancelearn

Northampton offers several courses in journalism, each three credits each. Courses available include: Journalism and Society; Copyediting; News Writing; Feature Writing; Reporting in the Information Age; and Writing for Public Relations. Tuition: $100/credit.

Editorial Practices Courses, USDA Graduate School Correspondence Program, Room 1112S, 14th and Independence Avenue, Washington, D.C. 20250; (888) 744-GRAD or (202) 314-3670; Web: http://grad.usda.gov, E-mail: self-paced@grad.usda.gov

The USDA Graduate School formerly offered a certificate in Editorial Practices, but their certificates have been discontinued. They still offer the individual courses, however. Courses available include: Advanced Practices in Editing; Applied Indexing; Basic Indexing; Intermediate Editing—Principles and Practices; Introduction to the Editing Process; Proofreading; Effective Writing for Professionals; Letter Writing Workshop; Practical Writing; Put It in Writing; Report Writing; Travel Writing; Writing for Government and Business; and Writing Short Informational Reports. Course fees: Each course is between $200-$300 each.

Freelance Writer Program, Education Direct, 925 Oak Street, Scranton, PA 18515, Tel: 800-275-4410, Web: www.educationdirect.com, E-mail: info@ educationdirect.com

You can earn this career diploma within 9 months, or take up to two years to complete it. This program will teach you how to market your work, deal with editors and publishers, and polish your work so that it's ready for submission. You'll also get a copy of the latest edition of *Writer's Market* (see "Books," below) included in your program. Subjects covered in the program include: The Writing Habit, Parts 1-2; The Business of Writing; Reference Sources for Writers; Using the *Writer's Market*; Becoming a Professional; and Becoming a Specialist. Course fee: $599.

> "I was working on the proof of one of my poems all the morning, and took out a comma. In the afternoon I put it back again."—Oscar Wilde

Professional Children's Writer Program, Professional Career Development Institute (PCDI), 430 Technology Parkway, Norcross, GA 30092-3406, Tel: 800-223-4542 or 770-729-8400, Web: www.pcdi-homestudy.com, E-mail: info@pcdi.com

The Professional Children's Writer Program from PCDI provides you with a wide range of skills in children's literature. It teaches 19 lessons by several children's writing professionals. The lessons include: The World of Children's Literature; Assessing Your Writing Skills; Beginning the Writing Process; Analyzing Your Audience; Writing Skills I—Creating Characters; Writing Skills II—Developing Plot; Writing Skills III—Saying It with Style; Writing the First Draft; Picture Books; Easy Readers; Chapter Books; Specialty Books; Writing Non-Fiction and Writing for Magazines; Developing a Writing Project Proposal; Revising and Rewriting Part I and II; Editing and Proofreading; Submitting Your Manuscript; and Preparing the Manuscript for Publication. Course Fee: $689. A payment plan is available.

Writing & Language Courses, Barnes & Noble University, www.bn.com

Barnes & Noble—the bookstore, of course—offers online courses in writing and languages, as well as other subjects, from their Web site, www.bn.com. They range in price from free to $99 each. Writing classes they currently have available include: Grammar Fitness, Start Writing Fiction, Thinking Like an Editor: How to Get Published, and Writing for Children.

Freelance Writing 101, Online Course from BizyMoms, Web: www.bizymoms.com
This 4-week online class from Bizy Moms focuses on setting up a writing business at home and finding markets for writing by improving writing skills, polishing book proposals, and brainstorming new ways to generate more writing. Lessons will include discussions on magazine, newspaper, newsletter, and Web writing markets for both non-fiction and fiction writing. Instructor Pamela White is a freelance writing with 8 years of experience, and has published an e-book at www.fabjob.com entitled *Be a Food Writer*. Course fee: $60.

For More Information...

Books

The Elements of Style, 3rd edition, by William Strunk, Jr. and E.B. White (Macmillan, 1979).

The Chicago Manual of Style (University of Chicago Press, 1993).

MLA Style Manual, by Joseph Gibaldi (The Modern Language Association of America, 1998).

Copyediting: A Practical Guide (3rd edition), by Karen Judd (Crisp Pub., 2001).

The Well-Fed Writer: Financial Self-Sufficiency as a Freelance Writer in Six Months or Less, by Peter Bowerman (Fanove Publishing, 2000).

How to Start a Home-Based Writing Business, by Lucy Parker and Karen Ivory (Globe Pequot Press, 2000).

How to Start and Run a Writing & Editing Business, by Herman Holtz (John Wiley & Sons, 1992).

The 2003 Writer's Market, edited by Katie Struckel Brogan and Robert Brewer (Writer's Digest Books, 2002).

Publish Your Own Magazine, Guidebook, or Weekly Newspaper: How to Manage and Profit from Your Own Homebased Publishing Company, by Thomas A. Williams (Sentient Publications, 2002).

Developing Proofreading and Editing Skills, by Sue C. Camp (McGraw-Hill, 2000).

How to Get Happily Published (5th edition), by Judith Appelbaum (HarperCollins, 1998).

E-books

Bizy's Guide to Web Site Editing and Proofreading as a Business, by Bruce Noeske, www.bizymoms.com ($17.95).

Fabjob's Guide to Becoming a Book Editor, by Jodi L. Brandon, www.fabjob.com ($14.95).

<u>Organizations</u>

Editorial Freelancers Association, 71 West 23rd Street, Suite 1910, New York, NY 10010-4102, Tel: 212-929-5400 or 866-929-5400, Web: www.the-efa.org, E-mail: info@the-efa.org.

American Society of Journalists and Authors (ASJA), 1501 Broadway, Suite 302, New York, NY 10036, Tel: 212-997-0947, Web: www.asja.org.

National Writer's Union, 113 University Place, 6th Floor, New York, NY 10003, Tel: 212-254-0279, Web: www.nwu.org, E-mail: nwu@nsu.org.

The Reporter's Network, P.O. Box 920868, Houston, TX 77292, Web: www.reporters.net, E-mail: reporter@reporters.net.

<u>Web Sites</u>

www.copydesk.net—outsourcing and placement agency that provides businesses with professional writers

www.writing-world.com—writing tips and resources

www.freelanceworkshop.com—online magazine article writing workshop

www.coffeehouseforwriters.com—tips, resources, and workshops

www.publishingbiz.com—The Publishing Business Group

www.happilypublished.com—the Web site of Judith Appelbaum, author of *How to Get Happily Published*

www.copyeditor.com—language newsletter and job search site for copyeditors

www.elance.com—freelance opportunities

www.ipl.org—The Internet Public Library

www.iuniverse.com and www.1stbooks.com—self-publishing companies

Financial Planner

Financial planning is defined as "the development and implementation of total, coordinated plans designed to achieve an individual's financial objectives." With more and more people living longer, financial planning is more important than ever. Financial planners work with individuals, families, and small businesses to help them analyze, set, and achieve financial goals. You need expertise in accounting, taxation, finance, and business law. A good sense of ethics also helps. You need to be good with people, and able to explain financial matters.

While most planners offer advice on a wide range of topics, some specialize in areas such as estate planning or risk management. According to the *Occupational Outlook Handbook (OOH)* (Jist Works, 2003), approximately one-fourth of financial planners are self-employed. In addition, *OOH* states that financial planning is projected to experience "faster-than-average" employment growth (increase 21-35%) through 2010 as the baby boomer generation saves for retirement and a better-educated and wealthier population requires investment advice.

> ## "I have enough money to last me the rest of my life, unless I buy something."—Jackie Mason

In order to become a Certified Financial Planner (CFP™), which is awarded by the Certified Financial Planner Board of Standards, Inc., you need to complete an educational program that is approved by them, and then take their certification exam. Even certificates can qualify you to sit for the exam. Be sure and verify which programs meet their educational requirements.

At-Home Training Programs

Financial Planning (Undergraduate certificate, Master degree, and Graduate certificate), Golden Gate University, Cyber Campus, 536 Mission Street, San Francisco, CA 94105, Tel: 415-369-5263, Web: www.ggu.edu, E-mail: cybercampus@ggu.edu

Golden Gate University offers several programs in financial planning: an undergraduate certificate, graduate certificate, and a Master of Science degree. Completion of the graduate or undergraduate certificates meets the educational requirement of the Certified Financial Planner (CFP®) designation, and allows students to sit for the exam. The undergraduate certificate (UFPC) requires completion of six courses (18 semester units), plus any necessary prerequisite courses. These courses include: Personal Financial Planning; Federal Income Tax I; Investments; Insurance Planning; Retirement and Employee Benefits Planning; and Estate Planning. The graduate certificate (GFPC) also requires six courses (18 semester units), which include: Personal Financial Planning; Personal Investment Management; Retirement & Employee Benefits Planning; Income Tax Planning; Estate Planning; and Insurance Planning. The Master of Science in Financial Planning (MSFP) requires 42 semester units, and courses taken as part of the graduate certificate can transfer into this program. Scholarships are available for

Continuing Cyber Students. Tuition: $400/credit for undergraduate credits; $613/credit for graduate credits.

Personal Financial Planning (Graduate certificate, MBA), City University, 11900 N.E. First Street, Bellevue, WA 98005, Tel: 888-42CITYU, Web: www.cityu.edu, E-mail: info@cityu.edu

City University offers an MBA in Personal Financial Planning, as well as a graduate certificate. The graduate certificate consists of five classes (15 credits) that include: Financial Planning, Insurance and Risk Management; Investment Management; Employee Benefits and Retirement Planning; Taxation and Planning; and Estate Planning. The MBA in Financial Planning combines financial history, risk management, business disciplines and other specialized aspects of financial planning. While working toward the MBA, each student completes eight financial planning courses, earning the graduate certificate, and qualifying to sit for the certification exam. Courses in the MBA program include the courses for the certificate, as well as: Managerial Economics; Legal Systems in a Global Economy; Marketing Management; High Performance Organizations; Managerial Communication & Research Methods; Management Information Systems; Management Accounting; Principles of Finance; Introduction to Personal Financial Planning; and the Personal Financial Planning/Capstone Course. Tuition: $342/credit.

Personal Financial Planning Programs, University of California, Los Angeles (UCLA), University of California, Los Angeles (UCLA), 10995 Le Conte Avenue, Los Angeles, CA 90024-2883, 310-206-1654, Web: www.uclaextension.edu, E-mail: business@uclaextension.edu

UCLA offers three programs in financial planning: 1) Award in General Business Studies with concentration in Personal Financial Planning, 2) Certificate in Business with concentration in Personal Financial Planning, and 3) Professional Designation in Personal Financial Planning. The Award in General Business is 36 credits, the certificate is 68 courses, and the professional designation is 36 credits. Courses include: Introduction to Computing for Business; Principles of Accounting; Business Economics; Survey of Personal Financial Planning; Pension and Other Retirement Benefit Plans; and many more. Tuition: $300-$500/course.

"I'm living so far beyond my income that we may almost be said to be living apart."—ee cummings

Family Financial Planning & Counseling (Undergraduate certificate, Graduate certificate), The University of Alabama, College of Continuing Studies, Division of Distance Education, Box 870388, Tuscaloosa, AL 35487-0388, Tel: 800-452-5971 or 205-348-9278, Web: http://bama.disted.ua.edu, E-mail: disted@ccs.ua.edu

The University of Alabama's undergraduate certificate in family financial planning and counseling requires 21 credits (7 courses). Courses are available online and via videotape. Required courses include: Introduction to Personal Financial Planning; Personal Insurance Planning and Management; Personal Investment Planning and Management; Personal Retirement Planning and Employee Benefits; Personal Estate Planning; Personal Income Tax Management and Planning; and Personal Financial Planning and Counseling Techniques. Students must be admitted to the University to be admitted into the program. Students who successfully complete the certificate may sit for the Certified Financial Planner (CFP®) exam. The graduate certificate in family financial planning and counseling also consists of 21 credits (7 courses)—all the same courses as the undergraduate certificate, except on the graduate level. Tuition: $445/course (3 credits each).

The Certified Financial Planner® Professional Education Program, College for Financial Planning, 6161 South Syracuse Way, Greenwood Village, CO 80111-4707, Tel: 800-237-9990, Web: www.fp.edu, E-mail: enroll@fp.edu

The Certified Financial Planner® Professional Education Program covers the knowledge and skills necessary to objectively assess financial status, identify problem areas, and provide comprehensive, client-based financial planning. Successful completion of the program fulfills the educational requirements to sit for the CFP® certification exam. The college also offers a M.S. in Financial Planning.

The standard curriculum delivery includes print, CD-ROM, and online. You also have the option to receive the program via the Internet only. The required courses include: Financial Planning Process & Insurance; Investment Planning; Income Tax Planning; Retirement Planning and Employee Benefits; and Estate Planning. From time of enrollment, students have five years to complete the program. Program fee: $2,295.00.

Certificate in Financial Planning, Florida State University Online, Center for Professional Development, 555 West Pensacola Street, Tallahassee, FL 32306-1640, Tel: 850-644-3801, Web: http://learningforlife.fsu.edu

The certificate program in financial planning at FSU aims to provide accurate and timely information in key areas of financial planning. It consists of six classes: Introduction to Financial Planning; Insurance Planning; Investment Planning; Income Tax Planning; Retirement Planning; and Estate Planning. At least one new course begins on the first Friday of every month—all course are online. The program is registered with the CFP Board, and graduates may sit for the exam. Tuition: $450/course.

Family Financial Planning (Graduate certificate and Master degree), Great Plains Interactive Distance Education Alliance (GPIDEA), Web: www.gpidea.org

A consortium of ten universities—Colorado State University, Iowa State University, Kansas State University, Michigan State University, Montana State University, University of Nebraska, North Dakota State University, Oklahoma State University, South Dakota State University, and Texas Technical University—named the Great Plains Interactive Distance Education, offers a Master of Science in Family Financial Planning, as well as a Graduate Certificate in Family Financial Planning. Upon completion of the curriculum, students are eligible to sit for the CFP® exam. The Master degree is 42 credits. Courses include: Family Systems; Family Economics; Fundamentals of Family Financial Planning; Financial Counseling; Estate Planning for Families; Housing and Real Estate in Family Financial Planning; Families, Employment Benefits, and Retirement Planning; Insurance Planning for Families; Personal Income Taxation; Professional Practices in Financial Planning; Investing for the Family's Future; Practicum; and Financial Planning Case Studies.

The Family Financial Planning Graduate Certificate has also been registered with the CFP® Board. The program consists of six courses (18 credits). Courses include: Fundamentals of Family Financial Planning; Estate Planning for Families; Retirement Planning, Employee Benefits and the Family; Insurance Planning for Families; Personal Income Taxation; and Investing for the Family's Future. Tuition: $350/credit.

"My problem lies in reconciling my gross habits with my net income."—Errol Flynn

Financial Planning (Undergraduate certificate), Kaplan College, 6409 Congress Avenue, Boca Raton, FL 33487, Tel: 866-523-3473 or 561-981-7300, Web: www.kaplancollege.edu, E-mail: infokc@kaplancollege.edu

Kaplan College's online certificate in financial planning consists of six subject area courses, each with ten lessons and quizzes, as well as a comprehensive Review Course containing extensive topic outlines and a simulation of the CFP® Certification Exam. Students complete one exam at the end of each of the six courses and may progress in the courses at their own pace. The program is designed to be completed in 18 months, but may be completed more quickly. Courses include: Fundamentals of Personal Financial Planning; Insurance and Employee Benefits; Investment Planning; Income Tax Planning; Planning for Retirement; Estate Planning; and Financial Planning Review Course. Tuition: $2,895 for entire program or $450/course. Financing options are available.

Personal Financial Planning (Certificate of Achievement), Metropolitan Community College, P.O. Box 3777, Omaha, NE 68103-0777, Tel: 800-228-9553 or 402-457-2400, Web: www.mccneb.edu

The Financial Planning certificate from Metropolitan Community College is designed to provide the student with practical experience in the fields of personal investment strategies related to retirement planning, estate planning, and tax-advantaged investments. Upon completion of the program, graduates are eligible to sit for the CFP® exam. The certificate consists of 49.5 credit hours, with 18 hours of general education courses (English, Math, and Social Sciences). The remaining credits are courses: Business Finance; Investments; Financial Planning Principles and Insurance; Investment Strategies and Portfolio Management; Income Tax Planning; Retirement Planning and Employee Benefits; and Estate Planning. Tuition: $33.50/credit for Nebraska residents; $48/credit hour for non-residents.

Professional Financial Planning Specialist Program, Professional Career Development Institute (PCDI), 430 Technology Parkway, Norcross, GA 30092-3406, Tel: 800-223-4542 or 770-729-8400, Web: www.pcdi-homestudy.com, E-mail: info@pcdi.com

The Professional Financial Planning Specialist program at PCDI is designed to help prepare students to do paraprofessional work in investment companies, banks, insurance companies, or corporations, or to be an assistant to Financial Planners. This course *does not* train for the specific career designation of Financial

Planner. Lessons include: The Financial Services Industry; What is Personal Financial Planning?; Money Management Strategy; Home and Auto Insurance; Health and Disability Insurance; Life Insurance; Income Tax Planning; Banking Services of Financial Institutions; Consumer Credit; Choosing a Source of Credit; Consumer Purchasing Strategies and Legal Protection; Finances of Housing; Investing Fundamentals; Investing in Stocks; Investing in Bonds; Investing in Mutual Funds; Real Estate and Other Investments; Retirement Planning; and Estate Planning. Course Fee: $689.

For More Information...

Books

How to Become a Successful Financial Consultant, by Jim Ainsworth (John Wiley & Sons, 1997).

Getting Started in Financial Consulting, by Edward Stone (John Wiley & Sons, 2000).

Getting Started as a Financial Planner, by Jeffrey Rattiner (Bloomberg Press, 2000).

Organizations

Certified Financial Planner Board of Standards, Inc., 1700 Broadway, Suite 2100, Denver, CO 80290, Tel: 800-487-1497 or 303-830-7500, Web: www.cfp-board.org, E-mail: mail@cfp-board.org.

International Association of Registered Financial Consultants (IARFC), The Financial Planners Bldg., P.O. Box 42506, Middletown, OH 45042-0506, Web: www.iarfc.org, E-mail: director@iarfc.org.

The Financial Planning Association (FPA), 5775 Glenridge Drive NE, Suite B-300, Atlanta, GA 30328 Tel: 800-322-4237, Web: www.fpanet.org.

National Association of Personal Financial Advisors (NAPFA), 3250 North Arlington Heights Road, Suite 109, Arlington Heights, IL 60004, Tel: 800-366-2732, Web: www.napfa.org, E-mail: info@napfa.org.

Society of Financial Service Professionals (SFSP), 270 S. Bryn Mawr Avenue, Bryn Mawr, PA 19010-2195, Tel: 610-526-2500, Web: www.financialpro.org.

Association for Financial Counseling and Planning Education, 2121 Arlington Ave., Suite 5, Upper Arlington, OH 43221-4339, Tel: 614-485-9650 Web: www.afcpe.org.

www.smartmoney.com—dow jones info

www.consumerreports.org—*Consumer Reports*

www.businessweek.com—*BusinessWeek* Online

Gift Basket Business

When you think about home business, you can't help but think of a gift basket business. Is everyone doing it? Seems like it, but there *is* a huge market out there—people love giving gift baskets. The gift basket industry is a $2.8-billion dollar industry! (*Entrepreneur* magazine, 2001).

I think particular opportunities exist in specialty gift baskets—something unique. See "Web Sites" below for some examples of some gift basket retailers who have made their services something special. There are a wide range of programs here too. They vary in the type of gift basket business they will teach you, first of all. Then, some offer only videos that teach you how to assemble a gift basket, and others provide a turn-key business system with affiliation with their company and logos. Do your research before investing any money in these programs. Some of these educational materials were developed by gift basket entrepreneurs them-selves, and will vary with the amount of help and support they give you.

At-Home Training Programs

The Basket Connection, 20959 S. Springwater Road, Estacada, OR 97023, Tel: 503-631-7288, Web: www.thebasketconnectioninc.com, E-mail: info@ thebasketconnectioninc.com

The Basket Connection is a company that helps people begin businesses in the basket industry. They offer complete business plan packages that include every-thing you need to start and run your own basket and gift basket business. They also offer ongoing consulting and a client Web site. Joanne Winthrop is the founder of the company, as has even been featured on the *Oprah Winfrey* show. The Basket Connection is also the only gift basket company endorsed by the Mother's Home Business Network (www.homeworkingmom.com). Joanne has different packages for different budgets.

The Value Package includes demonstration videos (Start-up video; Booking Home Parties; Gift Basket videos 1 & 2; and *Bowdabra Bow Making* video), the *Basket Training Manual*, the *Gift Basket Guide, Gift Basket Supply Manual, Gift*

Basket trade magazine, a Value Basket Kit, a Gift Basket Starter Kit, subscription to their quarterly newsletter, TBC Client-Only Web-site access, and 3 years of unlimited support and consultation. Value Package: $3,495. They also offer financing with a down payment of $1,000. The Professional Package includes all of the above, plus some extra videos, a Professional Basket Kit, and Professional Gift Basket Kit. Professional Package: $5,495. Financing available on this package with $3,500 down. A free video and information pack are available for both packages.

The Gift Basket Mentor, Inc., 3035 S. Elmira Court, Denver, CO 80231, Tel: 800-431-4510, Web: www.giftbasketmentor.com, E-mail: rita@giftbasketmentor.com

Rita Wilhelm has packaged together a bunch of supplies and educational tools to learn the basket industry. She offers the Gift Basket Business Start-Up Kit, which includes: The BowDabra bow-making tool, two-speed heat gun, shrink wrap, *The Key to Success Operations Manual,* the *Six Week Success Guide,* instructional videos (*Designing Beautiful Baskets* and *Corporate Sales* video), a list of wholesale suppliers, and professional consultation. Option 1 (full kit): $349. Option 2 (manuals and videos only): $249.

GiftBaskets 101, Tel: 800-700-7940, Web: www.giftbaskets101.com, E-mail: info@giftbaskets101.com

This gift basket package was created by Lucy Hicks, a 15-year veteran gift basket entrepreneur. It includes three books: *Gift Baskets 101, Gift Baskets 201: Advanced Marketing Concepts,* and *Gift Basket Supply Resource Directory.* Also included is the Gift Baskets 101 instructional video and 17 marketing flyer templates on CD-ROM. Topics included in the books and video include: standardizing your inventory; printed materials; pricing guidelines; mechanics; how to identify your target market; how to reach decision makers; and how to design a gift basket from start to finish. Gift Basket Business Package: $199.

BasketBusiness.com, Newport Media, 2973 Harbor Blvd., Suite 641, Costa Mesa, CA 92626, Web: www.basketbusiness.com, E-mail: newportmedia949@yahoo.com

Ron and Tara Perkins founded Newport Media in 1989, when the company published the first edition of *How to Find Your Treasure in a Gift Basket* start-up manual. Their special "Intro Pack" includes the manual, plus two instructional videos. The manual teaches all the do's and don'ts of setting up your company, and how to build a solid base of repeat business. It also includes an extensive directory of suppliers, a detailed description of theme baskets, tips on how to price baskets, and ways to promote your gift basket service. Intro Pack: $39.95.

> "Imagination is more important
> than knowledge."—Albert Einstein

Sweet Florals, 3936 S. Semoran Blvd., Suite 1308, Orlando, FL 32822, Tel: 800-693-1662, Web: www.sweetflorals.com, E-mail: sales@sweetflorals.com

Sweet Florals offers a unique take on the gift basket industry. This company teaches you how to make and sell "candy bouquets," decorative gifts of candy and florals. They have several packages, depending on your budget. Package I, the Online Biz Kit, is their entry level offering, and includes an online tutorial manual, authorized merchant list, online business marketing guide, online recipe guide, online color catalog, and ad samples. Package I is only $45.

Package II, the Starter Kit, adds many supplies to the mix. It includes supplies for 50 different bouquets, a Business Marketing Guide, an assortment of artificial SweetFloral Bouquets, and a Floral Wholesale List. Package II: $999. Package III, the Standard, adds bouquet kits, brochures, and business cards for $2,595. And the Premium Kit, Package IV, is their "ultimate e-business solution." It includes everything from the Standard Package with an e-commerce ready Web Site for $7,995.

***Gift Basket Review* magazine training videos, Festivities Publications, Inc., 815 Haines Street, Jacksonville, FL 32206, Tel: 800-729-6338, Web: www. festivities pub.com**

Gift Basket Review magazine offers a learning library of resources for gift basket entrepreneurs. Books include: *The National Gift Basket Design Book, The Best of Holiday Gift Baskets, Building a Better Gift Basket Business*, and *Guide to Corporate Sales*. Videos include: *The 4 Basic Building Methods; Five Ways to Make a Better Basket; Cheaper, Better, Faster Basket Mechanics; Efficiency Parking; Make-in-a-Minute Gift Baskets;* and *Publicity Power.* Books range in price from $9.95-$29.95 each. Each video is $39.95.

Le Gourmet Gift Basket Inc., 723 Anderson Street, Castle Rock CO. 80104, Tel: 800-93-GIFT-6 or 303-623-0500, Web: www.legift.com, E-mail: Cynthia@ legift.com

Cynthia McKay began Le Gourmet Gift Basket, Inc. as a small home-based business in Denver, Colorado in 1992. Since then, she has expanded the company across several states with 410 operating distributorships. Le Gourmet Gift Basket, Inc. teaches you the artistic ability and creativity you will need to begin a successful gift basket business. They do not charge any royalty fees after the one-time start-up fee, and the package includes full-time, continuous support. Once they have helped you obtain a business license, they then set you up with the tools of the trade and give you step-by-step instructions in setting up your business, marketing techniques, and basket assembly. They have a variety of business deals with UPS®, delivery services, credit card suppliers, equipment rentals, and gift basket products all on your behalf. In addition to gift baskets, they will show you how to market flowers and balloon arrangements, as well as specialty baskets for the new car owner, pet owner, real estate professionals, and others.

For a one-time fee of $3,995, you get: a comprehensive manual on how to successfully run your business from your home, storefront, or warehouse, and how to achieve the highest possible profit margin; a complete list of wholesalers across the nation who will deliver (at their cost) to your home; brochures to immediately market your new company; flyers for all holidays and specials throughout the year; updates on newly negotiated buys, designs and new marketing techniques; all order forms, stationery formats, gift card formats; and much more. Don't forget to check out *The Business of Gift Baskets: A Guide for Survival* by Cynthia McKay (See "Books," below).

Sweet Survival, P.O. Box 31, River Street Station, Paterson, NJ 07544, Tel: 973-279-2799, Web: www.giftbasketbusiness.com/startkit.htm or www.sweetsurvival. com, E-mail: questions@sweetsurvival.com

Shirley Frazier, author of *How to Start a Home-Based Gift Basket Business* (see "Books," below) offers a start-up kit for gift basket entrepreneurs, as well as a lot of nice information about conventions and classes around the country. The Gift Basket Starter Kit contains everything you need to create your first basket: one medium/large basket; six food/beverage products; one Sahara foam brick; one sheet tissue paper and newspaper section; one bow and yards of curling ribbon; one basket bag; enhancements (star spray and flowers); shred; one roll of transparent tape; and step-by-step instructions with pictures and text. Cost: $75. Shirley also sells instructional videotapes, books, reports, directories, and even an article, "How and Where to Find Gift Basket Classes," for $5.

A Guide to Making Money with Gift Baskets, Online Class from BizyMoms, Web: www.bizymoms.com, E-mail: birwin56@frontiernet.net

This online class from BizyMoms.com is taught by Bonnie Irwin-Pocock, owner of Baskets and More (www.bonniesbasketsandmore.com). The 4-week class will guide you through the process of starting and running your own business. You will learn: how to set up a work area in your home; how to select baskets and practical products using the *Wholesale and Reference Guide*; design and create themed gift baskets; and the tools to help your business succeed. Questions about the class can be e-mailed to Bonnie at birwin56@frontiernet.net. Cost: $60.

For More Information…

Books

How to Start a Home-Based Gift Basket Business, by Shirley Frazier (Globe Pequot Press, 1998).

The Business of Gift Baskets: A Guide for Survival, by Cynthia McKay and Carol Dorris (1601 S. Holdings Inc., 1998).

Start and Run a Gift Basket Business, by Mardi Foster-Walker (Self Counsel Press, 2000).

How to Start a Gift Basket Service: Your Step-by-Step Guide to Success, by Jacquelyn Lynn and *Entrepreneur* magazine (Entrepreneur Media, Inc., 2003).

The Business of Gift Baskets: How to Make a Profit Working from Home, by Camille Anderson (Camille Anderson, 1993).

Organizations

Gift Basket Professionals Network (GBPN), 446 South Anaheim Hills Road, Suite 167, Anaheim Hills, CA 92807, Tel: 714-254-7891, Web: www.giftbasketbusiness. org, E-mail: giftsbyj9@msn.com.

Gift Association of America, 172 White Pine Way, Harleysville, PA 19438-2851, Tel: 610-584-3108, Web: www.giftassn.com.

National Specialty Gift Association (NSGA), 7238 Bucks Ford Drive, Riverview, FL 33569, Tel: 813-671-4757, Web: www.giftprofessionals.com, E-mail: nsga@giftprofessionals.com.

Web Sites

www.locategiftbaskets.com—directory of gift basket retailers

www.fantastic-baskets.com—directory of gift basket retailers

www.autumnwinds.com—Gift Basket Exchange and Gift Basket Resource Center

www.festivities-pub.com—*Gift Basket Review* magazine

www.giftline.com—*GiftwareBusiness* magazine

www.surplus.net—wholesale supplies

www.wholesalecentral.com—wholesale supplies

www.basketbizhelp.com—tons of resources for the basket professional

www.baskware.com—software for the gift industry

www.giftbasketjubliee.com—the annual convention of *Gift Basket Review* magazine, with lots of classes to attend

Michelle's Favorite Gift Basket Sites:

www.thesmilebox.com

www.babybookbaskets.com

www.designerbaskets.com

www.cookiebouquet.com

Graphic Designer (*see also* Desktop Publisher)

Graphic design is a world beyond basic desktop publishing—where desktop publishing revolves basically around knowing different software, graphic design is the domain of the art-inclined. Not that you need to know how to draw—no. Graphic designers design everything from billboards to advertisements to letterhead to magazine covers to book jackets. Even candy bar wrappers are designed by a graphic designer. Graphic design has a strong art component to it, as well as an academic aspect to it—you need a degree to be taken seriously in this field.

A working knowledge of a variety of software is necessary to stay current in graphic design. Successful graphic designers have good design sense and fresh ideas, can interact easily with clients and associates, can handle stress, pay attention to detail, and understand the importance of meeting deadlines. Graphic designers charge anywhere from $10-$25 per hour. A typical day may include: project reviews; scheduling for the next day; updating a log of completed project tasks; preparing invoices for completed projects; returning calls and e-mail; working on project tasks; client meetings; subcontractor meetings; and computer system backups. This home career is computer-intensive, and you need to have a great computer and the required software. You may spend around $5,000 for the bare minimum equipment.

At-Home Training Programs

Graphic Design (Diploma, Associate degree, Bachelor degree), The Art Institute International (AII), 420 Boulevard of the Allies, Pittsburgh, PA 15219, Tel: 412-291-5100 or 877-872-8869, Web: www.aionline.edu, E-mail: aioadm@aii.edu

The Art Institute Online, a division of The Art Institute of Pittsburgh, offers three degrees in graphic design: a Diploma in digital design, and an Associate degree and a Bachelor degree in graphic design. In these programs, students develop an understanding of color and composition, design and typography, and drawing board skills. As they progress through the program, students are trained in creative problem solving and learn to offer solutions that are effective in the business world. By graduation, students in the graphic design programs have acquired the training and the portfolio necessary for entry-level positions in advertising agencies, design studios, publishing houses, and corporate communications departments. The digital design diploma teaches design fundamentals, typography, and graphic design in a six-week intensive format. The Associate degree is 105 credits; the Bachelor degree is 180 credits. Tuition: $1,135/course ($345/credit).

Foundations in Graphic Design (Undergraduate certificate) Academy of Art College, 79 New Montgomery Street, San Francisco, CA 94105, Tel: 800-544-ARTS or 415-274-2200, Web: www.academyart.edu, E-mail: info@academyart.edu

The Foundations in Graphic Design Professional Certificate of Continuing Education is for students interested in acquiring a basis of knowledge and skills necessary to the graphic designer. The certificate requires completion of 8 undergraduate courses (24 credits) in graphic design, including: Sketching for Communication; Color and Design; Materials, Tools, and Comping Techniques; Fundamentals of Graphic Design; Typography I; Digital Design I; Digital Tools I; and Digital Tools II. The school also has a bunch of program in Computer Arts, specializing in animation, 3D modeling, games, and more. Tuition: $550/credit.

Professional Designation in Computer Graphics and Graphic Design (Undergraduate certificate), University of California, Los Angeles (UCLA), 10995 Le Conte Ave, Los Angeles, CA 90024-2883, Tel: 310-206-1422, Web: www.uclaextension.edu/visualarts, E-mail: visualarts@uclaextension.edu

The Professional Designation in Computer Graphics and Graphic Design from UCLA is streamlined and customizable, integrating multidisciplinary art training with exposure to internships, mentorships, presentation skills, and portfolio development. Participants in the program can complete the course sequences by following either a two- or three-year plan. Students can begin the program during any quarter throughout the year. Course include: Drawing I; Production; Color; Design I, II & III; Typography I; Design History; Animation I; Multimedia I; Photoshop I; Illustrator I; QuarkXPress; Dreamweaver I; Flash I; Design Project Management; Specialization courses; and a Final Project. Specialization courses can be chosen from across multiple disciplines, or may concentrate on an intensive series of courses. Tuition: $300-$500/course.

For More Information...

<u>Books</u>

Pocket Pal: A Graphic Arts Production Handbook (18th ed.), edited by Michael H. Bruno (GATFPress, 2000). Check www.charrette.com (art supply store) for a copy of this essential graphic design book.

The Business Side of Creativity: The Complete Guide for Running a Graphic Design or Communications Business, by Cameron Foote (W.W. Norton & Co., 2002).

Graphic Artist's Guild Handbook of Pricing and Ethical Guidelines (Graphic Artists Guild, 2001).

Starting Your Career as a Freelance Illustrator or Graphic Designer, by Michael Fleishman (Allworth Press, 2001).

AIGA Professional Practices in Graphic Design, by the American Institute of Graphic Arts (Allworth Press, 1997).

By Design: The Graphic Designer's Essential Handbook—A Gallery of Professional Design, Popular Techniques, and Designer's Templates, by Octogram Publishing (Hearst Books, 2001).

2004 Artist's & Graphic Designer's Market, by Mary Cox (F&W Publications, 2003).

<u>Organizations</u>

Graphic Artists Guild, 90 John Street, Suite 403, New York, NY 10038-3202, Tel: 212-791-3400, Web: www.gag.org.

American Institute of Graphic Arts (AIGA), 164 Fifth Ave, New York, NY 10010, Tel: 212-807-1990, Web: www.aiga.org, E-mail: comments@aiga.org.

<u>Web Sites</u>

www.elance.com and www.creativemoonlighter.com—freelance opportunities

www.commarts.com—*Communication Arts* magazine

www.graphic-design.com—Design & Publishing Center

www.robinsdesign.com—a graphic designer who added *lots* of start-up information on her site

Home Inspector

If you ever bought or sold a house, you know what a home inspector is: a professional with a broad range of skills who inspects homes for sale and lets the potential buyers know what may need work in the house. If you're handy around the house and enjoy helping people, home inspection may be a good career for you. Home inspections are in constant demand, as are trained, experienced, and qualified home inspectors.

Home inspectors can operate out of their home, and a majority of their clients are homebuyers, but banks and realty companies also need their services. To get started, you need some basic inspection and testing tools ($200-$275), business cards, and a business phone line. As in any field, experience helps, but some of the most experienced engineers and construction people don't make good home inspectors. You need the ability to be meticulous and consistent while inspecting and report writing, to make judgment calls, handle people, and be able to communicate effectively verbally and in writing.

Home inspection is still a fairly small and new field, so you should watch for state legislation on licensing and regulation of home inspectors. Sooner or later, all states will require licensing, certification, or regulation. *The Occupational Outlook Handbook* (Jist Works, 2003) projects "above average growth" for inspectors through the year 2005 and beyond.

At-Home Training Programs

Carson Dunlop, 120 Carlton Street, Suite 407, Toronto, Ontario, Canada M5A 4K2, Tel: 800-268-7070, Web: www.carsondunlop.com, E-mail: hss@carsondunlop.com

Carson Dunlop has a 28-page brochure about their home inspection program that you can download from their Web site in PDF (Adobe Acrobat) format. The course system contains 10 modules, each of which features between 250 and 500 pages of course text and up to 250 illustrations. Each module also contains detailed study instructions to walk students through the steps necessary to complete each section. Module topics include: roofing; electrical; structure; heating; air conditioning and heat pumps; plumbing; exterior; insulation; interior; and communications and professional practice. Field exercises in each module direct students to visit and inspect local homes, which enables them to relate what they have just learned to real-world experience. The course also includes nine video training tapes that contain hundreds of real-world inspection scenes, narrated by professional home inspectors. Each section within the modules end with a multiple-choice exam that determines whether or not the student has mastered the material and is ready to move on. Upon completion of the program, graduates earn a certificate of completion. Course fee: $2,995 for home inspection training with technical support; $2,495 for training without technical support. Individual modules are available from $75-$400 each.

HomePro Systems, Inc., 2841 Harland Road, Suite 201, Falls Church, VA 22043, Tel: 800-HOME-PRO or 703-560-4663, Web: www.home-pro.com

HomePro Systems, Inc. offers a correspondence course in home inspection. You can study all the components of home inspection, or select any subject area to study. The course includes books, 19 hours of video, CD-ROMS, and computer testing software and is broken down into these components: structures; mechanical systems; electrical & plumbing; interiors; exteriors; and business administration. Course fee: $2,995. Books and videos only: $1,214.

Inspection Training Associates (ITA), 1016 S. Tremont Street, Oceanside, CA 92054-5051, Tel: 800-323-9235, Web: www.home-inspect.com, E-mail: ita@ home-inspect.com

ITA's correspondence course has been designed to aid home inspectors in their quest for information and training. The course has been tailored from their in-depth 11-day school, using the same curriculum and study materials, plus additional videotapes. It consists of 11 modules: The Home Inspection Business; Inspection Techniques; Foundations and Structures; Exteriors; Roofs; Building Codes; Plumbing; Electrical; Heating; Interior and Insulation; and Air Conditioning and Heat Pumps. You can study at your own pace and order each module as required, or order them all at once and save $300. The modules are designed to be completed one at a time. Textbooks, study guides, and tests are parceled with each corresponding module, along with detailed instructions on how to work through each module. Upon completion and upon request, students receive the Final Exam on floppy disk, a full "Matrix" Inspection Report Form set, and a Report Field Folder. After your final exam is graded, you receive a certificate of completion. Course fee: $1,495 for modules purchased separately; $1,195 to purchase all modules at once.

"There's no place like home."
—Dorothy, *The Wizard of Oz*

HE School of Building Inspection, P.O. Box 1986, Salt Lake City, UT 84110, Tel: 888-466-4677, Web: www.hometraining.com

HE School of Building Inspection offers a 4-Point Package that includes their Jump Start™ Video Training Series, 500-page manual, two exams—one covering the videos and the other covering the manual. The videos cover: heating, ventilation and air conditioning; structures; home inspector liability; electrical; plumbing;

exteriors; basic roof evaluation; inspection procedures; advanced roof evaluation; steam, hot water and oil fired heating; and wood destroying insects and organisms. The video training exposes the student to close to 2,000 building evaluation scenes. The manual provides detailed information on these topics, designed to be used in tandem with the videos. HE also offers a "6-Day Live Course on Video," where you will see hands-on exercises, see in-the-field training, hear pertinent lecture topics, and listen to Q&As. Four-Point Package: $599. Six Days of Video: $1,145. Or you can purchase the Six Days of Videos plus the Four-Point Home Study Package for $1,495.

Accu-Spect Home Inspector Institute, 95 Keddy Blvd., Chicopee, MA 01020-3919, Tel: 800-233-2758, Web: www.accuspect.net

Accu-Spect has been training home inspectors since 1985. They primarily use videotapes to teach in this program. The program consists of 11 videos, a printed manual, CD-ROMs, unlimited tech support, home inspector tips, and a marketing package. Videos may be purchased individually and run from $50-$170 each. Video topics include: Conducting a Home Inspection; Inspection Terminology; Probing Specific Areas & Visual Accessibility; Pre-Inspection Contract & Disclaimer; Tools for Conducting a Home Inspection; Electrical; Common & Uncommon Defects; Plumbing; Heating; Understanding Structural Components; and Sea Walls & Retaining Walls. When purchasing this program, Accu Spect offers $50 off your NAHI (see "Organizations," below) membership fee. Plus, once you join NAHI, you can also earn 20 NAHI continuing education credits. An Accu-Spect certificate of completion is available when the full series is purchased and you pass the test. Total program: $975.

Building Specs Inc. Inspection Systems, 423 Thompson Creek Road, Stevensville, MD 21666, Tel: 800-217-7979 or 410-604-2700, Web: www.buildingspecs.com, E-mail: info@buildingspecs.com

The Building Specs Home Study Course manual covers every aspect of home inspection, and comprehensive checklists make sure you are retaining what you read. Also included are a report writing critique, sales and marketing tips and information, and environmental concerns. *The Building Specs Inc. Training Manual, Code Check Reference Book*, and *Trouble Shooters Guide to Residential Construction.* Course fee: $395.

Courses in Home Inspection, National Institute of Building Inspectors® (NIBI), 424 Vosseller Ave, Bound Brook, NJ 08805, Tel: 888-281-6424, Web: www.nibi.com/online, E-mail: info@nibi.com

NIBI's online courses in home inspection are designed to provide access to a compendium of information and resources related to residential construction and home inspections. Students can use this information to prepare for a career in home inspections or related fields. The same course material also provides continuing education credits for ASHI (see "Organizations" below). Courses change routinely, but classes have included: Roofing Systems; Plumbing Systems; Hot-Water Supply Systems; Exterior Elements; Interior Elements; Cooling Systems; Structure; Electrical Systems; Heating Systems; and Introduction to Home Inspection. Courses range in price from $50-$150 each.

> "A man builds a fine house; and now he has a master, and a task for life; he is to furnish, watch, show it, and keep it in repair, the rest of his days."—Ralph Waldo Emerson

Home Inspection Course, Allied Business Schools, 22952 Alcalde Drive, Laguna Hills CA 92653, Tel: 888-501-7686, Web: www.alliedschools.com, E-mail: allied@alliedschools.com

Allied's Home Inspection Course is available online or through traditional correspondence. The course has 13 comprehensive lessons which provide instruction on: Establishing a Business; The Inspection Representative; Soils and Foundations; Wood and Construction; Roofing; Plumbing; Electricity; Heating and Ventilation; Air Conditioning and Heat Pumps; Appliances; Swimming Pools and Spas; Termites and Wood Destroying Insects; and Environmental Considerations. In addition to the textbook, students inspect their own homes and fill out an inspection report based on findings. Also included "Real Homes—Real Inspections" video, Porter Valley Software's Inspect Vue R3 demo software, inspection mirror, clipboard, lead paint test kit, mechanical pencil and a special report on starting your own business. Course fee: $688.

Home Inspector Course, Education Direct, 925 Oak Street, Scranton, PA 18515, Tel: 800-275-4410, Web: www.educationdirect.com, E-mail: info@educationdirect.com

The Home Inspector Course at Education Direct teaches: Inspection Standards; Interior, Exterior, and Structure Inspection; Heating and Air Conditioning; and Starting a Home Inspection Business. Also included in the program are tools, such as wire gauges, a circuit analyzer, pocket caliper, a tape measure, a four-in-one screwdriver, an awl, and a pair of professional quality binoculars. Course fee: $489.

Professional Home Inspection Program, Professional Career Development Institute (PCDI), 430 Technology Parkway, Norcross, GA 30092-3406, Tel:

800-223-4542 or 770-729-8400, Web: www.pcdi-homestudy.com, E-mail: info@pcdi.com

PCDI's Professional Home Inspection Program consists of 16 lessons: Roofs; Roof-Mounted Structures; Paved Areas, Lots, and Landscaping; Walls, Windows, and Doors; Garages; Wood-Destroying Insects and Rot; Attics and Interior Rooms; Basements and Crawl Spaces; The Electrical System; Domestic Water Heaters; Air Conditioners; Energy Considerations; Environmental Concerns; Plumbing Systems; and Heating Systems Part I and II. As part of the program, you receive a 12-page inspector's checklist and a starter kit of inspection tools, including an awl, 25-foot measuring tape, dial thermometer, circuit tester, penlight, and screwdriver set. Course fee: $689.

For More Information...

Books

Become a Home Inspector! by Michael Pompeii (Pompeii Publications, 2001).

How to Start a Home Inspection Service: Your Step-by-Step Guide to Success, by Claire Gunther and *Entrepreneur* magazine (Entrepreneur Media, Inc., 2003).

Home Inspection Business from A to Z, by Guy Cozzi (Nemmar Real Estate Training, 2002).

Organizations

American Society of Home Inspectors (ASHI), 932 Lee Street, Suite 101, Des Plaines, IL 60016, Tel: 847-759-2835, Web: www.ashi.com.

National Association of Home Inspectors (NAHI), 4248 Park Glen Road, Minneapolis, MN 55416, Tel: 952-928-4641 or 800-448-3942, Web: www.nahi.org, E-mail: info@nahi.org.

The Housing Inspection Foundation (HIF), 1224 North Nokomis NE, Alexandria, MN 56308, Tel: 320-763-6350, Web: http://www.iami.org/hif.html, E-mail: hif@iami.org.

Web Sites

www.hmteam.com—The Home Team Inspection Service, franchise opportunity

www.housemaster.com—HouseMaster, franchise opportunity

www.wini.com—World Inspection Network, franchise opportunity

www.inspectionworld.com—AHSI's annual convention

Image Consultant

Did you see that Disney movie, *The Kid* with Bruce Willis? His character was an image consultant! An image consultant is a person who specializes in visual appearance and verbal and non-verbal communication. An image consultant counsels individual and corporate clients on appearance, behavior, and communication skills through consultations, coaching, presentations, seminars, and workshops. Services in visual appearance would include body and color analysis, wardrobe development and management, and personal shopping. Behavior and communication skills they teach include social etiquette skills. In short, an image consultant can help clients look, sound, and interact more effectively with those around them so that they can achieve their specific personal or professional goals with authenticity, credibility, and confidence.

> ### "I'm going to be a lady if it kills me."
> —Jean Harlow in *Dinner at Eight*, 1933

Image consultants come from a variety of backgrounds. Many specialize in a particular field of image consulting. Some are color specialists, others wardrobe specialists. There are even fashion feng shui specialists! People attracted to this profession are usually artistic, business-oriented, entrepreneurial, self-starters, helpers to others, have a good professional image, are confident, persuasive, convincing, and are sales-oriented. Image consulting has been identified as one of the top home-based professions for the new millennium—probably because it's in demand, but not many people know how to become one. Image consultants are employed by a variety of clients—from business executives to movie stars—who want to put their best foot forward. A great place to start is here: *The Perfect Fit: How to Start an Image Consulting Business,* by Lynne Henderson Marks and Dominique Isbecque (FirstPublish LLC, 2001).

At-Home Training Programs

The Image Maker Inc., Dr. Joyce Knudson, AICI Master, 348 Cool Springs Blvd., Franklin, TN 37067, Tel: 888-845-5600 or 615-309-8168, Web: www.imagemaker1.com, E-mail: joyce@imagemaker1.com

The home study program from The Image Maker, Dr. Joyce Knudson, is designed for the learner who wants to enter the image profession and learn from a mentor/coach with the advantage of individual personal attention. Dr. Joyce Knudson was the first ever in the history of the AICI (see "Organizations" below) to receive the highest achievement in the image industry—Master Status Distinction. The program is self-paced through telephone, fax, e-mail, or mail. Subjects covered include: fashion & style; wardrobe basics; makeup & skin care; figure analysis; color analysis; nonverbal communication; business strategic planning; consulting; etiquette, posture & poise; speech presentation; voice & diction; marketing promotion; seminar production; and business casual. Also included is "How to Do a Color Analysis and Makeover" video tape, two revised and updated *From Head to Soul* books, an audio tape series, a 200-page manual, unlimited mentoring during after your course is completed, and a certificate from The ImageMaker, Inc., signed by Dr. Knudsen. Course fee: $2,700 available in three payments.

"Beauty is how you feel inside, and it reflects in your eyes. It is not something physical."—Sophia Loren

Color Profiles, Ltd. dba Lindquist Associates, 3011 South Josephine Street, Denver, CO 80210, Tel: 303-759-8471, Web: www.lindquistassociates.com, E-mail: debra@lindquistassociates.com

Debra Lindquist, AICI, CIP, principal of Lindquist Associates, is the owner and innovator of Color Profiles, Ltd., a sophisticated color system created in 1974. She offers classes to trainees so that they can learn at home working at their own pace, with one-on-one attention from Debra. Debra is a professional member of the Association of Image Consultants International (AICI), and has been an image consultant for more than thirty years. She has a B.S. degree from Iowa State University with emphasis on clothing and art, and an M.S. degree from Ball State University in education. The home study course is divided into four modules. A certificate of completion is issued for each module completed.

Module one explores the concepts of color theory. Actual color selections are made for photographs of people with an emphasis upon choosing skin tones and appropriate red hues. In module two, students build upon their initial color selections by exploring the relationships of eye and hair color to the color selection process. In module three students learn how intuitive judgments and the psychological aspects of color can impact the process of making color choices for clients. And module four covers design elements and design principles and their application to creating wardrobes. Course fee: $500-$2,500 depending upon number of completed modules.

Image Resource Group, Inc., 7804 Wincanton Court, Falls Church, VA 22043, Tel: 703-560-3950, Web: www.professionalimagedress.com, E-mail: info@professionalimagedress.com

A complete program of consultant materials is available from Image Resource Group that allows you to plan and teach business etiquette seminars and presentations. The program includes a manual, masters for handouts, a sample workbook, and 40 slides on body language and dining etiquette. Also available is "How to Teach a Seminar" audiocassette album and workbook, 6 audiotapes and a 50-page workbook. Cost: $125.

For More Information...

Books

The Perfect Fit: How to Start an Image Consulting Business, by Lynne Henderson Marks and Dominique Isbecque (FirstPublish LLC, 2001).

The New Professional Image: From Business Casual to the Ultimate Power Look, by Susan Bixler (Adams Media Corp., 1997).

5 Steps to Professional Presence, by Susan Bixler and Lisa Scherrer (Adams Media Corp., 2000).

Color with Style, by Donna Fujii (Graphic-Sha Publishing, 1992).

Triumph of Individual Style: A Guide to Dressing Your Body, Your Beauty, Yourself, by Carla Mathis (Fairchild, 2002).

Business Etiquette Mastery: The Power of Executive Leadership, by Joli Andre (Polished Professionals, 1997).

40 Over 40: 40 Things Every Woman Over 40 Needs to Know About Getting Dressed, by Brenda Kinsel (Wildcat Canyon Press, 2000).

In the Dressing Room with Brenda, by Brenda Kinsel (Wildcat Canyon Press, 2001).

The Ultimate Plus-Size Modeling Guide, by Catherine Schuller (Emerging Visions Enterprise, 1997).

Image Matters! First Steps on the Journey to Your Best Self, by Lauren Solomon (E-Squared Publications, 2002).

Organizations

Association of Image Consultants International (AICI), 12300 Ford Road, Suite 135, Dallas, TX 75234, Tel: 972-755-1503, Web: www.aici.org, E-mail: info@aici.org .

Colour Designers International, 1035 Minnesota Ave. Suite D, San Jose, CA 95110, Tel: 408-920-8025, Web: www.colourdesigners.org, E-mail: abrie@ix.netcom.com.

Web Sites

www.fit.edu—Fashion Institute of Technology, check out their in-person certificate in image management

www.donnafujii.com—Donna Fujii Institute, offering in-person training by Donna Fujii, author of *Color with Style*

www.carlamathis.com—The ColorStyle Institute, training by Carla Mathis, author of *Triumph of Individual Style*

www.londonimageinstitute.com—London Image Institute, training by Lynne Marks in New York and Atlanta

www.conselle.com—Conselle Institute of Image Mangement

Indexer

Indexers are growing in demand—from indexing books to Web sites. Book indexers usually work as freelance contractors for publishing houses to create the indexes for their books. It requires attention to detail, analytical skills, and a love of books. Indexers must have an instinct for how people will seek out material so they can create user-friendly indexes. The best place to find out about indexing is the American Society of Indexers (www.asindexing.com), which offers an abundance of informational materials, local chapters, and conducts professional development workshops, in addition to an annual convention. In general, indexers usually charge from $3 to $5 per printed book page they read to produce the index, or from $20 to $50 per hour. Additional opportunities exist for indexers of documentation and Web sites, who may get a higher hourly rate.

Traditionally, book indexing has a fast turnaround. Indexes are the last part of the book to be created, and often are needed to be done quickly, especially if the publishing house is running behind schedule. So, in addition to being analytical and detail-oriented, indexers need to be flexible and able to work on a tight deadline. And because freelancers do all back-of-book indexing, to start your business you need to be able to network with publishing houses and book packagers and have a strong drive to market and promote yourself.

At-Home Training Programs

Book Indexing Postal Tutorials (BIPT), The Lodge, Sidmount Avenue, Moffat, Scotland DG10 9BS, Tel: 011-44-01683-220440, Web: www.lodge-moffat. co.uk/bipt.htm/, E-mail: bipt@lodge-moffat.co.uk

BIPT is a practical course, consisting of five tutorials involving the compilation of indexes to short texts, chosen to represent most of the problems an indexer is likely to meet. A sixth optional tutorial is the creative of an index to a complete book. The first tutorial with booklets costs 60 UK pounds. If you decide to continue, the remaining four tutorials cost 150 UK pounds. (Due to high airmail costs, students from the U.S., Canada, and Australia pay 68 UK pounds for Tutorial 1 and booklets and 175 UK pounds for Tutorials 2-5.) For U.S. and Canadian students, you must make payments in British currency—you can call Ruesch International at 800-424-2923 to order a sterling cheque made payable to Ann Hall. There will be a fee per check. Also, double check the amount of sterling to pay her—e-mail Ann (bipt@lodge-moffat.co.uk) to verify course fees before you order the cheque. Ruesch International also has branches in New York, Los Angeles, Chicago, Atlanta, and Boston.

USDA Graduate School Correspondence Program, Room 1112S, 14th and Independence Avenue, Washington, D.C. 20250; (888) 744-GRAD, (202) 314-3670; Web: http://grad.usda.gov, E-mail: selfpaced@grad.usda.gov.

The USDA Graduate School offers two paper-based courses, *Basic Indexing* and *Applied Indexing*. *Basic Indexing* offers 12 lessons focusing on back-of-the-book indexing techniques and covers the style of the University of Chicago Press, the most common style used by U.S. publishers. In addition to topics such as alphabetizing, headings, and index preparation methods, the course also covers current information regarding the use of computers and allows the student hands-on training in actual index design. Course fee: $300.

Applied Indexing offers 12 lessons focusing on simulating the indexing experience as closely as possible, but in a learning environment. Students will learn how to analyze a book index, edit a first-draft index, and apply indexing and business principles to project-related situations that working indexers encounter (proposing and justifying bids, submitting invoices, estimating length of time for specific projects, producing indexes to size requirements, handling misrepresented projects, treating special problems in indexes, and designing indexes that satisfy readers and publishers). Students will practice on a variety of different kinds of nonfiction books. *Basic Indexing* is a prerequisite. Course fee: $300.

"I find that a great part of the information I have
was acquired by looking up something and
finding something else on the way."—Franklin P. Adams

Web Indexing Course, Broccoli Information Management, 735 Willet Ave, Suite 206, E. Providence, RI 02915, Tel: 877-205-9259, Web: www.bim.net, E-mail: broccoli@bim.net

Broccoli Information Management offers Web-based training in indexing of Web and intranet documents. Kevin Broccoli, President of Broccoli Information Management, who has written indexes for magazines, books, and Web sites, teaches the course. The course, *Web Site Indexing*, is for freelance indexers, in-house indexers, technical writers with indexing experience, and online help authors with indexing experience, because it assumes that you already have a basic knowledge of HTML. If you do not know how to create a simple Web site, you can take *Web Site Indexing with HTML Primer* (see Web site for details).

The course spans 11 weeks with approximately 1-2 hours of work per week. You will learn how to create indexes for Web site pages in a variety of formats, how to use Web site indexing software, and how to market your services. Web indexing is quite different from indexing books, and other topics will cover hand coding, Web site indexing tools, applying search engine technology to human indexing, and getting work as a Web Indexer. The course is not an online book; rather, it follows a timeline over the 11 weeks, in which you can practice the skills you learn, as well as submit practice assignments to the instructor. A course discussion board is available for questions and answers. Unlike book indexing, Web site indexing does not have an established set of rules and guidelines. In this course you are encouraged to brainstorm, be creative, and think of alternative ways of doing things. Course fee: $250.

Back-of-the-Book Indexing Course, Susan Holbert Indexing Services, 24 Harris Street, Waltham, MA 02452-6105, Tel: 877-408-7299 or 781-893-0514, Web: www.abbington.com/holbert, E-mail: susan.h@rcn.com

A professional back-of-the-book indexer with 17 years of experience, Susan Holbert has produced a 5+ hour video entitled *How to Index Books: A Practical Workshop on Freelance Indexing*. The workshop contains information on how to index (with hand-on practice), how to find clients, how to market your services, how to negotiate fees, and descriptions of indexing software. The package includes the videotaped workshop (with a question and answer session), a 30-page course book, extensive class materials, sample resumes, software reviews, and networking information. Course fee: $159.

Training in Indexing, Society of Indexers, Blades Enterprise Centre, John Street, Sheffield S24SU UK, England, Tel: +44 (0) 114-292-2350, Web: www.indexers.org.uk, E-mail: admin@indexers.org.uk

The Society of Indexers offers a self-paced, open learning course leading to accreditation with the Society of Indexers in Great Britain. The five units cover documents, authors, users, and indexers; choice and form of entries; arrangement and presentation of indexes; information sources and reference tools; and the business of indexing. Tutorial support is available to members of the Society. Members also receive a substantial discount on the cost of the units. The 3rd edition of the course was being published in 2002 in both printed and electronic format. Each unit takes about 45-50 hours of study and is based on British and International Standard guidelines. Each unit costs between 40-60 UK pounds each, with discounts for members of the society. Contact admin@indexers.org.uk for payment options for U.S. students.

For More Information...

Books

Starting an Indexing Business—Second Edition, edited by Enid L. Zafran (Information Today, 1998).

Running Your Indexing Business, edited by Janet Perlman (Information Today, 2001).

Marketing Your Indexing Services—Second Edition, edited by Anne Leach, (Information Today, 1998).

Can You Recommend a Good Book on Indexing? by Bella Hass Weinberg (Information Today, 1998).

Beyond Book Indexing: How to Get Started in Web Indexing, Embedded Indexing, and Other Computer-Based Media, edited by Diane Brenner and Marilyn Rowland (Information Today, 2000).

Directory of Indexing and Abstracting Courses and Seminars, edited by Maryann Corbett, (Information Today, 1998).

Handbook of Indexing Techniques: A Guide for Beginning Indexers, by Linda K. Fetters (Fetters Information Management, 2001).

Indexing Books, by Nancy Mulvany (University of Chicago Press, 1994).

Organizations

American Society of Indexers (ASI), 10200 West 44th Ave, Suite 304, Wheat Ridge, CO 80033, Tel: 303-463-2887, Web: www.asindexing.org, E-mail: info@asindexing.org.

The Indexing and Abstracting Society of Canada, P.O. Box 664, Station P, Toronto, ON, Canada, M5S 2Y4, Web: www.indexingsociety.org.

The Society of Indexers in Britain, Blades Enterprise Centre, John Street, Sheffield S24SU UK, England, Tel: +44 (0) 114-292-2350, Web: www.indexers.org.uk, E-mail: admin@indexers.org.uk.

<u>Web Site</u>

http://groups.yahoo.com.group/IndexCafe—an unmoderated discussion group open to all indexers

Information Broker

Information brokering is a popular new field that has grown dramatically during the information explosion of the last 10 years. A growth in online databases, personal computers, and telecommunications technology with high-speed modems has made all kinds of information available right into your home office. There is also a growing market for information brokers due to the explosion of information—somebody has to filter through all this stuff for clients. Information is now an essential commodity.

> "No matter how cynical you get, it is
> impossible to keep up."—Lily Tomlin

Before pursuing an information brokering career, consider some of the financial costs of getting set up: various online databases charge for access to their servers, setting up a powerful home computer is a must, and of course, there are the skills you need to learn. Some traits helpful in this career are: creativity, an inclination to take calculated risks; the ability to define and implement goals; being aware and open to new business opportunities; and entrepreneurial skills. You need to have the drive to operate a small business and market and sell your services. You also need to develop skills in research, and be able to assist clients in finding solutions through the use of information. Liking research (and being good at it), as well as being comfortable with computers, are also helpful attributes. Special opportunities exist for people who specialize in certain topics.

At-Home Training Programs

Information Brokering Course, University of Maine-Augusta, 46 University Drive, Augusta, ME 04330-9410, Tel: 877-UMA-1234 or 207 621-3000, Web: www.uma.maine.edu, E-mail: lnit@maine.edu

The University of Maine-Augusta offers a 3-credit online information brokering course as part of Bachelor of Science in Library Science entitled *Information Brokering and Other Entrepreneurial Options for Library/Media Professionals* (LIB441). This course explores the creative side of the library career market. Utilizing the new technologies that are available to library professionals have made careers in the free enterprise system possible. Establishing a business plan and how to market yourself in the information age will be part of the class. Students will create a business plan that shows how they will merge the information age with the business community. Contact the Library and Information Science Coordinator, Jean Thomas, for more information at lnit@main.edu. Tuition: $114/credit for Maine residents; $277/credit for non-residents.

Information Brokering Program, MarketingBase Mentor, Tel: 800-544-5924 or 707-829-9421, Web: www.marketingbase.com, E-mail: amelia@marketingbase.com

Developed by a professional information broker, Amelia Kassel, the MarketingBase Mentor Program teaches market planning, marketing strategies, pricing, how to construct a search, what databases to use, and the essentials you need to get started in the information business. The program is tailored to your needs, based on your interests and strengths. Your assignments are reviewed on a personal basis using the same tools you need for information brokering via your computer and phone. Course topics include: Introduction and the Market; Information Brokers Definition; A Home-Based Business and a Small Business; A New and Exciting Career Opportunity; Online Databases; The Market for Information Brokers; The Value-Added Characteristic of Information Brokers; Services Offered by Information Brokers; Specialized Information Brokering Services; Earnings Capacity and Other Rewards; Education and Credentials; What about a Library Science Degree; Future Growth in Information Brokering; Start-up Needs/Costs; Online Database Training; Online Searching; Leading Online Database Vendors; Consumer-Oriented Online Services; Internet; Memberships; E-mail; Legal, Copyright, and Ethical Issues; How to Find Clients; The Market Plan; Marketing Strategies that Work; Industry Standards for Pricing; Setting Budgets; and Subcontracting. Amelia Kassel has a Master of Library Science and has been president and owner of MarketingBase, a successful information brokering company, since 1984. Course fee: $3,000.

For More Information...

<ins>Books</ins>

The Information Broker's Handbook (3rd edition), by Sue Rugge and Alfred Glossbrenner (McGraw-Hill, 1997).

Start Your Own Information Broker Service, by Y. Company Pfeiffer, Susan Rachmeler, and National Business Library (Pfeiffer & Co., 1995). This title is out of print, but check for used copies on amazon.com.

Sawyer's Survival Guide for Information Brokers, by Deborah Sawyer (Burnell Enterprises, 1995).

The Infopreneurs: Turning Data into Dollars, by H. Skip Weitzen (John Wiley & Sons, 1991).

Infopreneurs Online and Global: Taking the Hottest Business of the '90s into the 21st Century, by H. Skip Weitzen and Rick Parkhill (John Wiley & Sons, 1996).

<ins>Organizations</ins>

Association of Independent Information Professionals, Inc. (AIIP), 8550 United Plaza Blvd., Suite 1001, Baton Rouge, LA 70809, Tel: 225-408-4400, Web: www.aiip.org, E-mail: info@aiip.org.

The American Society for Information Science (ASIS), 1320 Fenwick Lane, Suite 510, Silver Spring, MD 20910, Tel: 301-495-0900, Web: www.asis.org.

Special Libraries Association (SLA), 1700 18th Street NW, Washington, D.C. 20009-2514, Tel: 202-234-4700, Web: www.sla.org, E-mail: sla@sla.org.

<ins>Web Sites</ins>

www.supersearchers.com—a growing collection of links to subject-specific Web resources recommended by leading online searchers

www.infotoday.com—Information Today, Inc.

www.batesinfo.com—links to search engines and databases, selected articles, and a newsletter

Interior Designer/Decorator

You know, even an interior designer's career options have exploded—one of my favorite shows is *Trading Spaces* on the cable channel TLC (neighbors trade a room in each other's home to redecorate with the help of an interior designer). But for most designers not on TV, it's all about making homes and businesses more comfortable, attractive, and functional for their clients. Interior designers need to be creative, imaginative and artistic. They also need to be disciplined, organized, and skilled business people.

There is a difference between an interior *designer* and an interior *decorator*. Interior designers are professionally trained in space planning. In 18 states, they must pass a strict exam and be licensed. While both designers and decorators are concerned with aesthetics, style, and mood, interior designers have comprehensive training and that includes an understanding of: space planning for public and private facilities; building codes; standards regarding the needs of disabled or elderly persons; ergonomics; lighting quality and quantity; and acoustics and sound transmission. An interior decorator works only with surface decoration— paint, fabric, furnishings, lighting and other materials. No license is required to be a interior decorator. Note that the programs listed here include *both* interior design and interior decorating programs.

Interior designers provide various services. They may generate ideas for the functional and aesthetic possibilities of the space; create illustrations and renderings; allocate, organize and arrange a space to suit its function; monitor and manage construction and installation of design; select and specify fixtures and furnishings; and even build or make custom furnishings and interior details.

Many interior designers/decorators are self-employed—according to the *Occupational Outlook Handbook* (Jist Works, 2003), 3 out of 10 designers work for themselves.

At-Home Training Programs

Interior Design (Bachelor degree), The Art Institute International (AII), 420 Boulevard of the Allies, Pittsburgh, PA 15219, Tel: 412-291-5100 or 877-872-8869, Web: www.aionline.edu, E-mail: aioadm@aii.edu

The Interior Design Bachelor of Science degree program is part art, part science—going far beyond decorating. In this program students study computer aided drafting and design, 3D design, space planning, problem solving, and the history of design and architecture. Coursework also covers specialty design, including exhibit design, hospitality design, retail store design, and corporate design. In addition, students learn how to communicate their design solutions through a variety of visual media. The Bachelor degree is 180 credits (60 courses). Note: Be sure and verify the technical requirements for this program (see Web site)—you need a certain type of computer and software to begin the program. Tuition: $345/credit or $1135/course.

Interior Architecture and Design (Undergraduate certificate, Associate degree, Bachelor degree, Master degree) Academy of Art College, 79 New Montgomery Street, San Francisco, CA 94105, Tel: 800-544-ARTS or 415-274-2200, Web: www.academyart.edu, E-mail: info@academyart.edu

The Academy of Art College Online offers four degrees in Interior Architecture and Design—an undergraduate certificate, an Associate of Art (AA) degree, a Bachelor of Fine Arts (BFA) degree, and a Master of Fine Arts (MFA) degree. The programs integrate theory, design, and technology in tandem with industry standards. Students develop the intellectual, artistic, and ethical abilities necessary for professional practice. Students are encourage to achieve a balance between mastery of design skills and creativity that will lead to innovative thinking about our inner and outer environment. Concern for spatial issues, design innovation, and attention to detail are emphasized. The certificate is 120 credits, the AA is 66 credits, the BFA is 132 credits, and the MFA is 63 credits. Tuition: $550/credit for undergraduates; $600/credit for graduate students.

Interior Design (Undergraduate certificate), University of California, Los Angeles (UCLA), 10995 Le Conte Ave, Los Angeles, CA 90024-2883, Tel: 310-825-9061, Web: www.uclaextension.edu

UCLA offers a certificate program in interior design, a 30-course sequence. The courses are aimed at assessing client needs, determining safety requirements, conceiving an aesthetic design that meets function and safety criteria, selecting materials and furnishings, preparing and administering bids as the client's agent, working with other licensed contractors, and monitoring design implementation through completion. Students can complete the program in as little as 2½years. The curriculum satisfies the educational requirements for the American Society of Interior Designers and the International Interior Design Association (see "Organizations," below), and enables students to qualify for the National Council for Interior Design Qualification Examination. Course include: Fundamentals of Interior Design; Design Communications; Surface Materials; Digital Communication; Lighting Design; CAD; Building Codes; Public Speaking for Designers and Architects; Interior Design Studio; and more. Tuition: $300-$500/course.

> "You can dream, create, design and build the most wonderful place in the world, but it requires people to make the dream a reality."—Walt Disney

Interior Design Course, Sheffield School of Interior Design, 211 East 43rd Street, New York, NY 10017, Tel: 212-661-7270, Web: www.sheffield.edu, E-mail: info@sheffield.edu

Sheffield School of Interior Design course in interior design consists of 30 lessons, each of which is supplemented by page-by-page guidance on Sheffield audiocassettes and step-by-step demonstrations on training videotapes. The lessons include: Eye of the Designer; Planning for People; Sketching a Room; Drawing a Floor Plan; Planning a Furniture Layout; Lighting a Room; Fabrics; Window Treatments; Wall Treatments; Flooring Treatments; Color Schemes; Harmony and Accessories; Rooms of the House; Kitchens and Baths; Period Furniture; Finished Presentation; and Business Methods. Sheffield also includes a Business Set-Up Kit with the forms and guidance to run your own business. Students have up to 3 years to complete the program, and a trial enrollment period is offered. Full payment: $848. Monthly payment plan: $998 ($35 each with down payment of $28).

Professional Interior Decorator Program, Professional Career Development Institute (PCDI), 430 Technology Parkway, Norcross, GA 30092-3406, Tel: 800-223-4542 or 770-729-8400, Web: www.pcdi-homestudy.com, E-mail: info@pcdi.com

The PCDI program in interior decorating is made up of 18 lessons: The Decorating Process; The Measuring Process; Design Elements and Principles; Color and Design Part 1 & 2; Windows, Doors, and Fireplaces; Furniture Selection; Furniture Styles 1 & 2; Space Planning; Color and Lighting; Textiles 1 & 2; Floors and Stairways; Walls and Ceilings; Special Considerations in Room Planning; Residential Planning; Accessorizing; and Decorators and Careers. Course fee: $789. A payment plan is available.

Interior Decorator, Education Direct, 925 Oak Street, Scranton, PA 18515, Tel: 800-275-4410, Web: www.educationdirect.com, E-mail: info@educationdirect.com

Education Direct's program for interior decorator teaches: Meeting Your Client's Needs; Designing with Furniture; Windows; Walls; Floors; Lighting and Accessories; and Starting Your Own Business. Tools included in the program are a fabric estimator, style wheel, template, rules, and more. This program can be completed in 6 months. Course fee: $589.

For More Information...

<u>Books</u>

How to Start a Home-Based Interior Design Business, by Suzanne DeWalt (Globe Pequot Press, 2003).

Start Your Own Interior Design Business and Keep it Growing: Your Guide to Business Success, by Linda Ramsay and Faren Maree Bachelis (Touch of Design, 1994).

Business and Legal Forms for Interior Designers, by Tad Crawford and Eva Doman Bruck (Allworth Press, 2001).

How to Prosper as an Interior Designer: A Business and Legal Guide, by Robert L. Alderman, Esq. (John Wiley & Sons, 1997).

<u>E-book</u>

Fabjob's Guide to Becoming an Interior Designer, by Debbie Travis, et al., www. fabjob.com ($29.95).

<u>Organizations</u>

American Society of Interior Designers (ASID), 608 Massachusetts Ave., Washington, D.C. 20002-6006, Tel: 202-546-3480, Web: www.asid.org, E-mail: asid@asid.org.

International Interior Design Association (IIDA), Headquarters, 13-122 Merchandise Mart, Chicago, IL 60654-1104, Tel: 888-799-4432 or 312-467-1950, Web: www.iida.org, E-mail: iidahq@iida.org.

Interior Design Educator's Council (IDEC), 9202 North Meridian Street, Suite 200, Indianapolis, IN 46260-1810, Tel: 317-816-6261, Web: www.idec.org, E-mail: info@idec.org.

National Council for Interior Design Qualification (NCIDQ), 1200 18th Street NW, Suite 1001, Washington, D.C. 20036, Tel: 202-721-0220, Web: www.ncidq.org, E-mail: info@ncid.org.

Paint and Decorating Retailers Association (PDRA), 403 Axminister Drive, St. Louis, MO 63026-2941, Tel: 636-326-2636, Web: www.pdra.org, E-mail: info@pdra.org.

<u>Web Sites</u>

www.interiordesign.net—*Interior Design* magazine

www.archdigest.com—*Architectural Digest* magazine

www.i-d-d.com—Interior Design Directory

Medical Billing and Coding

Medical billing and coding are long-time work-at-home careers, as the need for medical services is always growing. Because physicians are overwhelmed with insurance paperwork, medical claims processing and medical billing has become big business. Training in medical billing teaches you to process medical claims efficiently, handle patient invoices, and obtain reimbursements for both patients and doctors. Training in medical coding teaches you how to properly code insurance claims.

The medical reimbursement process includes descriptions of procedures and services the physician provides. As you can imagine, these would be terribly long and confusing left in narrative form. Someone was wise enough to realize that. They devised a system of code numbers representing each procedure and service a physician is likely to provide and another to represent each disease, disorder, or injury. The physician's computerized billing software sends information showing what was done and the insurance company's software interprets it accurately, since they use the same coding system. This speeds up the reimbursement process so doctors are paid faster and better *if* the medical coding and billing is done correctly. Physicians entrust their medical reimbursement responsibilities to medical coders and billers who can speak their language—medical terminology, anatomy & physiology, and disease processes. They want medical coders who understand CPT-4, ICD-9-CM, Evaluation & Management, HCPCS, and much more. They want someone they can depend on for knowledge, high quality of skills and excellence of work habits.

At-Home Training Programs

Medical Coding Specialist (Undergraduate certificate), Medical Reimbursement Specialist (Undergraduate certificate), and Health Information Technology (Associate degree), Santa Barbara City College, 721 Cliff Drive, Santa Barbara, CA 93109-2394, Tel: 805-965-0581, Web: http://online. sbcc.edu

Santa Barbara City College offers three online degrees in this field: a Medical Coding Specialist certificate, a Medical Reimbursement Specialist certificate, and an Associate degree in Health Information Technology. The Medical Coding certificate is 28 credits, with classes including Introduction to Health Information Management, ICD-9 Coding, Basic Medical Terminology, and Medical Insurance Billing. The Medical Reimbursement certificate is 27 credits, including the same classes, with additional courses in Basic Pathophysiology, Pharmacology for Allied Health, and Reimbursement Method. And the Health Information

Management Associate degree is 46 credits, with similar classes, but with additional courses in Human Anatomy & Physiology, Legal Aspects of Health Care, Introduction to Management, and Statistical Applications in Health Care. Courses are instructor-led, and all online. Tuition: $141/credit.

Medical Coding Specialist (Undergraduate certificate), Southwest Wisconsin Technical College, 1800 Bronson Blvd., Fennimore, WI 53809, Tel: 800-362-3322, Web: www.swtc.edu, E-mail: student-services@swtc.edu

The Medical Coding Specialist certificate from Southwest Wisconsin Technical College is offered online, and is comprised of 7 classes (16 credits), including ICD-9-CM Coding; CPT Coding; Medical Business Issues Records/Insurance; Health & Disease; Pharmacology; Medical Terminology; and Body Structure & Function. Tuition: $72/credit for residents of Wisconsin; $478/credit for non-residents.

Health Information Technology (Associate degree), Pitt Community College, P.O. Box Drawer 7007, Greenville, NC 27835-7007 (Physical address: 1986 Pitt Technology Road, Highway 11-South, Winterville, NC 28590), Tel: 252-321-4371, Web: www.pitt.cc.nc.us, E-mail: hitinfo@pcc.pitt.cc.nc.us

The Associate degree in Health Information Technology from Pitt Community College allows candidates to sit for the national certification exam administered by AHIMA (see "Organizations," below) to become a Registered Health Information Technician (RHIT). Total credits for the program total 76. Major courses include: Anatomy & Physiology; Health Information Orientation; Record Systems/Standards; Health Care Statistics; Coding/Classification; Computers in Health Care; Medical Terminology; and more. Tuition: $34.25/credit for residents of North Carolina; $190.75/credit for non-residents.

Health Care Coding & Classification (Undergraduate certificate), Health Information Technology (Associate degree), and Health Administrative Services with emphasis in Health Information Management (Bachelor degree), Weber State University, Dumke College of Health Professions, 3907 University Circle, Ogden, UT 84408-3907, Tel: 801-626-7242, Web: www.weber.edu/ ce/dl, E-mail: healthprofessions@weber.edu

Weber State University offers three degrees in medical coding/health information: an Institutional Certificate in Health Care Coding and Classification; an Associate of Applied Science (AAS) degree in Health Information Technology; and a Bachelor of Science (BS) in Health Administrative Services with emphasis in Health Information Management. The certificate is 21 credits, the AAS is 63 credits, and the BS is 120 credits. Classes available include: Introduction to Health Information Systems & Settings; Health Information Statistics; Diagnosis

Coding; Information Technology in Health Care Management; Medical Terminology; Computer Applications in Health Care; Health Care Marketing; Health Communication, and more. Tuition: $180/credit for Utah residents; $630/credit for non-residents.

> "People who work sitting down get paid more
> than people who work standing up."—Ogden Nash

Coding Specialist (Undergraduate certificate) and Health Information Technology (Associate degree), Rochester Community & Technical College, 851 30th Avenue SE, Rochester, MN 55904-4999, Tel: 507-285-7456, Web: www.rctc.edu

Rochester Community & Technical College offers two degrees in this field: a Coding Specialist certificate and an Associate of Applied Science (AAS) degree in Health Information Technology. The Coding Specialist certificate is comprised of 5 classes (13 credits) including: Coding I, II, and III; Alternative Health Record Systems; and Legal Aspects of Health Information. The Health Information Technology associate degree is 59 credits, with classes including Coding I, II, and II; Computer Voice Technology; Introduction to Medical Terminology; Pathophysiology; Computerized Health Information; HIT Internship; and more. Tuition: $104/credit for Minnesota, Iowa, and North Dakota approved residents; $192/credit for non-residents.

Medical Coding Certificates, Association of Registered Medical Professionals (ARMP), 11405 Old Roswell Road, Alpharetta, GA 30004, Tel: 800-334-5724, Web: www.aormc.com, E-mail: armp@ipractice.md

The AARMP offers two certificate programs in medical coding: Registered Medical Coding Associate and Registered Medical Coding Certification. The Registered Medical Coding Associate consists of three classes: Introduction to Medical Coding, Introduction to Medical Terminology, and Introduction to Medical Anatomy. The Associate is 4 CEUs and costs $200. The Registered Medical Coding Certification consists of five classes: CTP Coding; ICD-9 Coding, HCPCS Coding, Evaluation and Management Coding, and Medicare Essentials. The Certification is 15 CEUs and costs $800.

Professional Medical Coding Curriculum, American Academy of Professional Coders (AAPC), American Academy of Professional Coders (AAPC), 309 West

700 South, Salt Lake City, UT 84101, Tel: 800-626-2633, Web: www. aapc.com, E-mail: info@aapc.com

The Professional Medical Coding Curriculum from the AAPC is broken up into two parts: CPC (Physician Coding) and CPC-H (Hospital Coding). Students have 12 months to complete each section. The first six months, students complete the first three modules, and the second six months, students complete the remaining two or three, depending on which section it is. (The CPC had 5 modules and the CPC-H has 6 modules.) The program is paper-based—students study and complete the workbooks to return to the AAPC for grading. CPC course fee: $1,005/members; $1,105/non-members. CPC-H course fee: $1,165/members; $1,265/non-members.

Study materials for AMBA certification exam and *AMBA Training Seminar* on video, American Medical Billers Association (AMBA), 4297 Forrest Drive, Sulphur, OK 73086, Tel: 580-622-2624, Web: www.ambanet.net/amba.htm, E-mail: amba@webcom.com.

AMBA offers a voluntary exam to obtain the national credential for the medical billing profession—Certified Medical Reimbursement Specialist (CMRS). To prepare for the exam, they offer study materials in e-book format that cover medical terminology, anatomy and physiology, ICD-9-CM coding, CPT-4 coding, and more. Study materials: $199. AMBA also offers a 3-volume video program in medical billing & training: $225.

"Be careful about reading health books.
You may die of a misprint."—Mark Twain

Online Coding Classes and Certified Medical Billing Specialist (CMBS), Medical Association of Billers (MAB), 2441 Tech Center Court, Suite 108, Las Vegas, NV 89128, Tel: 800-207-6966 or 702-240-8519, Web: http://www. physicianswebsites.com, E-mail: medassocb@aol.com

The Medical Association of Billers offers online coding classes, as well as a Certified Medical Billing Specialist program. The online coding classes come in introductory, intermediate, and advanced levels. They are not self-paced, but instructor-led, with start-dates and assignments due weekly. The introductory level includes classes: Introduction to Medical Office Insurance; Proper Billing for Medicare; Introduction to ICD-9-CM Coding; Medical Billing Center marketing; Anatomy & Medical Terminology; Proper Use of Modifiers; Introduction to CPT Coding; and Introduction to HCPCS Coding. Each class is $169/members;

$185/non-members. The MAB also has a Medical Billing Specialist Certification Program, which is a self-paced. Cost: $179/members; $199/non-members.

Medical Billing Course and Marketing Your Medical Billing Business Course, National Electronic Billers Alliance (NEBA), 2226-A Westborough Blvd. PMB 504, South San Francisco, CA 94080, Tel: 650-359-4419, Web: www. nebazone.com, E-mail: merry@nebazone.com

NEBA offers two courses, *Medical Billing as a Business* and *Marketing Your Medical Billing Business.* In addition, NEBA offers the Healthcare Reimbursement Specialist Exam (HRS), available to NEBA members only, for a fee ($200). *Medical Billing as a Business* is $995 and covers: Business Basics; How Health Insurance Works; ICD-9 Coding; Medicare Coding; Medicare Billing; 1998 E&M Guidelines; Collecting Medical Claims Information; Processing Claims Manually; Processing Claims Electronically; Credit Policies, Billing Procedures, and Making Collections; and Ancillary Services. *Marketing Your Medical Billing Business* is $495 and covers: Marketing Mindset; Positioning; Researching Your Market; Defining Your Target Market; Developing a Marketing Plan; Charting Your Progress; Understanding the Benefits EMC Provides; Publicity and Public Relations; Marketing Materials Design & Production; and Additional Tips.

Certified Medical Biller Certification Course, Electronic Medical Billing Network of America (EMBN), 51 Eton Court, Bedminster, NJ 07921, Tel: 908-470-4100, Web: www.medicalbillingnetwork.com, E-mail: merl@medicalbillingnetwork.com

This course is designed for individuals desiring to earn the designation of Certified Electronic Medical Biller (CEMB). Upon successful completion of the course, a final exam is presented, and a passing grade distinguishes the certification. Course topics include: Setting Up Your Medical Billing Business; Insurance for the Medical Office; Medical Marketing Success; Success in Management and Business Strategies; Success in Marketing and Consulting; and MediSoft Patient Account Software. Included in the program is a one-year membership in the EMBN (see "Organizations," below) and unlimited phone support. Cost of program: $655.

Medical Coding/Billing Program, Andrews School, 5601 NW 72nd, #167, Oklahoma City, OK 73132, Tel: 405-721-3555, Web: www.andrewsschool. com, E-mail: Linda@andrewsschool.com

The Medical Coding/Billing Program from the Andrews School is comprised of 77 lessons in three modules covering ethics in coding, medical terminology, ICD-9-CM, medical abbreviations, hospital coding, hospital procedural coding, insurance and reimbursement methodologies, case studies, and more. The program takes approximately one year to complete. Tuition: $3,800. A payment plan is available.

Medical Billing at Home Starter Program, Claims Transit, 4297 Forrest Drive, Sulphur, OK 73086, Tel: 580-622-5809, Web: www.webcom.com/medical/ info.htm, E-mail: larry@brightok.net

A program developed by Larry and Cyndee Weston, professional medical billers since 1990. Included in the Starter Program is MediSoft Patient Accounting Software; software owner's manual; an e-book, *Advanced Claims Processing Comprehensive Training Manual*; *Claims Wizard* cost analysis software; a Web site for ongoing support; and unlimited e-mail support for one year. When you purchase the program you'll also get AMBA's *Medical Billing Training Seminar* on video (see AMBA in "Organizations," and below). Program cost: $499.

> "It's not the hours you put in your work that counts,
> it's the work you put in the hours."—Sam Ewing

Medical Coding and Billing Program, Meditec, 190 S. Fort Lane, Suite 5, Layton, UT 84041, Tel: 877-335-4072 or 801-593-0663, Web: www.meditec. com, E-mail: info@meditec.com

Meditec offers a Medical Coding and Billing program, consisting of 4 volumes (including the CPT and ICD coding books), or is available totally online. In order to take this program, you need to have medical terminology training or experience, or you can add a medical terminology course to the program. Meditec's program qualifies you to sit for the certification exam from AHIMA (see "Organizations," below). Completion of the program also certifies you through the AAPC, for an additional examination fee ($375). The program covers: ICD and CPT coding books; ICD codes, CTP codes, and HCPCS codes; liability and legal issues; 200 pages of exercises from actual hospital documentation; and more. Course fee: $1,047. Without Medical Terminology course: $748. Without Billing Module: $599.

Professional Medical Billing Program, Professional Career Development Institute (PCDI), 430 Technology Parkway, Norcross, GA 30092-3406, Tel: 800-223-4542 or 770-729-8400, Web: www.pcdi-homestudy.com, E-mail: info@pcdi.com

PCDI's program in medical billing includes a set of audio tapes; *Medical Terminology for Health Professionals* textbook; the *Signet/Mosby Medical Encyclopedia*; *Medicode's Physician ICD-9-CM*, Volumes 1 & 2; and *Current Procedural Terminology* (CPT). The program is comprised of 22 lessons:

Introduction to the World of Medical Insurance; Medical Terminology for the Human Body; Skeletal and Muscular Systems; The Cardiovascular, Lymphatic, and Immune Systems; Respiratory and Digestive Systems; Urinary and Nervous Systems; Eyes, Ears, and Integumentary Systems; Endocrine and Reproductive Systems; Diagnosis, Imaging, and Enteral Medical Terminology; Health Insurance and Managed Health Care; An Insurance Claim's Life Cycle; Common Claims; Commercial Claims; Blue Cross/Blue Shield Plans; Medicare; Medicaid; Tricare/Champus; Workers' Compensation; Diagnosis Coding; CPT Procedure Coding; HCPCS and HCFA Coding; and Coding from Source Documents. Course fee: $989.

Medical Billing & Coding Course, Allied Business Schools, 22952 Alcalde Drive, Laguna Hills CA 92653, Tel: 888-501-7686, Web: www.medicalbillingcourses. com, E-mail: allied@alliedschools.com

Allied's program in Medical Billing & Coding has 10 comprehensive areas of study: Types of Medical Insurance; Records Management; Understanding Fees and Co-Pay Schedules; Standardized Coding; Medical Terminology; Computerized Billing; Preparing and Reviewing Claims; Handling Rejected Claims; How to Explain Insurance Benefits to Patients; Bookkeeping and Office Duties; and Finding Potential Employment. The course includes Allied's workbook, MediSoft Patient Accounting Software, *The Current Procedural Terminology* text, *The Essentials of Medical Terminology* text, ICD-9-CM Code Book, a medical dictionary, *American Century Dictionary*, a personal journal, and Allied special reports about home-based business. Upon passing the course, students receive a one-year membership to the Medical Association of Billers (MAB) (see "Organizations," below). Course fee: $788.

Claims Assistance Professional (CAP) Business Kit, Claims Security of America, P.O. Box 23863, Jacksonville, FL 32241-3863, Tel: 800-400-4066, Web: www.claims-security.com

Claims Security of America offers a Claims Assistance Professional (CAP) Business Kit that includes two bound and tabbed volumes, a computer disk, *Medicare Handbook*, and *The Successful Presenter* by William Draves. The bound volumes contain more than 500 pages covering: Introduction to the Health Insurance Industry; The Medicare Maze; Medical and Insurance Programs; The Health Insurance Claims Process; The Claims Professional's Tracking System; Case Studies; General Business Planning; Pricing the Service; and Marketing the Business. The computer disk contains ready-to-use templates of forms, contracts, letters, and agreements. *The Successful Presenter* will help prepare you to make presentations to individuals and groups. In addition, bonuses are available, including two videocassettes, a business development start-up kit, free telephone

technical support, *The Entrepreneur's Guide to Busine.*
Understanding Financial Statements. Course fee: $495.

For More Information...

<u>Books</u>

Medical Billing Home-Based Business, Success in Management and Business
by Merlin Coslick (Electronic Medical Billing Network of America, 1999).

*Setting Up Your Medical Billing Bu*siness, by Merlin Coslick (Electronic Med.
Billing Network of America, 1999).

Medical Billing: The Bottom Line, by Claudia Yalden (CAY Medical Management,
1999).

Understanding Medical Insurance: A Guide to Professional Billing, by Jo Ann
Powell (Delmar Learning, 1999).

A Basic Guide to Starting Your Own Medical Billing Business, by Darlene Collings
(Darlene Collings, 1999).

Start Your Own Medical Claims Auditor/Transcriptions Business, by Business
Concepts (Prentice Hall Press, 1999).

How to Start a Medical Claims Billing Service: Your Step-by-Step Guide to Success,
by *Entrepreneur* magazine (Entrepreneur Media, Inc., 2003).

*Independent Medical Coding: The Comprehensive Guidebook for Career Success as a
Medical Coder*, by Donna Avila-Weil and Rhonda Regan (Rayve Productions,
1998).

*Codebusters: A Quick Guide to Coding and Billing Compliance for Medical
Practices*, by Patricia Aalseth (Jones & Bartlett, 1999).

Step-by-Step Medical Coding, by Carol J. Buck (W.B. Saunders, 2002).

<u>E-book</u>

*1-2-3 Guide to Medical Billing: Start and Market Your Own Medical Billing
Business*, by Beth Coats, www.bizymoms.com ($29.95).

<u>Organizations</u>

American Medical Billers Association (AMBA), 4297 Forrest Drive, Sulphur, OK
73086, Tel: 580-622-2624, Web: www.ambanet.net/amba.htm, E-mail: amba@
webcom.com.

can Health Information Management Association (AHIMA), 233 N.
igan Avenue, Suite 2150, Chicago, IL 60601-5800, Tel: 312-233-1100,
: www.ahima.org, E-mail: info@ahima.org.

ctronic Medical Billing Network of America (EMBN), 51 Eton Court,
edminster, NJ 07921, Tel: 908-470-4100, Web: www.medicalbillingnetwork.
com, E-mail: merl@medicalbillingnetwork.com.

National Electronic Billers Alliance (NEBA), 2226-A Westborough Blvd. PMB
504, South San Francisco, CA 94080, Tel: 650-359-4419, Web: www.nebazone.
com, E-mail: merry@nebazone.com.

Medical Association of Billers (MAB), 2441 Tech Center Court, Suite 110, Las
Vegas, NV 89128, Tel: 702-240-8519, Web: http://www.physicianswebsites.
com, E-mail: medassocb@aol.com.

American Association of Medical Billers (AAMB), Tel: 323-778-4352, Web:
www.billers.com, E-mail: aamb@aol.com.

American Academy of Professional Coders (AAPC), 309 West 700 South, Salt
Lake City, UT 84101, Tel: 800-626-2633, Web: www.aapc.com, E-mail:
info@aapc.com.

Web Sites

http://boards1.ivillage.com/cgi-bin/boards/wfmed—iVillage.com's discussion board
for medical billers

www.billerswebsite.com—subscription Web site of resources and information

www.medicalrepublic.com—services for medical billers

www.hiaa.org—Health Insurance Association of America

www.donnellybenefits.com—seminars offers in Pennsylvania

Medical Transcription

Medical transcriptionists type medical reports from doctors' dictation that document a patient's medical care and condition. These may include office chart notes, history and physical examinations, consultations, letters, memos, admission notes, emergency medicine reports, operative reports, discharge summaries, x-rays, pathology reports, and many laboratory tests and diagnostic studies. The medical transcriptionist takes care to transcribe this information, demonstrating a knowledge of medical terminology, anatomy, pharmacology, human diseases, surgical procedures, and laboratory tests to produce an accurate and complete permanent patient record. A medical transcriptionist must have a mastery of English grammar, structure and style; a knowledge of medical transcription practices; skill in word processing, spelling, and proofreading; and high professional standards that contribute to their ability to interpret, translate, and edit medical dictation for content and clarity.

Medical transcriptionists work in various kinds of places, from medical centers to hospitals to doctors' offices, but opportunities abound for full-time and part-time positions, as well as flexible work schedules. Many experienced medical transcriptionists work from home via computer and modem. People who are successful in this profession as a home career typically like to help others; have an interest in medicine; have above-average skills in spelling, grammar, and punctuation; enjoy typing and transcribing; work independently; are self-starters; care about quality and excellence; enjoy reading; and desire a professional career in medicine. Note: Check with each individual program for prerequisites. Some require you pass a keyboarding test, and others offer a keyboarding course as part of the program. Also, technical requirements are important here (the type of computer required).

At-Home Training Programs

Career Studies—Medical Transcription (Undergraduate certificate), Patrick Henry Community College, 64 Patriot Avenue, P.O. Box 5311, Martinsville, VA 24115, Tel: 800-232-7997 or 276-638-8777, Web: www.ph.cc.va.us

The undergraduate certificate in medical transcription from Patrick Henry Community College is comprised of 11 courses (a total of 29 credits). Courses include: Keyboarding I & II; Word Processing; Medical Machine Transcription; Medical Office Procedures; Technical Report Writing; Medical Terminology; Introduction to Microcomputer Software & Lab; International Classification of Diseases I; and College Survival Skills. Tuition: $52.71/credit for Virginia residents; $198.64/credit for non-residents.

Medical Transcription (Associate degree), California College for Health Sciences (CCHS), 2423 Hoover Avenue, National City, CA 91950, Tel: 800-221-7374, Web: www.cchs.edu, E-mail: cchsinfo@cchs.edu

The CCHS Associate of Science in Medical Transcription is divided into three parts: MT Fundamentals; MT Core Curriculum; and Advanced Medical Transcription. Students may choose to enter at any one of the three points consistent with their skill level. The distance-learning program uses the System Unit Method (SUM) tapes as part of your lesson plan. The tapes contain carefully selected, authentic physician dictation, sequenced by medical specialty, for practical, hands-on training. Tuition: $1900 (18 credits); advanced courses $399 each.

Medical Transcription (Undergraduate certificate), Northwest Technical College, 150 2nd Street, SW, Suite B, Box 309, Perham, MN 56573, Tel: 877-598-8523, Web: www.ntcmn.edu, E-mail: info@ntcmn.edu

The Medical Transcription certificate from Northwest Technical College is made up of 28 credits (11 courses). Courses include: Keyboarding I; Word Processing; Business Communications; Intro to Anatomy & Physiology; Intro to Computer Tech; Medical Terminology; Medical Transcription; Medical Language Applications; Advanced Medical Transcription; Skill Building; and Pathophysiology. Tuition: $3,500 (11 courses, 28 credits).

"Don't live in a town where there are no doctors."—Jewish proverb

Medical Transcription (Undergraduate certificate), Southwest Wisconsin Technical College, 1800 Bronson Blvd., Fennimore, WI 53809, Tel: 800-362-3322, Web: www.southwest.tec.wi.us

This intensive online one-year program provides hands-on experience transcribing a variety of medical reports of many specialties from actual dictation. Students have one year to complete the program, but it can be completed in two semesters. The program is made up of 33 credits (13 courses), including: Medical Transcription; Microsoft Word; Health & Disease; Pharmacology for Medical Transcription; Medical Terminology; Body Structure & Function; Fundamentals of English; Advanced Medical Transcription; Medical Business Issues; Advanced Clinical Medical Terminology; Technical Communication for Health Occupations; Graduate Orientation; and Psychology of Human Relations. Tuition: $72/credit for Wisconsin residents; $478/credit for non-residents.

Medical Transcription (Undergraduate certificate and Diploma), Rochester Community & Technical College, 851 30th Avenue SE, Rochester, MN 55904-4999, Tel: 507-280-3107, Web: www.rctc.edu

The online Medical Transcription certificate from Rochester Technical and Community College is made up of 6 courses (15 credits). Courses include: College English; Introduction to Medical Transcription; Medical Transcription I & II; Body Systems/Diseases; and Medical Specialties/Pharmacology. This abbreviated online program is designed to train or retrain students for basic medical transcription skills. Students should have an entrance level keyboarding skill of at least 45 words per minute, current office technology skills, and a high level of

English reading and writing skills. A keyboarding course is offered for students needing keyboarding skills, which does not count toward the certificate.

The Diploma program in Medical Transcription consists of 15 courses (35 credits), which is an intensive program for medical transcription training. It stresses extensive building of medical terminology and a highly developed skill in transcription, office skills, and technology training. Courses are the same as in the certificate program but add: general education courses; Word Processing I; Employment Strategies; Business Communications; Microcomputer Business Applications; PowerPoint; Medical Word Processing; and Medical Office Procedures. Tuition: $103/credit for Minnesota and North Dakota-approved residents; $192-$232/credit for non-residents.

Beginning Medical Transcription (BMT), Health Professions Institute, P.O. Box 801, Modesto, CA 95353-0801 (Physical address: 2105 Lancey Drive, Suite 1, Modesto, CA 95355), Tel: 209-551-2112, Web: www.hpisum.com, E-mail: hpi@hpisum.com

The Health Professions Institute uses the SUM program of tapes, which uses authentic physician-dictated transcription for hands-on experience. The beginning program includes: 12 hours of dictation on CD-ROM for Windows (or on 12 audio cassette tapes); transcript keys to correct your work; step-by-step reading assignments; *The Medical Transcription Workbook; Human Diseases; H&P: A Nonphysician's Guide to the Medical History and Physical Examination; Laboratory Medicine: Essentials of Anatomic and Clinical Pathology*; and word-and-phrase books. Advanced training using the SUM program is also available. Beginning training: $840. Advanced training modules: $210-$280 each.

> "It's no longer a question of staying healthy. It's a question of finding a sickness you like."—Jackie Mason

Medical Transcription Program, Andrews School, 5601 NW 72nd, #167, Oklahoma City, OK 73132, Tel: 405-721-3555, Web: www.andrewsschool. com, E-mail: Linda@andrewsschool.com

The Andrews School self-paced medical transcription program takes an average of 9-12 months to complete, and includes 3,412 minutes of physician-dictated medical reports. Students are required to transcribe 2,122 minutes of dictated material. The school provides a full-featured standard cassette transcription machine, as well as all training tapes and reference books, including *Medical Terminology for Health Professions, Medical Phrase Index, AAMT Book of Style,*

Surgical Word Book, and more. The program is comprised of 84 lessons in three modules covering medical terminology, anatomy & physiology, medical grammar, pharmacology, proofreading, and more. In addition, advanced specialty materials are available to meet the specific needs of each student, as well as a video library of how to build and sustain a successful medical transcription business. Tuition: $3,800. A payment plan is available.

Medical Transcription Training Program, Career Step, 1220 N. Main #6, Springville, UT 84663, Tel: 800-246-STEP or 801-489-9393, Web: www. careerstep.com, E-mail: info@careerstep.com

The online course of medical transcription from Career Step includes software and a PC transcription foot pedal as part of the enrollment price, which turns the PC into a "transcriber." During the program, students download and transcribe 22 hours of clinic notes and intermediate and advanced physician-dictated reports right at your computer. The curriculum includes: Keyboard Kinetics—Techniques for Building Speed and Efficiency on the Keyboard; Grammar and Style English; Human Anatomy, Physiology and Disease Processes; Medical Word Building (with two sets of flash cards); Abbreviations, Medical Plurals, How to Look Up Words, Word Differentiation; Focus on Medial Specialties; Test Packet and Answer Key; Making Your Career Step; and Clinic Notes—Intermediate and Advanced Transcription. Students work from a library of 26 cassettes. Gold Level enrollment includes all of the above for $1,320. Platinum Level enrollment includes all the Gold features, plus a graduate support package—an employment and referral directory; personal employment consultations; contracts and pricing guide; "Start Your Own Medical Transcription Business;" an evaluation of your resume or sales letter; a help hotline for one year after graduation; and a referral letter for $1,560. A payment plan is available for both programs.

The course is also available in paper-based format. Gold Level Paper-Based Course: $1,080. Platinum Level Paper-Based Course: $1,360.

Medical Transcription Education, Medical Transcription Education Center, Inc. (M-TEC), 3634 West Market Street, Suite 103, Fairlawn, OH 44333, Tel: 877-864-3307 or 330-670-9333, Web: www.mtecinc.com, E-mail: mtec@ mtecinc.com

M-TEC has 4 programs in medical transcription. Tier I, Premier, is for people with no previous experience and for home-based opportunities. Tier I, Basic, is for those who have a job lined up or someone to mentor them. Tier II, Premier, is for the health care professional changing careers. Tier II, Basic, is for the health care professional changing careers, but who already has a job as an MT. Coursework includes: Anatomy/Physiology; Laboratory Medicine; English/

Medical Grammar & Editing; Medical Science/Human Disease Processes; Medical Language/Terminology; Pharmacology; Medicolegal Concepts & Ethics/Professional Development; Fundamentals of Medical Transcription; and Fundamentals of Technology. Tier I, Premier: $2,795. Tier I, Basic: $1,550. Tier II, Premier: $2,695. Tier II, Basic: $1,450.

Medical Transcription Training, Meditec, 190 S. Fort Lane, Suite 5, Layton, UT 84041, Tel: 877-335-4072 or 801-593-0663, Web: www.meditec.com, E-mail: info@meditec.com

Meditec offers a Medical Transcription program online or in paper-based format. The online program covers English spelling, usage, grammar, and style; derivation of medical terminology; medical terminology vocabulary builder; anatomy & physiology; body planes & movements; laboratory analyses, terminology & abbreviations; radiology terminology & abbreviations; and medical specialties and specialists. Also included are more than 100 patient reports for interactive analysis and interpretation; online interactive medical transcription training tools (online dictionaries, abbreviations listings, terms, and more); CD-ROMs with physician dictation; a pharmacological compendium; a surgical compendium; and *The Professional HomeBiz Book*. You can also add to your enrollment the WavePlayer footpedal and software so you can play the dictations directly from your computer ($160 extra). Tuition for online or paper-based program: $829.

Medical Transcription Course, MedTrans, 1255 W. Baseline Road, Suite 155, Mesa, AZ 85202, Tel: 877-331-4222 or 480-777-9110, Web: www.medtrans. net or www.learn2workathome.com, E-mail: customerservice@ learn2workathome.com

The MedTrans course in Medical Transcription covers anatomy; formats for transcription; English terms and formats; general medical terminology; and specialty and pharmaceutical terminology. The course is available in three formats: a text workbook with CD; by digital download; or a text workbook with cassette tapes. All programs: $467. Optional additions include various textbooks for $49.95-$79.95, a SpellCheck software program for $105, and an Olympus Transcription Kit Foot Switch for $145. Note: For the digital download option, you must have a broadband or better Internet connection, as well as the software/foot pedal.

> "Far and away the best prize that
> life offers is the chance to work hard
> at work worth doing."—Theodore Roosevelt

Medical Transcription Program, Global Medical Transcription Inc., P.O. Box 1421, 241 Beach Place, Kaunakakai, HI 96748, Tel: 877-779-8779, Web: www.medicaltrans.net, E-mail: info@medicaltrans.net

This is a two-phase program consisting of a self-paced independent study course followed by an intense apprenticeship. The first phase includes many hours of practice transcriptions of medical reports, anatomy and medical terminology courses, plus medical and transcription reference books. All the necessary hardware and software (transcription foot pedal and software) is included. Four to six months to complete the first phase is typical. The second phase of the program is an apprenticeship. The 9-week apprenticeship is real world training covering a broad spectrum of medical specialties under the supervision and guidance of the apprentice coordinator and her editors. The apprentices transcribe assigned dictations daily, which are edited and returned with feedback and encouragement. Program fee: $2,650.

Medical Transcription Program, Laird's School of Medical Transcription, 1565 Highway 37 West, Suite 2, Toms River, NJ 08755, Tel: 800-209-9899, Web: www.lairdsschool.com, E-mail: info@lairdsschool.com

The Laird's program is organized into 13 Study Units: Introductory Studies; Reproduction and Development; Digestion, Metabolism, and Nutrition; The Urinary System and Body Fluids; The Heart, Blood, and Blood Vessels; Respiratory System; The Musculoskeletal System; The Nervous and Sensory Systems; Psychiatry; The Endocrine System; Skin and Plastic Surgery; The Lymphatic System, Body Defense, and AIDS; and Oncology and Radiology. Each study unit includes a study unit guide; Laird's Student Feedback Form; medical terminology building blocks; reference material; practice audiocassettes of instructor-dictated medical reports with answer key; practice audiocassettes of physician-dictated medical reports; and a final exam. A standard-sized cassette transcriber with headset and foot pedal is included in the program. Other materials included are: *Stedman's Concise Medical Dictionary; Laird's Student Handbook; Laird's Quick Reference Abbreviations and Acronyms; Laird's Quick Reference Laboratory Terminology; Laird's Quick Reference Surgical Terminology; Laird's Manual of Drugs and Pharmaceuticals; Laird's Manual of Diseases; Laird's Manual of Laboratory Tests and Diagnostic Procedures; Laird's Manual of Style; Laird's Psychiatry Reference Book;* and *Laird's Oncology Reference Book.* Tuition: $2,085.

Professional Medical Transcription Program, Professional Career Development Institute (PCDI), 430 Technology Parkway, Norcross, GA 30092-3406, Tel: 800-223-4542 or 770-729-8400, Web: www.pcdi-homestudy.com, E-mail: info@pcdi.com

PCDI's program in medical transcription consists of 21 lessons. Included in the program are audiotapes for practice transcription and an audio tape player with a digital counter and headset. Lessons include: Introduction to Medical Terminology and Structure of the Human Body; Skeletal System and Muscular System; Cardiovascular, Lymphatic, and Immune Systems; Respiratory and Digestive Systems; The Urinary and Nervous Systems; Eyes, Ears, and Skin; The Endocrine and Reproductive Systems; Diagnostics, Imaging, and Pharmacology; Knowing Your Equipment and English Grammar; Punctuation, Capitalization and Numbers; and Hillcrest Medical Center, Cases 1-10 (practice transcription). Course fee: $989.

Is Medical Transcription the At-Home Business for You? Online Course from BizyMoms, Web: www.bizymoms.com, E-mail: LJAandRGA@aol.com

This online 4-week course will teach you what is involved with doing medical transcription from home, including what skills and training are necessary, types of work available, what you can reasonably expect to earn, what the day-to-day work of a transcriptionist is like, and how you can best get started. After completing this course you will *not* be prepared to begin work in the field of medical transcription, but you should have an idea if this is a career you would like to pursue. Course fee: $60.

For More Information...

<u>Books</u>

How to Become a Medical Transcriptionist, by George Morton (Medical Language Development, 1998).

Medical Transcription Career Handbook, by Keith Drake (Prentice Hall, 1999).

The Independent Medical Transcriptionist: The Comprehensive Guidebook for Career Success in a Medical Transcription Business, by Donna Avila-Weil and Mary Glaccum (Rayve Productions, 2002).

Medical Transcription: Fundamentals and Practice, by Health Professions Institute (Prentice Hall, 1999).

The AAMT Book of Style for Medical Transcription, by Claudia Tessier (American Association of Medical Transcriptionists, 1995).

Organization

American Association of Medical Transcriptionists (AAMT), 100 Sycamore Avenue, Modesto, CA 95354-0550, Tel: 800-982-2182 or 209-527-9620, Web: www.aamt.org, E-mail: aamt@aamt.org.

American Health Information Management Association (AHIMA), 233 N. Michigan Avenue, Suite 2150, Chicago, IL 60601-5800, Tel: 312-233-1100, Web: www.ahima.org, E-mail: info@ahima.org.

Web Sites

http://messageboards.ivillage.com/iv-wftrans—iVillage.com's medical transcription discussion board

http://mtdaily.com—Medical Transcription Networking Center

www.mtdesk.com—medical transcription resources

www.medword.com—more resources

Paralegal Service

A paralegal performs specifically delegated legal work for which a lawyer is required. Paralegals work for attorneys, corporations, governments, court systems, and can specialize in real estate, criminal law, estate planning, family law, labor law, litigation, or corporate law, to name a few. Law firms are hiring more and more paralegals in recent years, but some attorneys choose to outsource their paralegal duties, rather than hiring a full-timer. Many paralegals are going into business for themselves, helping people process legal paperwork for routine transactions, such as incorporations and uncontested divorces. But, warns author Dorothy Secol, "It is also not a field for someone who has just graduated from a paralegal program." Being a freelance paralegal is much more than being a paralegal. It is also being a business owner, and with that comes the responsibility of owning a business, having assets, liabilities, insurance, employees, and payroll. Secol recommends that you have at least 5-7 years of experience as a paralegal before venturing out on your own.

For the nuts-and-bolts of operating a freelance paralegal business, see *Paralegal's Guide to Freelancing* by Dorothy Secol and *Independent Paralegal's Handbook*, by Ralph Warner (see "Books," below). The paralegal profession is projected to grow "faster than average," (21-35%), according to the *Occupational Outlook Handbook* (Jist Works, 2003). In the same breath, however, the handbook states that competition for jobs in on rise too, as the number of graduates of paralegal training programs outpaces job growth.

At-Home Training Programs

Attorney Assistant Training Program, Litigation Option (Undergraduate certificate) and Corporate Option (Undergraduate certificate), University of California, Los Angeles (UCLA), 10995 Le Conte Ave, Los Angeles, CA 90024-2883, Tel: 310-825-0741, Web: www.uclaextension.edu/aatp

UCLA offers two certificates with different concentrations: an Attorney Assistant, Litigation Option certificate and an Attorney Assistant, Corporate Option certificate. The litigation option is designed to train persons interested in working as paralegals in law firms specializing in litigation, and covers: drafting complaints and answers; preparing motions to dismiss and demurrers; preparing motions for summary judgment; preparing affidavits and declarations; preparing memoranda of points and authorities; summarizing and indexing depositions; preparing and organizing trial exhibits; preparing judgments; researching and abstracting public records; and performing legal research. The corporate option covers preparing and filing articles of incorporation and certificates of amendment; drafting and amending bylaws; assisting in drafting shareholder agreements for close corporations; composing notices, agenda, waivers, resolutions, minutes of meetings, and actions of boards of directors and shareholders; drafting proxy statements and scripts for shareholder meetings; preparing stock certificates; drafting bankruptcy petitions, schedules, and proofs of claim; drafting complaints and answers; summarizing and indexing depositions; and performing legal research. AATP Program: $3,750.

Paralegal Studies (Associate degree), Ashworth College, P.O. Box 92307, Norcross, GA 30010-3087 (Physical address: 430 Technology Parkway, Norcross, GA 30092-3406), Tel: 800-223-4542 or 770-729-8400, Web: www.ashworthcollege.com, E-mail: info@ashworthcollege.com

The Associate degree in Paralegal Studies at Ashworth College is comprised of 20 courses, including: Introduction to Business; Business Communications I &II; Business Law; Introduction to Paralegalism I & II; Torts; Personal Finance; Civil Litigation; American Government; Introduction to Psychology; Business Mathematics; Law Office Management; Criminal Law and Procedures; Real Estate Law; Introduction to Computers; The Administration of Wills, Trusts, and Estates; Family Law; Income Tax Fundamentals; and Legal Research and Writing. Tuition: $1,289 for the first semester (4-semester program). A payment plan is available.

Legal Assistant/Paralegal (Certificate) and Paralegal Studies (Associate degree), The Paralegal Institute, Inc., 2933 West Indian School Road, Drawer 11408, Phoenix, AZ 85061-1408, Tel: 800-354-1254, Web: www.theparalegalinstitute. com, E-mail: paralegalinst@mindspring.com

The Paralegal Institute has two programs: a certificate in Legal Assistant/Paralegal (LAP) and an Associate degree in Paralegal Studies. The certificate consists of: Legal Research; Ethics; Court Systems; American Law; Substantive Litigation; Criminal Law; Trial Procedure; Interviews and Investigations; and other basic skills. The Associate degree consists of the LAP program, plus a choice of two special courses in English, Writing, Mathematics, Psychology, and Business Management. Tuition: LAP—$2,150; Associate degree—$3,510. A payment plan is available.

Paralegal Studies (Undergraduate certificate, Associate degree, and Bachelor degree), Saint Mary-of-the-Woods College, Women's External Degree Program (WED), St. Mary-of-the-Woods, IN 47876, Tel: 812-535-5151, Web: www. smwc.edu, E-mail: smwc@smwc.edu

St. Mary-of-the-Woods College offers a certificate, an Associate degree, and a Bachelor degree in Paralegal Studies. The Bachelor degree is 125 credits, the Associate degree is approximately 69 credits (depending on your general studies requirements), and the certificate is 27 credits. Courses available include: Law, Ethics and Society; Legal Communication; Computers in Law; Theories in Liability; Advanced Legal Research and Writing; Civil Litigation; Commercial Transaction; Women and the Law; Bankruptcy; Family Law; Death and Taxes; and more. Tuition: $307/credit.

"It is the spirit and not the form of law that keeps justice alive."—Earl Warren

Paralegal Studies (Associate degree) Tompkins Cortland Community College, 170 North Street, Dryden, NJ 13053, Tel: 888-567-8211, Web: www.sunytccc. edu, E-mail: admissions@sunytccc.edu

The Associate of Applied Science in Paralegal Studies at Tompkins Cortland Community College provides a basic orientation and academic exposure to a variety of subjects, including legal research and drafting, civil litigation, real estate law, wills and estate planning, family law, and legal ethics. The entire program may be completed online in two or three semesters. The total program is 76 credits. Tuition: $104/credit for New York residents; $218/credit for non-residents.

Paralegal Studies (Associate degree, Bachelor's degree) University of Great Falls, UGF Telecom, 1301 20th Street South, Great Falls, MT 59405-4996, Tel: 800-856-9544 or 406-761-8210, Web: www.ugf.edu

The University of Great Falls has an Associate of Applied Science and a Bachelor of Arts in Paralegal Studies. Each course starts with a video lecture with a follow-up live audio conference with the instructor and other students. Courses include: Introduction to Paralegalism; Introduction to Legal Analysis; Legal Research & Writing; Litigation & Trial Practice; Field Experience in Legal Assistance; Current Issues in Paralegalism; and Business Law I. Electives available include: Criminal Law; Criminal Evidence & Procedure; Commercial Transactions; Domestic & Family Law; Property Law; Estate Law; Debtor-Creditor Law; Office Systems; and Legal Research Institute. The Associate of Applied Science is 64 credits; the Bachelor's degree is 128 credits. Tuition: $340/credit.

Paralegal Technology (Associate degree), Western Piedmont Community College, 1001 Burkemont Avenue, Morganton, NC 28655-4511, Tel: 828-438-6165, Web: www.wp.cc.nc.us

The Paralegal Technology curriculum at Western Piedmont Community College includes substantive and procedural legal knowledge in civil litigation, legal research and writing, real estate, family law, wills, estates, trusts, and commercial law. Required courses also include subjects in English, mathematics, and computers. The program is a total of 68 credits. Tuition: $31/credit for North Carolina residents, $173.25/credit for non-residents.

National Paralegal Certificate, The Washington Online Learning Institute, 111 Main Street, Nanuet, NY 10954, Tel: 800-371-5581, Web: www.theparalegalschool.com, E-mail: info@theparalegalschool.com

The National Paralegal Certificate Program is an online 10-month course of study designed to prepare the future of paralegal professional with the theoretical understanding and the practical skills of the world of law. The program is equivalent to 35 semester hours. Upon completion of the program, students will be awarded a Certificate of Paralegal Studies from the Institute. Courses include: Introduction to the World of Law; Legal Research and Writing; Bankruptcy; Criminal Law; Ethics; The Law of Real Estate; Civil Litigation; Personal Injury Law (Torts); Corporate Law; Family Law; and Wills, Trusts and Estates. Tuition: $4,990 for entire program, including texts and a Lexis/Nexis account.

"A jury consists of twelve persons chosen to
decide who has the better lawyer."—Robert Frost

**Paralegal Certificate, American Paralegal Institute (API), 2 Perlman Drive,
Spring Valley, NY 10977, Tel: 800-371-6105, Web: www.paralegaltech.com, E-mail: info@paralegaltech.com**

API offers a 10-month certificate in Paralegal Studies, a total of 32 credits. All
courses are online with live lectures and interaction with the instructor. Courses
include: Legal Research & Writing; Estates, Trusts & Probate; Introduction to
Litigation; Real Property; Professional Responsibility & Legal Ethics;
Constitutional Law; Torts & Personal Injury; Contracts; Corporate Law; Criminal
Law; and Bankruptcy. Tuition: $4,995 for entire program or $595/course.

**Paralegal Studies (Certificate, Associate degree, and Bachelor degree), Kaplan
College, 6409 Congress Avenue, Boca Raton, FL 33487, Tel: 888-887-6494 or
561-981-7300, Web: www.kaplancollege.edu, E-mail: infokc@kaplancollege.edu**

Kaplan College offers three degrees in paralegal studies: A Pathway to Paralegal
Studies certificate; an Associate of Applied Science; and a Bachelor of Arts degree
in Management/Applied Management with a Law Office Management
Emphasis. The certificate is 36 credits, the Associate degree is 90 credits, and the
Bachelor degree is 180 credits. Courses available include: Paralegalism Today;
Civil Litigation I & II; Contracts; Legal Research; Legal Ethics; and electives. The
Associate degree requires all these courses, plus courses in college composition,
human dynamics, software applications and electives in social science, humani-
ties, and mathematics. Tuition: $235/credit.

**Paralegal Studies Courses, USDA Graduate School Correspondence Programs,
14th and Independence S.W., Room 112S, Washington, D.C. 20250, Tel: 888-744-GRAD, Web: grad.usda.gov, E-mail: selfpaced@grad.usda.gov**

The USDA Graduate School formerly offered a certificate program in paralegal
studies, but as you may have read already, they discontinued their certificate pro-
grams. But, the courses are still available individually. Courses available include:
Administrative Law and Procedure; Business Law I & II; Constitutional Law;
Criminal Law; Family Law; Freedom of Information Act and The Privacy Act;
Legal Ethics; Legal Literature; Legal Research; Legal Writing; Torts Law, and
Wills, Trusts and Estate Administration. All paralegal courses are paper-based.
Each course: $200-$300 each.

Legal Secretary Program, Allied Business Schools, 22952 Alcalde Drive, Laguna Hills CA 92653, Tel: 888-501-7686, Web: www.alliedschools.com, E-mail: allied@alliedschools.com

With the Legal Secretary Program at Allied students learn about the inner workings of the law office, handling confidential information, verbal communications court filing procedures, legal terminology, marketing your skills for employment, an overview of the court system, preparing legal documents, and the litigation process. The textbooks are *Introduction to Legal Secretary, Volumes I & II*, and additional materials include the text *Legal Research*, a legal dictionary, and a course in College Keyboarding for no extra charge. Plus, students receive a copy of Allied's Special Report covering how to start your own home-based business. Course fee: $788.

> ## "I have never let my schooling interfere with my education."—Mark Twain

Professional Paralegal Program, Professional Career Development Institute (PCDI), 430 Technology Parkway, Norcross, GA 30092-3406, Tel: 800-223-4542 or 770-729-8400, Web: www.pcdi-homestudy.com, E-mail: info@pcdi.com

The Professional Paralegal Program from PCDI is paper-based program comprised of 20 lessons, including: Paralegals and the Legal Profession; Paralegals and Legal System; Criminal Law; Constitutional Law; Contract Law; Tort Law; How to Study Law; Introduction to the Legal System; Assisting in Litigation; Legal Analysis; Legal Interviewing; Investigations; Computer Literacy; Law Office Management Techniques; Informal and Formal Advocacy; Regulation of Paralegals; Ethics; Legal Research Part A & B; and Legal Writing. Course fee: $1,089.

Paralegal Program, Education Direct, 925 Oak Street, Scranton, PA 18515, Tel: 800-275-4410, Web: www.educationdirect, E-mail: info@educationdirect.com

The Paralegal Program from Education Direct is a CD-ROM program covering Legal Terminology; Law Office Computing; Computer-Assisted Legal Research; Business Law; Conducting Legal Investigations and Interviews; and more. Lessons and supplements are included, as well as a legal dictionary and Microsoft® Office XP. Double check their technical requirements, as you need a specific kind of computer and operating system for this program. Course fee: $799.

For More Information...

<u>Books</u>

Paralegal's Guide to Freelancing: How to Start and Manage Your Own Legal Services Business, by Dorothy Secol (John Wiley & Sons, 1996).

Paralegal Career Guide, by Chere Estrin (Prentice Hall, 2001).

Independent Paralegal's Handbook: Everything You Need to Run a Business Preparing Legal Paperwork for the Public, by Ralph Warner (Nolo Press, 1999).

Legal Research for Beginners, by Sonja Larsen and John Bourdean (Barrons Educational Series, 1997).

<u>Organizations</u>

National Association of Legal Assistants (NALA), 1516 S. Boston #200, Tulsa, OK 74119, Tel: 918-587-6828, Web: www.nala.org, E-mail: nalanet@nala.org.

National Paralegal Association, Box 406, Solebury, PA 18963, Tel: 215-297-8333, Web: www.nationalparalegal.org, E-mail: admin@nationalparalegal.org.

National Federation of Paralegal Associations, Inc. (NFPA), P.O. Box 33108, Kansas City, MO 64114, Tel: 816-941-4000, Web: www.paralegals.org, E-mail: info@paralegals.org.

Standing Committee on Legal Assistants, American Bar Association, 541 North Fairbanks Court, Chicago, IL 60611, Web: www.abanet.org.

American Association for Paralegal Education, 407 Wekiva Springs Road, Suite 241, Longwood, FL 32779, Tel: 407-834-6688, Web: www.aafpe.org, E-mail: info@aafpe.org.

<u>Web Sites</u>

www.officemoonlighter.com—freelance opportunities

www.findaparalegal.com—directory of paralegals

www.paralegal-plus.com—an example of a paralegal firm

www.forparalegals.com—lots of resources and info for paralegals

Personal/Life Coach

Personal/life coaching is one of the fastest growing home professions—second only to the IT industry according to some studies. A personal/life coach is someone who helps people achieve their goals and dreams. She helps her clients to define and clarify their goals in life and then works with them toward achieving the desired outcome, such as starting a business, becoming financially secure, leading a balanced life, or enjoying a successful relationship. A personal coach helps her clients set goals, manage time, stay motivated, and even build their dreams. There are many types of personal coaches, such as career coaches, life purpose coaches, and corporate coaches, with many combining these specializations. In addition, personal/life coaches can also specialize in particular areas such as time management, weight-loss management, parenting, relationships, small business, financial management, and more.

Coaches can earn anywhere from $50-$150 per hour or more. You set your own rates as a coach. Setting rates depends on your level of experience and the type of coaching you offer. Most personal coaches are in private practice in their homes. You don't even necessarily need a separate home office to make a living as a coach. Coaching can take place over the phone and even via e-mail, so you can coach anyone where there is a telephone.

> ## "I think self-awareness is probably the most important thing towards being a champion."—Billie Jean King

You don't need any one particular piece of education or experience to become a coach. Although there are no standard regulations at this time, coach-training programs are the main avenues for education. They provide solid skills in the field and provide an opportunity for certification, which gives the coach credibility and validation. Plus, most coach training is available via distance learning.

For more in-depth descriptions of each program—there's a lot of them—you can refer to my book, *Train at Home to Become a Certified Personal/Life Coach: The Essential Guide to Becoming a Personal Coach in Your Spare Time…and Before You Quit Your Day Job* (Writer's Club Press, 2003).

At-Home Training Programs

Abundant Practice: A Program for Coaches, P.O. Box 30523, 4567 Lougheed Hwy, Suite 201, Burnaby, British Columbia V5C 2J6, Tel: (604) 473-9884, Toll-Free Tel: (800) 610-0970, Web site: www.tlcsuccess.com. A series of courses for coaches who want to learn how to build their practice using solid business strategies. Completion time: 4 months. Tuition: $1,295.

Academy for Coach Training, 16301 NE 8th Street, Suite 216, Bellevue, WA 98006, Tel: (425) 401-0309, Fax: (425) 401-0311, E-mail: info@coachtraining.com, Web Site: www.coachtraining.com. Provides comprehensive coaching skills training. Completion time: 24 weeks. Tuition: $6,913.

ADD Coaching Academy, 17 Googas Road, Slingerlands, NY 12159, Tel: (518) 482-3458, Fax: (518) 482-1221, E-mail: david@addca.com, Web Site: www.add-coachacademy.com. Provides training for coaches to work with persons with attention deficit disorder. Completion time: 9 months. Tuition: $3,695.

Advantage Coaching, 324 E. Roosevelt Rd, Suite 206, Wheaton, IL 60187, Tel: (630) 682-8447, Toll-free: (800) 657-5904, Fax: (630) 681-9233, E-mail: info@advantagecoaching.com, Web Site: www.advantagecoaching.com. Offers two corporate coach training programs through the National Association of Business Coaches. Completion time: 3 months. Tuition: $1,100.

Career Coach Institute, 10299 Scripps Trail E-214, San Diego, CA 92131, Toll-free: (866) CCOACH-4, Fax: (208) 692-0574, E-mail: info@careercoachinstitute.com, Web Site: www.careercoachinstitute.com. A career coach-training program resulting in certification. Completion time: 6 months. Tuition: $1,295-$4,995.

Ciris Alliance: Power Coach Network, 208/15 Albert Avenue, Broadbeach, Queensland 4218, Australia, E-mail: executive@cirisalliance.com, Web: cirisalliance.com/opportunities/trainingprograms.html. Power coach training and membership in the Ciris Alliance. Completion time: 3-4 weeks. Tuition: Australian $500-$1,800.

Coach for Life, 6343 El Cajon Blvd. #138, San Diego, CA 92115, E-mail: coaching@coachforlife.com, Web: www.coachforlife.com. Coaching training based on the Fulfillment Coaching Model.™ Completion time: 9-21 months. Tuition: $3,395-$10,495.

Coach University (CoachU), P.O. Box 2124, Salina, KS 7402-2124, Toll-free: 800-482-6224, E-mail: info@coachu.com (automated brochure), help@coachu.com (questions), Web: www.coachu.com. Provides coaching courses for novice or experienced coaches with in-house CoachU certification. Completion time: 2 years. Tuition: $4,795.

The Coaches Training Institute (CTI), 1879 Second Street, San Rafael, CA 94901, Tel: 415-451-6000, Toll-free: 800-691-6008, E-mail: info@thecoaches.com, Web: www.thecoaches.com. ICF accredited certification program using the Co-Active Coaching Model. Completion time: 6 months. Tuition: $3,395.

Coaching from Spirit, P.O. Box 836, Saxonburg, PA 16056, E-mail: admissions@coachingfromspirit.com, Web: www.coachingfromspirit.com. Training to become a Spirit Coach. Completion time: 4-12 months. Tuition: $1,300-$2,600.

"I've failed over and over and over again in my life and that is why I succeed."—Michael Jordan

Coachville, Tel: 866-Coachville, E-mail: help@coachville.com, Web: www. coachville.com. Free coach training, resources, and referral service. Completion time: 6+ months. Tuition: Free.

College of Executive Coaching, 3875 Telegraph Road PMB A115, Ventura, CA 93003, Tel: 805-647-7760, Toll-free: 888-764-8844, E-mail: info@executive-coachcollege.com, Web: www.executivecoachcollege.com. Offers a 72-hour executive coach certification program. Completion time: 72 hours. Tuition: $565/course.

Comprehensive Coaching U, 727 Mallard Place, North Wales, PA 19454, Toll-free: 877-401-6165, E-mail: contact@coachinginstruction.com, Web: www. comprehensivecoachingu.com. A holistic approach to coaching skills. Completion time: 12-24 months. Tuition: $3,000-$8,000.

Corporate Coach University International, P.O. Box 2800-331, Carefree, AZ 85377, Tel: 719-266-8057, Toll-free: 800-482-6224, E-mail: admissions@coach-inc.com, Web: www.ccui.com. Certification program in business coaching for managers and professionals. Completion time: 6-12 weeks. Tuition: $3,595.

EDUCOACH, 16697 North 108th Way, Scottsdale, AZ 85259, Tel: 480-515-5220, E-mail: director@educoach.com, Web:www.educoach.com. Coach training using the Totally Coached School™ Model. Completion time: 12 weeks. Tuition: $1,500.

Executive Coach Academy, 201 West 74th Street, Suite 14F, New York, NY 10023, Tel: 212-501-7666, E-mail: programquestions@executivecoachacademy.com, Web: www.executivecoachacademy.com. Sixteen-week executive coaching program. Completion time: 16 weeks. Tuition: $1,950-$2,100.

Fill Your Coaching Practice, Web: www.fillyourpractice.com. Condensed training program in obtaining clients for your coaching practice. Completion time: 8 weeks. Tuition: $97.

International Coach Academy, P.O. Box 307272, Columbus, OH 43230-9998, Tel: 866-476-9655, E-mail: info@icoachacademy.com, Web:www.icoachacademy. com. Coach training for both the beginner and practicing coach. Completion time: 6-24 months. Tuition: $2,624-$3,800.

Institute for Life Coach Training, 2801 Wakonda Drive, Fort Collins, CO 80521, Tel: 888-267-1206, E-mail: info@lifecoachtraining.com, Web: www. lifecoachtraining.com. A program for therapists, counselors, human services professionals, and others who want to learn coaching skills. Completion time: 15 weeks-6 months. Tuition: $1,695.

Kadmon Academy of Human Potential, Box BCM-3695, London EX1N 3XX, United Kingdom, Tel: (020) 7919 6032, E-mail: lifecoaching@ ukprofessionals.com, Web: www.lifecoaching.ukprofessionals.com. Coach training with a holistic approach. Completion time: 12 months. Tuition: GBP 995 (approx. US$1,500).

Life on Purpose Institute, 1160 W. Blue Ridge Road, P.O. Box 834, Flat Rock, NC 28731, Tel: 828-697-9239, E-mail: brad@lifeonpurpose.com, Web: www.lifeonpurpose.com/coachtrain.html. Training and certification as a Life on Purpose Coach. Completion time: 12 months. Tuition: $2,950.

Life Purpose Institute, 8775 Aero Drive, Suite 233, San Diego, CA 92123-1779, Tel: 858-573-0888, E-mail: information@lifepurposeinstitute.com, Web: www.lifepurposeinstitute.com. Coach training in life purpose and career coaching using the Life Purpose Process©. Completion time: 13 weeks. Tuition: $2,295.

Live Your Dream by Joyce Chapman, PMB #111, 826 Orange Avenue, Coronado, CA 92118-2698, Tel: 541-994-9971, Web: www.joycechapman.com. Dream and journaling coaching based on Joyce Chapman's bestselling books. Completion time: 3-6 months+. Tuition: $1,000-$1,500.

"The great aim of education is not knowledge but action."—Herbert Spencer

MentorCoach4400 East West Highway #1104, Bethesda, MD 20814, Tel: 304-986-5688, E-mail: info@mentorcoach.com, Web: www.mentorcoach.com. Provides working, licensed therapists with knowledge and skills to add coaching to their practice. Completion time: 6 months. Tuition: $1,995.

Optimal Functioning Institute, 903 Luttrell Street, Suite 1, Knoxville, TN 37917, Tel: 423-524-9549, Web: www.addcoach.com. A comprehensive ADD coach-training program. Completion time: 15-18 months. Tuition: $3,250.

Parent as Coach Academy, P.O. Box 14032, Portland, OR 97293, Tel: 503-236-6103, E-mail: info@parentascoach.com, Web: www.parentascoach.com. Coach training for working with parents, teens and families. Completion time: 6 months. Tuition: $2,700.

Relationship Coaching Institute, P.O. Box 111783, Campbell, CA 95011, Tel: 408-261-3332, Web: www.relationshipcoachinginstitute.com. Relationship coach training and membership support. Completion time: Varies by class. Tuition: One-time enrollment fee of $495. Monthly membership dues: $29-$49 month.

Results Life Coaching, US Operations, 47 Clive Street, Metuchen, NJ 08840-1060, Tel: 866-854-5433, E-mail: rlcnj@resultslifecoaching.com, Web: www.resultslifecoaching.com. A life coach training program. Completion time: 12 weeks. Tuition: $2,995.

For More Information...

Books

Train at Home to Become a Certified Personal/Life Coach, by Michelle McGarry (Writer's Club Press, 2003).

Co-Active Coaching: New Skills for Coaching People Toward Success in Work and Life, by Laura Whitworth, Henry House, Phil Sandahl, and Henry Kimsey-House (Davies-Black Publishers, 1998).

The Portable Coach: 28 Surefire Strategies for Business and Personal Success, by Thomas Leonard and Byron Larson (Scribner, 1998).

Take Time for Your Life: A Personal Coach's Seven-Step Program for Creating the Life You Want, by Cheryl Richardson (Broadway Books, 1999).

Take Yourself to the Top: The Secrets of American's #1 Career Coach, by Laura Berman Fortgang (Warner Books, 1998).

Get Clients Now! A 28-Day Marketing Program for Professionals and Consultants, by C.J. Hayden (AMACOM, 1999).

Masterful Coaching, by Robert Hargrove (Jossey-Bass/Pfeiffer, 2002).

Executive Coaching with Backbone and Heart: A Systems Approach to Engaging Leaders with Their Challenges, by Mary Beth O'Neill (Jossey-Bass, 2000).

Therapist as Life Coach: Transforming Your Practice, by Patrick Williams and Deborah C. Davis (W.W. Norton & Co., 2002).

Organizations

International Coach Federation (ICF), 1444 I Street NW, Suite 700, Washington, D.C. 20005, Tel: 888-423-3131 or 202-712-9039, Web: www.coachfederation.org, E-mail: icfoffice@coachfederation.org.

Worldwide Association of Business Coaches (WABC), 8578 Echo Place West, Sidney, BC V8L 5E2 Canada. Web: www.wabccoaches.com, E-mail: member-support@wabccoaches.com.

International Association of Personal and Professional Coaches (IAPBC), One Royce Plaza, P.O. Box 300089, Houston, TX 77230-0089, Tel: 713-436-4334, Web: www.iapbc.org.

International Consortia of Business Coaches (I-CBC), Web: www.i-cbc.com.

Professional Coach and Mentors Association (PCMA), Tel: 800-979-7262, Web: www.pcmaonline.com, E-mail: info@pcmaonline.com.

Christian Coaches Network (CCN), Tel: 425-558-1845, Web: www. christiancoaching.com, E-mail: director@christiancoaching.com.

Web Sites

www.coachville.com—membership organization with free coach training

www.findacoach.com—directory and referral service for coaches

www.work2wealth.com—life coaching for home business entrepreneurs

www.electricenvisions.com—a weight management coaching practice

www.surpassyourdreams.com—a career coaching practice

www.thecoachinglounge.com—a home business coaching practice

Personal Trainer

If you're interested in becoming a personal trainer, there are bunch of distance-learning programs for you. Each has its own specialties and unique aspects. From strength training to sports conditioning to Pilates, you can learn it all from home. Personal training—one-on-one fitness training—is the fastest growing profession in the health and fitness field, and usually involves designing resistive exercise programs. There are some interesting specializations a personal trainer can choose, such as personal training for adolescents, pre-natal fitness, fitness for older adults, and many more.

Personal trainers do a variety of activities with clients, including: obtaining health/medical information; assessing client expectations, preferences, motivation, and readiness; obtaining a detailed lifestyle and exercise history; interpreting the results of client assessment; establishing client-specific goals and objective measures; determining appropriate fitness parameters; teaching safe and effective exercise technique; and teaching strategies that promote physical activity. They are knowledgeable in exercise physiology, kinesiology, anatomy, motor learning/control, nutrition, substance abuse, weight management, stress management, and basic behavioral sciences. Certification programs in personal training can also cover business strategies, legal and ethical responsibilities, and fair business practices.

At-Home Training Programs

Courses in Fitness and Conditioning, United States Sports Academy, One Academy Drive, Daphne, AL 36526, Tel: 251-626-3303. Web: www.ussa.edu, E-mail: academy@ussa.edu

The United States Sports Academy has various online courses in fitness and conditioning available. They also offer certificates as a Fitness Specialist and Athletic Training, but not all courses are online. Available online courses include: Psychological Aspects of Health and Fitness Programs; Sport and Fitness Nutrition; Aerobic Dance Exercise; Fitness Education for Children; Teaching Children Gymnastics; Sport Marketing; Sport Public Relations & Fundraising; Personal Training; Marketing of Leisure Services; and more. Tuition: $50-$100/course.

Fitness Instruction (Undergraduate Certificate), University of California, Los Angeles (UCLA), 10995 Le Conte Ave, Los Angeles, CA 90024-2883, Tel: 310-825-7093, Web: www.uclaextension.edu/fitness, E-mail: fitness@uclaextension.edu

The eight-course (24 credits) Fitness Instruction certificate from UCLA is designed for fitness instructors, personal trainers, sports and strength coaches, registered dietitians, nutritionists, and other allied health professionals who with to acquire specific knowledge in fitness instruction, health promotion, and disease prevention. The six core courses are: Applied Anatomy and Biomechanics for Fitness Instructors; Introduction to Human Nutrition; Exercise Physiology for Fitness Instruction; Resistance Training Fundamentals; Fitness Testing and Health Risk Appraisal; and Adult Fitness Instruction—Theory and Practice. Two electives and a comprehensive exam complete the program. Tuition: $300-$500/course.

> "Everywhere is walking distance if
> you have the time."—Steven Wright

Personal Training Certification Home Study Course, American Council on Exercise, 5820 Oberlin Dr., Suite 102, San Diego, CA 92121-3787, Tel: 800-825-3636, Web: www.acefitness.org, E-mail: support@acefitness.org

The Personal Training Certificate Home Study Course from the American Council on Exercise includes: *The Personal Trainer Manual: The Resource for Fitness Professionals (2nd edition)*; *Master the Manual—A Study Guide*; a sample test for the Personal Trainer Certification Exam with 60 questions representative of the actual ACE Personal Trainer exam; a 160-page personal trainer home study course guide with review questions to help you assess your progress; flashcards to help you review; six 30-minute instructional audiocassettes; 12- and 20-week planners to aid you in scheduling your home study program; free consultation with their resource center staff; and self-guided online review questions. Certification exam fees are extra. Course fee: $299.95.

Personal Fitness Trainer Certification, International Fitness Professionals Association (IFPA), 14509 University Point Place, Tampa, FL 33613, Tel: 800-785-1924 or 813-979-1925, Web: www.ifpa-fitness.com

The IFPA offers a Personal Fitness Trainer Program, as well as many others. The Personal Fitness Trainer Program teaches and tests on the essential information to train individuals in gyms, health clubs, and one-on-one fitness training environments. Subject areas include: basic muscle physiology; energy metabolism; exercise physiology training principles; strength and aerobic conditioning; safety guidelines; sports training; exercise testing; body composition analysis; safety, anatomy, and exercise; program design and development; documentation; nutritional considerations for the personal trainer; psychology, motivation, ethics, and success; and the business of fitness (marketing, law, finance). The program includes *The Book on Personal Training* textbook, study outline, review workshop, 2 instructional videos, and certification exam. Course fee: $429.

Other programs IFPA offers via distance learning include: Advanced Personal Trainer ($429), Sports Nutrition Specialist ($429), Weight Management Instructor ($699), Group Fitness Instructor ($399) Youth Fitness Instructor ($449), and Tai Chi Instructor ($299).

Personal Trainer Certification, National Association for Fitness Certification (NAFC), P.O. Box 67, Sierra Vista, AZ 85636, Tel: 800-324-8315 or 520-452-8712, Web: www.body-basics.com, E-mail: bodybasics@body-basics.com

NAFC offers a Personal Trainer Certification, as well as others. The Personal Trainer Certification consists of three courses: Weight Training, Fitness Assessment, and Lifestyle Consultant. Materials included in the course include textbooks and a workbook study guide, instructional videos, and hands-on assignments. A local librarian that the student chooses proctors the final exam. Course fee: $399. The Personal Trainer Certification can be combined with other certifications with reduced rates (Personal Trainer/Wellness Consultant: $599; Personal Trainer/Group Fitness Instructor: $599).

Other individual certifications offered include: Wellness Consultant Certification ($499); Group Fitness Instructor Certification ($399); Sport & Recreation Trainer Certification ($359); and Expecting Fitness—Pre- & Post-Natal Fitness Certification ($75).

Certified Fitness Trainer (CFT), International Sports Sciences Association (ISSA), 400 E. Gutierrez Street, Santa Barbara, CA 93101, Tel: 805-884-8111, Web: www.issaonline.com

The ISSA offers a Certified Fitness Trainer program, as well as a variety of other certifications. The Certified Fitness Trainer program covers information on designing resistive exercise programs, nutrition, sports medical issues, business and marketing skills, anatomy, kinesiology, injury prevention, supplementation and nutrition, and all aspects of weight training and strength conditioning. The course includes the ISSA textbook, *Fitness: The Complete Guide*, an online interactive teaching program, CFT video, business guide, toll-free technical support, online technical support, a free weekend seminar, and an ISSA certificate upon completion. Course fee: $595.

Also offered by the ISSA certifications as: Fitness Therapist ($595); Specialist in Performance Nutrition ($550); Specialist in Fitness for Older Adults ($595); Specialist in Sports Conditioning ($550); Youth Fitness Trainer ($595); Endurance Fitness Trainer ($495); Specialist in Martial Arts Conditioning ($495); Water Fitness Trainer ($495); Specialist in Adaptive Fitness ($495); and Golf Fitness Trainer ($495).

Personal Trainer Certification, National Endurance Sports Trainers Association (NESTA), 31441 Santa Margarita Parkway, Suite A-140, Rancho Santa Margarita, CA 92688-1835, Tel: 877-348-6692 or 949-589-9166, Web: www.nestacertified.com

NESTA offers a Personal Trainer Certification and a host of other certifications as well. The Personal Trainer certification covers weight training; warm-ups and stretching; client evaluations; safety; starting your business—marketing/advertising techniques; ethics/legal issues; basic anatomy & physiology; personal image for success; networking; nutrition; and more. Materials included are: 2 instructional videos; 3 audio CD lessons; workbook and course instructions; test & answer sheet; and additional instructions for student help, e-mail support, and use of their online learning system. Group pricing is available if two or more students want to share materials. Course fee: $179. For combination of Certified Personal Trainer and Certified Advanced Personal Trainer: $259. A special CD-ROM, *Jump Start Your Fitness Business*, is available for $29.95.

Additional certifications available include: Advanced Personal Trainer ($125); Holistic Fitness Practitioner ($299); Sport Yoga™ Instructor ($299); Fitness Management/Marketing Certification ($75); Speed, Agility & Quickness Trainer ($199); Mind-Body Fitness Specialist ($75); Kick Boxing Certification ($229); Lifestyle and Weight Management Specialist ($75); and more.

"The road to success is always
under construction."—Arnold Palmer

Certified Personal Trainer Program, St. Augustine School of Medical Assistants and Health Sciences, 1455 Tallevast Road, Dept. L0130, MedAssistant.org Project, Sarasota, FL 34243, Web: www.medassistant.org, E-mail: info@ medassistant.org

St. Augustine School of Medical Assistants and Health Sciences offers a Certified Personal Trainer Program, as well as a Nutrition Specialist Program. This online program uses the textbook, *Program Design for Personal Trainers*, and teaches the courses: Introduction to Exercise and Personal Training; Basic Fitness Program Design; Medical and Health History; Health Risk Factors; Introduction to Exercise Physiology; The Cardiorespiratory System; Exercise Monitoring; Basic Exercise Physiology; Interval Conditioning; Exercise Equipment; Special Client Needs; and Nutrition and Personal Fitness. All courses are online and self-paced. An open-book online exam completes the program. Tuition: $345. A payment plan is available.

Personal Trainer Certification, NDEITA, 5955 Golden Valley Road, Suite 240, Minneapolis, MN 55422, Tel: 800-237-6242 or 763-545-2505, Web: www.ndeita.com

NDEITA offers a Personal Trainer Certification Program, as well as a Pilates Certification. The Personal Trainer Certification consists of 14 hours of lecture, demonstrations, and hands-on practical application. Extra materials (for extra cost) include *NDEITA Personal Trainer Manual* (required) and the *Personal Trainer Study Workbook* (recommended). Subjects covered include: exercise science refresher; health & fitness assignments; exercise programming for healthy adults; exposure to cardiovascular & strength training equipment; dynamics of communication & leadership skills; and a written exam/national certification. Course fee: $329. The Pilates Certification Program is also available for $329.

Fitness and Nutrition Course, Education Direct, 925 Oak Street, Scranton, PA 18515, Tel: 800-275-4410, Web: www.educationdirect.com, E-mail: info@ educationdirect.com

The Fitness & Nutrition program from Education Direct covers: Exercise and How it Affects the Body; Injury Prevention and First Aid; Nutrition and General Health; Sports Nutrition; Stress Management and Reduction; Designing a Conditioning/Fitness Program; and Business Skills for the Fitness Field. Materials included are a pair of 5-pound dumbbells, a fat calculator, and a pedometer. Course fee: $499.

Professional Fitness Specialist Program, Professional Career Development Institute (PCDI), 430 Technology Parkway, Norcross, GA 30092-3406, Tel: 800-223-4542 or 770-729-8400, Web: www.pcdi-homestudy.com, E-mail: info@pcdi.com

The PCDI Professional Fitness Specialist Program is comprised of 18 lessons: Fitness and Wellness; Preparing for Exercise, Training Threshold; Cardiovascular Fitness; Developing Flexibility; Developing Endurance and Strength; Strength and Endurance Exercises; Measuring and Controlling Body Fat; Skill-Related Fitness—Body Mechanics; Wellness and Fitness Nutrition; Managing Stress, Evaluating Fitness Facilities; Combating Threats to Your Health, Addiction; Combating Threats to Your Health, Physical and Mental Disorders; The Athlete's Diet; High-Impact Meals for Peak Performance; Sugar, Carbohydrates, Protein and Hydration; Eating for Exercise and Recovery, Dietary Supplements; Weight Management for Athletes—Lean Body Mass; and Weight Management for Athletes—Losing and Gaining Safely. Course fee: $789.

For More Information…

Books

The Personal Trainer Business Handbook, by Ed Gaut (Pierpoint Martin, 1994).

The Business of Personal Training, edited by Scott Roberts (Human Kinetics Publishing, 1996).

The Personal Trainer's Business Guide, by Craig Mastrangelo and Kirk Galiani (Exercise Science, 2001).

Program Design for Personal Trainers, by Douglas Brooks (Human Kinetics Publishing, 1998).

The Personal Trainer's Handbook, by Teri S. O'Brien (Human Kinetics Publishing, 2003).

E-book

Fabjob's Guide to Becoming a Personal Fitness Trainer, by Paige Wehner, www.fabjob.com ($14.95).

Organizations

International Association of Mind-Body Professionals (IAMBP), John Spencer Ellis Enterprises, Inc, c/o IAMBP, 31441 Santa Margarita Pkwy, Suite A140, Rancho Santa Margarita, CA 92688, Tel: 877-348-6692 or 949-589-9166 ext. 4, Web: www.mindbodypro.com.

International Fitness Professionals Association (IFPA), 14509 University Point Place, Tampa, FL 33613, Tel: 800-785-1924 or 813-979-1925, Web: www.ifpa-fitness.com.

National Association for Fitness Certification (NAFC), P.O. Box 67, Sierra Vista, AZ 85636, Tel: 800-324-8315 or 520-452-8712, Web: www.body-basics.com, E-mail: bodybasics@body-basics.com.

International Sports Sciences Association (ISSA), 400 E. Gutierrez Street, Santa Barbara, CA 93101, Tel: 805-884-8111, Web: www.issaonline.com.

National Endurance Sports Trainers Association (NESTA), 31441 Santa Margarita Parkway, Suite A-140, Rancho Santa Margarita, CA 92688-1835, Tel: 877-348-6692 or 949-589-9166, Web: www.nestacertified.com.

American Council on Exercise, 5820 Oberlin Dr., Suite 102, San Diego, CA 92121-3787, Tel: 800-825-3636, Web: www.acefitness.org, E-mail: support@acefitness.org

National Strength & Conditioning Association, P.O. Box 9908, Colorado Springs, CO 80932, Tel: 800-815-6826 or 719-632-6722, Web: www.nsca-lift.org.

American College of Sports Medicine, P.O. Box 1440, Indianapolis, IN 46206-1440, (317) 637-9200 Web: www.acsm.org.

Web Sites

www.jobsinsports.com—a subscription site of sports jobs

www.ptonthenet.com—lots of personal training info

www.ptconsultants.com—Personal Training Business Consultants International

www.ictraining.com—lots of info about certification and personal training

www.ideafit.com—IDEA Health & Fitness Association

Public Relations Specialist

Public relations takes time, skill, and patience. Training doesn't hurt, either. Even if you're not a PR guru, these courses could help you run the business you already have, or will begin soon. Public relations professionals know how to work with media in order to get publicity, run press conferences, plan special events, plan author tours—anything to promote their clients' wares. They work with all kinds of clients, from corporations to individuals. They write press releases and compile press kits, write speeches, plan events, prepare clients for interviews, and manage crises. Public relations professionals have to be extraordinarily good with people, and be gracious under pressure.

Public relations professionals help small businesses by providing a high-impact, low-cost way to get key messages to an intended audience. Public relations consultants have the opportunity to learn about a lot of different companies and industries. P.R. consultants are needed by all types and sizes of corporations in such diverse industries as entertainment, fashion, financial services, high tech, manufacturing, professional sports, retail, and transportation. Public relations is also used by non-profit groups, churches, universities, politics, healthcare, and even government entities.

> **"Some are born great, some achieve greatness,**
> **and some hire public relations officers."—Daniel Boorstin**

If you're going out on your own in P.R., the Public Relations Society of America (PRSA) maintains a database of freelance public relations professionals that you can list your business in. Also, check out their book, *How to Start Your Own P.R. Firm,* by John Gladstone and Edward Gillow (PRSA, 1998) (see "Books," below).

At-Home Training Programs

Public Relations (Undergraduate certificate), Rochester Institute of Technology (RIT), One Lomb Memorial Drive, Rochester, NY 14623-5603, Tel: 585-475-2234, Web: http://distancelearning.rit.edu, E-mail: online@rit.edu

The certificate in public relations from RIT consists of 20 credits. Courses include: Introduction to Public Relations; Strategic Public Relations; Speechwriting; Managing the Project; Media Relations; Writing for the Organization; Advertising Evaluation and Technology; Promotional Writing; and Scripting. Tuition: $307/credit.

Public Relations (Undergraduate certificates), University of California, Los Angeles (UCLA), 10995 Le Conte Ave, Los Angeles, CA 90024-2883, Tel: 310-825-0641, Web: www.uclaextension.edu

UCLA has three certificates in public relations—a general PR certificate (29 credits); a nonprofit public relations concentration (35 credits); and an entertainment publicity concentration (30 credits). Courses available include: Fundamentals of Public Relations; Writing for Public Relations; Elements of Publicity; Public Relations Management; Working with the Media; Special Events Planning; Writing the Feature Article; Newsletters—Writing, Editing, and Preparation; Crisis Management and Communications; Marketing Essentials for Successful Public Relations; The Art of Fundraising; Public Relations for Nonprofit

Organizations; Entertainment Public Relations; Publicity for the Entertainment Industry; and more. Tuition: $300-$500/course.

Not-for-Profit Public Relations (Bachelor degree), St. Mary-of-the-Woods College, Women's External Degree Program (WED), St. Mary-of-the-Woods, IN 47876, Tel: 800-926-SMWC or 812-535-5186, Web: www.smwc.edu, E-mail: smwc@smwc.edu

The Not-for-Profit Public Relations Bachelor degree consists of 125 credits, 41 of which are not-for-profit core courses that include: NFP Fundamentals; Macroeconomics; General Psychology; Principles of Management; Not-for-Profit Administration; Principles of Marketing; and more. The public relations courses include: Introduction to Mass Media; Graphic Design I; Consumer Behavior & Promotion Management; Public Relations; Salesmanship; Reporting; Principles of Public Relations Writing; and NFP Internship. Tuition: $307/credit.

For More Information...

Books

How to Start Your Own P.R. Firm, by John Gladstone and Edward Gillow (PRSA, 1998). Available at www.prsa.org.

Successfully Managing Your Public Relations Practice, by Public Relations Society of America (1998). Available at www.prsa.org.

The Associated Press Guide to News Writing, by Rene J. Word Cappon (Arco Publishing, 2000).

The Public Relations Writers' Handbook, by Merry Aronson and Don Spetner (Jossey-Bass, 1998).

Guerilla Publicity: Hundreds of Sure-Fire Tactics to Get Maximum Sales for Minimum Dollars, by Jay Conrad Levinson, Rick Frishman, and Jill Lublin (Adams Media Corp., 2002).

The Handbook of Strategic Public Relations and Integrated Communications, edited by Clarke L. Caywood (McGraw-Hill Trade, 1997).

Publicity and Media Relations Checklists, by David R. Yale (McGray-Hill Trade, 1995).

Writing Effective News Releases: How to Get Free Publicity for Yourself, Your Business, or Your Organization (Piccadilly Books 1992).

E-book

Fabjob's Guide to Becoming a Public Relations Specialist, by Lynne Bliss, www. fabjob.com ($14.95).

Organizations

Public Relations Society of America, 33 Irving Place, New York, NY 10003-2376, Tel: 212-995-2230, Web: www.prsa.org.

Entertainment Publicists Professional Society, P.O. Box 5841, Beverly Hills, CA 90209-5841, Tel: (888) 399-EPPS, Web: www.eppsonline.org, E-mail: info@ eppsonline.org.

International Public Relations Association (IPRA), Web: www.irpanet.org.

National Council for Marketing and Public Relations, P.O. Box 336039, Greeley, CO 80633, Tel: 970-330-0771, bolson@ncmpr.org, Web; www.ncmpr.org.

Web Sites

www.learnpr.com—an at-home self-paced course in public relations for freelancers

www.agencyfinder.com—searchable directory of certified agencies, including public relations firms

www.prmuseum.com—Museum of Public Relations

www.workinpr.com—career search site for P.R. professionals

www.prnewswire.com—access to breaking news from thousands of organizations

Scopist

Ever wonder what happens to that "ticker tape" transcript the court reporter types? It goes to a scopist. A scopist is a professional who provides computer-aided transcription services for court reporters. The scopist receives the reporter's unedited, unresearched notes on a computer disk or via modem or e-mail. Scopists take the stenotyped report typed by the court reporters and translate it into a legible transcript. With the aid of specialized software and the scopist's skills of translating undefined stenotype into English, punctuation, researching, and formatting, a complete transcript is produced.

The basic skills a scopist needs are stenotype reading, a good command of the English language, computer knowledge and specialized CAT software, transcript formatting, familiarity with legal terminology and a flexibility and willingness to work to a reporter's specifications.

At-Home Training Programs

Internet Scoping School, 7445 Cherokee Court, Lolo, MT 59847, Tel: 406-273-2892, Web: www.scopeschool.com, E-mail: info@scopeschool.com

Internet Scoping School is the first Internet-based online scopist training course, and has been in existence since 1998. As well as providing a comprehensive training course, the school actively advertises and provides marketing opportunities for its graduates. The course teaches: reading of stenotype notes; how to produce a high-quality, well-edited manuscript, meeting the requirements of a variety of vendors; lots of tips on everything from marketing to reference materials to the scoping profession; and training on Case CATalyst software, made by Stenograph Corporation, the largest provider of court-reporting software, servicing 60-65% of practicing court reporters. Registration for the course includes all the modules (six total), one year membership to the National Court Reporter's Association (NCRA), and references. Fees: Full course, one-time payment, $1,995; Full course, pay-as-you-go, $2,300.

BeST Scoping Techniques, Judy Rakocinski, 4111 Dahoon Holly Court, Bonita Springs, FL 34134, Tel: 239-949-3145, Fax: 239-949-0763, Web: www.bestscopingtechniques.com, E-mail: jcrinc@comcast.net, or Cathy Vickio, Tel: 281-277-3305, E-mail: vickhou@worldnet.att.net

Best Scoping Techniques is an online self-paced training course to teach you how to become a successful scopist. The complete course teaches: how to read stenotype, sharpen grammar and punctuation, familiarization with medical and legal terms, and how to research on the Internet; how to zip and e-mail jobs, including what RTF and ASCII files are and when to use them; and how to organize your scoping business, including dealing with client preferences, income/expenses, scheduling work, pacing yourself, invoicing your clients, and getting paid. BeST will also provide you with a starting supply of business cards, ideas for brochures, and a custom Web site for your services. Course fee: $1,495.

For More Information...

Books

Successful Freelance Court Reporting, by Dana Chipkin and Wendy Mapstone (Delmar Learning, 2000).

Alternative Realtime Careers: A Guide to Closed Captioning and CART for Court Reporters, by Gary Robson (National Court Reporters Association, 2000).

<u>E-book</u>

Scopistry, by www.scopists.com ($7.99).

<u>Organizations</u>

National Court Reporters Association (NCRA), 8224 Old Courthouse Road, Vienna, VA 22182-3808, Tel: 800-272-6272, Web: www.verbatimreporters.org, E-mail: msic@ncrahq.org. Offers distance learning seminars with legalspan.com, certification, an annual convention, and the *NCRA Scopist Directory*.

The U.S. Court Reporters Association (USCRA), P.O. Box 465, Chicago, IL 60690-0465, Tel: 800-628-2730, Web: www.uscra.org, E-mail: uscra@uscra.org.

<u>Web Sites</u>

www.scopists.com—freelance directory and resources

www.scopistssupportgroup.com—scopist directory and resources

www.reportersupport.com—scopist directory

www.machineshorthand.com—resources for court reporters

www.stenovations.com—info on software and a scopist directory

Virtual Assistant/Secretarial Services

The Virtual Assistant (VA) business is growing rapidly, as many companies—big and small—are outsourcing their secretarial needs. And with the Internet, it's possible to have a professional virtual assistant on the other side of the country. A virtual assistant work as executive assistants, secretaries, data entry personnel, clerks, tax advisors, medical transcriptions, even Web designers. VAs are small business owners who become an integral part of their clients' lives, rather than working from project to project. Communication between clients and VAs is accomplished using phone, fax, e-mail diskette transfer, cassette tape, overnight mail, and instant messaging.

VAs perform most of the same duties that in-person assistants perform, including information processing, Internet research, bill paying services, mail and e-mail services, event planning, as well as assisting with travel arrangements. Education levels of virtual assistants vary, but they are normally well educated and have a variety of skills and experience in office management and computer systems and hardware. VAs need to be self-starters; have great computer and office skills; be able to anticipate the needs of others; make a commitment to keeping up to date on new software; and be able to accept and work with different personality types.

At-Home Training Programs

Virtual Assistant Training, Virtual Assistance U, Janet L. Jordon, 517 Fairfield Drive, Corpus Christi, TX 78412, Tel: 361-993-0923, Web: www. virtualassistanceu.com, E-mail: jordan@virtualassistanceu.com

The VA training at Virtual Assistance U is a 16-week program covering setting up a virtual assistant practice. Classes, coaching exercise, simulation exercises, and peer discussions are integral to the program. Core topics include: Developing Action Plans; Toolkits for Excellence; Strategies for Success 1 & 2; Alliances and Resources; Expert Coach Action Plan with Q&A; and On Target for Launch. IAVOA (see "Organizations," below) members receive a 10% discount on tuition. Course fee: $375. Mini courses are also available.

Executive Secretarial (Diploma), University of Northwestern Ohio, 1441 N. Cable Road, Lima, OH 45805, Tel: 419-998-3120, Web: www.unoh.edu/ academics/collegedl/, E-mail: info@unoh.edu

The Executive Secretarial Diploma from Northwestern Ohio consists of 72 credit hours in four quarters. Major requirements include: Written Communications; Relational Databases Microcomputers; Developing Business Presentations; Spreadsheet Applications; Keyboarding; Notehand Theory; Notehand Dictation and Transcription; Records Management; Machine Transcription; Office Systems & Procedures; Word Processing; and Advanced Document Formatting. Tuition: $195/credit.

Administrative Assistant (Associate degree), Madison Area Technical College, 3550 Anderson Street, Madison, WI 53704, Tel: 800-322-6100 or 608-246-6336, Web: www.matcmadison.edu, E-mail: admissions@matcmadison.edu

The Associate degree program in Administrative Assistance is a collaborative effort of Madison Area Technical College and the International Association of Administrative Professionals (see "Organizations, below). Courses are taught online and designed for individuals employed in a business office. Fourth semester students are eligible to site for the CPS® exam through the IAAP. The program is 69 credits. Tuition: $70-$100/credit.

Administrative Assistant Course, Allied Business Schools, 22952 Alcalde Drive, Laguna Hills CA 92653, Tel: 888-501-7686, Web: www.secretarialcourses.com, E-mail: allied@alliedschools.com

The Administrative Assistant course from Allied includes the *Administrative Assistant's Student Workbook* and the *Administrative Assistant's & Secretary's Handbook*. Topics covered include: Overview for the New Secretary; Daily Routine; Telephone Usage; Mail Services and Shipping; Travel Arrangement; Keeping Accurate Records; Office Machines; Telecommunications Equipment; Computer Communications; Keyboarding Skills; Word Processing; Correct English Usage; Bookkeeping and Accounting; and more. Also included is "The Business Plan for Home-Based Business." Course fee: $688.

For More Information…

Books

The Virtual Assistant's Building Your Client Base and Marketing 101 Manual and Workbook, by Christine Durst and Michael Haaren (Entrepreneur Publishing, 2000).

The Virtual Assistant's Pre-Launch Manual and Workbook, by Christine Durst and Michael Haaren (Entrepreneur Publishing, 2000).

How to Start a Home-Based Secretarial Services Business, by Jan Melnik (Globe Pequot Press, 1994).

Merriam-Webster's Secretarial Handbook (Merriam-Webster, 1995).

The Professional Secretary's Handbook, by Mary DeVries (Houghton Mifflin, 1995).

Complete Typing Business Guide: Everything You Need to Know to Start and Successfully Operate a Home-Based Typing Business, by Frank Chisenhall (Supertest Publishing, 1990).

E-books

Bizy's Guide to: How to Start Your Own Virtual Assistant Biz, by Diana Ennen & Kelly Poelker, www.bizymoms.com ($24.95).

Bizy's Guide to Starting a Profitable Home-Based Word Processing Business, by Diana Ennen, www.bizymoms.com ($24.95).

Up Close and Virtual: A Practical Guide to Starting You Own Virtual Assistant Business, by Dianna Ennen and Kelly Poelker, www.another8hours.com ($24.95).

<u>Organizations</u>

International Virtual Assistants Association (IAVOA), 401 Virginia Drive, San Jacinto, CA 92583, Tel: 909-654-4326, Web: www.iavoa.com, E-mail: iavoa@aol.com.

International Virtual Assistants (IVA), 11024, Balboa Blvd., Suite 315, Los Angeles, CA 91344, Tel: 877-440-2750, Web: ww.ivaa.org.

International Association of Administrative Professionals (IAAP), 10502 NW Ambassador Drive, P.O. Box 20404, Kansas City, MO 64195-0404, Tel: 816-891-6600, Web: www.iaap-hq.org, E-mail: service@iaap-hq.org.

VACertification.com, Route 1 Box 275, Red Oak, OK 74563, Tel: 918-753-2716, Web: www.vacertification.com, E-mail: certification@vacertification.com. Offers certification options of Professional Virtual Assistant (PVA) and Master Virtual Assistant (MVA).

<u>Web Sites</u>

http://messageboards.ivillage.com/iv-wfoffice—message board on iVillage.com for VAs

www.svaclub.com—Specialist Virtual Assistant Club

www.virtualassistanttips.com—marketing and organizational tips for VAs

www.virtualbizgroup.com—membership and referral organization

www.innovativecoach.com—VA coaching

www.avirtualsolution.com—VA startup resources, directory of VAs

www.staffcentrix.com—Staff Centrix Employment Service

www.va4hire.com—Virtual Assistants for Hire

Web Site Designer/Webmaster

Web Site Designers and Webmasters need a variety of different skills these days. From learning different programming languages and software to understanding how the Internet works, Web designers have their work cut out for them. But it can be a fun, challenging, and creative career. There's no doubt that the Web is ever-expanding, so the need for talented and energetic Web designers will continue to rise. A Web designer can work for almost anyone—small businesses, individuals, non-profits, and even schools. Everyone needs a Web site these days.

Web designers can also offer a variety of services in addition, such as Internet consulting and training, Web site hosting, e-commerce development, search engine registration, and even marketing. Start-up concerns are similar to a graphic designer—a great computer is a must, plus all the additional software. For more information on starting a home-based Web design business, check out *How to Start a Home-Based Web Design Business*, by Jim Smith (Globe Pequot Press, 2001) (see "Books," below).

Some courses and degrees here cover HTML programming, software, multimedia, and JavaScript, while others teach you software programs like FrontPage. The type of business you will run will determine what kind of education you choose.

At-Home Training Programs

Web and Desktop Publishing (Undergraduate certificate), Minot State University, 500 University Avenue West, Minot, North Dakota 58707, Tel: 800-777-0750, Web: http://online.minotstate.edu, E-mail: msu@minotstateu.edu.

The Desktop and Web Publishing Certificate Program includes training in basic software programs, as well as specialized training in the design of business documents (letterhead, business cards, certificates, etc.) and Web pages. Newly acquired skills are further enhanced with actual application techniques in the E-Commerce Technology course. All course are available online and can be applied toward the MIS Bachelor of Science degree. Courses: Information Processing; Internet and World Wide Web; Desktop Publishing and Design; Website Design; JavaScript; and E-Commerce Technology (18 total credit hours). Students have 16 weeks in the fall/spring semesters to complete the course, or 8 weeks in the summer. Tuition: $126.83/credit hour.

Web Design (Diploma), The Art Institutes Institute Online, 420 Blvd. Of the Allies, Pittsburgh, PA 15219, Tel: 877-872-8869 or 412-291-5100, Web: www.aionline.edu, E-mail: aioadm@aii.edu

The Web Design Diploma is 36 credits (12 courses) and teaches the basics of working in the Web environment with emphasis on Web page design, page editing software, Web graphics, video production for the Web, and JavaScript. The Institute also offers a diploma in digital design. Courses for the Web Design Diploma include: Computer Literacy; Information Design; Fundamentals of World Wide Web; Digital Imaging for Web and Multimedia; Computer Animation for Multimedia and Web; Desktop Video; Web Site Development I & II; and more. Tuition: $1,135/course ($345/credit).

Web Page Design (Undergraduate certificate), Wytheville Community College, 1000 E. Main Street, Wytheville, VA 24382-3308, Tel: 800-468-1195 x4757 or 216-223-4757, Web: www.wc.cc.va.us

The Web Page Design certificate from Wytheville Community College consists of six courses (19 credits). Courses include: Survey of Internet Services; Web Page Design I; Internet Programming I & II; Database Management and File Structure; and a Capstone Project. Tuition: $59.71/credit for Virginia residents; $204.14/credit for non-residents.

Web Professional: Foundations (Undergraduate certificate), The Pennsylvania State University Park Campus, World Campus, 207 Mitchell Bldg., University Park, PA 16802, Tel: 800-252-3592, Web: www.worldwidecampus.psu.edu

Penn State offers three non-credit certificates in Web design: Web Professional: Foundations ($3,500); Web Professional: Design & Multimedia Principles ($2,950); and Web Professional: Usability Advocate ($869). Courses available include: Functional Web Site Design; Layout Design for the Web; Beyond HTML; Intro to Photoshop; Audio for the Web; Streaming Media; Web Animation; Advanced Web Graphics; HTML Level 1 & 2; JavaScript Level 1 & 2; Multimedia and the Web; Web Server Administration; and Security Issues & Basics.

> ### "The WWW is first and foremost an emotional experience. Few Web sites reflect this important priority."—Grant Fairley

Web/Multimedia Authoring (Undergraduate certificate), Bellevue Community College, Distance Education, Room D261, 3000 Landerholm Cr. SE, Bellevue, WA 98007-6484, Tel: 425-564-2438, Web: www.distance-ed.bcc.ctc.edu, E-mail: landerso@bcc.ctc.edu

This certificate is a combination of Web page design, scripting, and streaming media. Students will learn how to author dynamic Web pages using the most current technology. In addition to prerequisites in English and digital media (10 credits), the program requires an additional 48-50 credits. Courses include: Web Multimedia Foundations; Web Development Foundations; Video/Animation Foundations; Imaging Foundations; Client-Side Scripting; Web Multimedia Authoring I & II; Web Design and Development I& II; and a Portfolio or Internship. Tuition: $67.76/credit for Washington residents; $80.95/credit for non-residents.

Java Programming (Undergraduate certificate), Regis University, 3333 Regis Blvd., Denver, CO 80221-1099, Tel: 800-388-2366 or 303-458-4100, Web: www.regis.edu

The Java Programming certificate from Regis consists of four courses (12 credits). Courses include: C Programming; Systems Analysis and Design; Object Oriented Analysis and Design; and Java Programming. The certificate can be applied toward the university's degrees in Computer Information Systems, Computer Networking, or Computer Science. Tuition: $280/credit.

Web Developer (Undergraduate certificate), College of Southern Maryland, P.O. Box 910, La Plata, MD 20646-0910, Tel: 301-934-7765, Web: www.csmd.edu/distance/index.htm, E-mail: info@csmd.edu

The Web Developer certificate from College of Southern Maryland is 21 credits. Courses include: Composition and Rhetoric; The Information Age; The Internet and Web Application Essentials; Intro to Principles of OOP and JavaScript; Advanced Web Authoring; Basic Web Server Setup and Security; Intro to Java Programming; and Web Project-Based Learning Application. Tuition: $81/credit.

Web Developer (Diploma), National American University, 321 Kansas City Street, P.O. Box 1780, Rapid City, SD 57709, Tel: 800-770-2959, Web: www.national.edu

The Web Developer Diploma from National American University consists of 55 credits. Courses include: Principles of Programming; UNIX; Web Page Development I & II; Programming in C/C++; JAVA Programming; Internet Server; Server-side Scripting; and Advanced JAVA Programming. Tuition: $200/credit.

The university also offers a Bachelor of Science degree in Information Technology with emphasis in Web Developer/Webmaster (184 credits). Additional courses include: general education requirements; Visual Basic; Apache WebServer; Database for Windows; and more.

"We've heard that a million monkeys at a million keyboards could produce the complete works of Shakespeare; now thanks to the Internet, we know that is not true."—Robert Wilensky

Web Developer (Undergraduate certificate), Northwestern Michigan College, 1701 E. Front Street, Traverse City, MI 49686, Tel: 800-748-0566 or 231-995-2017, Web: www.nmc.edu, E-mail: welcome@nmc.edu

The Web Developer certificate from Northwest Michigan College is designed to teach students the knowledge necessary to analyze information and to apply graphic design techniques to develop effective, pleasing, and useful Web sites. The program is 22 credits, or more if you need to take prerequisites. Courses include: Programming Logic & Design; Visual Basic Programming; HTML Programming; Introduction to Database Management; Personal Computer Database Concepts; Photoshop; Web Publishing; Professional Communications; Business Communications; Internet Publishing II; JavaScript; and Web Programming. Tuition: $95/credit for in-district students; $135/credit for out-of-district students; and $175/credit for out-of-state students.

Web Site Development (Undergraduate certificate), Webster University, 470 E. Lockwood Avenue, St. Louis, MO 63119, Tel: 314-968-6900, Web: www.webster.edu/worldclasroom

The courses offered in the Web Site Development certificate provide students with the basic knowledge and skills necessary to design and develop professional Web sites. The certificate is 18 credits, and courses include: HTML Programming; Web Animation; Data Handling on the Web; Web Scripting; Dynamic HTML; and Interactive Site Development. Tuition: $430/credit.

Web Site Development & Management (Associate degree, Undergraduate certificate), Champlain College, 163 South Willard Street, Burlington, VT 05401, Tel: 800-570-5858 or 802-860-2727, Web: www.champlain.edu, E-mail: admission@champlain.edu

Champlain College offers an Associate degree (60 credits) and a certificate (24 credits) in Web Site Development & Management. Courses for the certificate include: Introduction to Web Page Development; Relational Databases with Web Applications; Advanced Web Page Development; Introduction to Data Communications; Implementing Web Media/E-Commerce Technologies; Internet & Web Architecture; Server-Side Scripting; and Designing Media for the Web. Additional courses available for the Associate degree include: general education courses; Web Storyboarding; Dreamweaver; Word Processing; Implementing Web Media; and an internship. Tuition: $380/credit.

Web Site Developer (Graduate certificate), East Carolina University, School of Industry and Technology, Office of Graduate Studies, Rawl 121, Greenville, NC 27858-4353, Tel: 800-398-9275 or 252-328-6321, Web: www.sit.ecu.edu/ gradprog, E-mail: options@mail.ecu.edu

The Web Site Developer graduate certificate from East Caroline University provides hands-on experience using industrial standard software through their virtual server lab. The certificate is 15 graduate credits, with courses in: Internet Research Methods; Network Media Services; Dynamic Web Services; Enterprise Web Services; and Web Site Development. Tuition: $183/credit for North Carolina residents; $1,166/credit for non-residents.

Digital Arts: Web Design and Development (Associate degree), Rochester Community and Technical College, 851 30th Ave SE, Rochester, MN 55904-4999, Tel: 507-280-2965 or 800-247-1296, Web: www.rctc.edu, E-mail: kevin.dobbe@roch.edu

The Associate degree in Web Design and Development at Rochester Community and Technical College is Web-delivered, and consists of 64 credits. Courses include: general education requirements; Introduction to E-Business; Basics of Project Management; Client-Side Scripting; Database Design and Management; Visual Basic Programming; Interactive Web Design; Digital Projects; Multimedia Production; Vector Graphics Animation; and Internet Networking Basics. Tuition: $103/credit for Minnesota and North Dakota-approved residents; $192-$232/credit for non-residents.

Professional Web Site Design Program, Professional Career Development Institute (PCDI), 430 Technology Parkway, Norcross, GA 30092-3406, Tel: 800-223-4542 or 770-729-8400, Web: www.pcdi-homestudy.com, E-mail: info@pcdi.com

The Professional Web Site Design Program from PCDI consists of 18 lessons, as well as the *Web Page Design* textbook, *New Perspectives on Creating Web Pages with HTML* textbook, and Microsoft FrontPage 2000 software. Lessons include: What's the World Wide Web?; Hypertext Markup Language; Web Design 1 & 2; Time Management; Text Writing and Graphic Design; The Web and HTML; Adding Hypertext Links to a Web Page; Advanced Web Page Design; Designing with Tables; Frames; Creating Forms; Programming with JavaScript; Multimedia Web Pages; Adding Style to Your Web Site; Images and Frames; Elements and Components; and Tables/Managing a Web Site. Course fee: $989.

Web Design Programs, Education Direct, 925 Oak Street, Scranton, PA 18515, Tel: 800-275-4410, Web: www.educationdirect.com, E-mail: info@ educationdirect.com

Education Direct offers several courses in Web Design. They have programs in Web Page Developer; Java Programmer; Web Programming; and Internet Multimedia & Design. Program fees: $599-$699 each.

Web design classes, Barnes and Noble University, www.bn.com

Graphic and Web design classes, including Web Pages Made Easy, Dreamweaver, Flash, QuarkXPress, and DHTML. Free: Ranges from free to $99 each.

Bizy Classes—Create Your Own Web Site, The Basics of HTML and Create Your Own Web Site, Going Beyond the Basics, Online Courses from BizyMoms, Web: www.bizymoms.com

This Basic 4-week online class gets you started with the very basics of HTML, with one-on-one assistance from Instructor Jen Czawlytko, Webmaster for Bizymoms.com. This course includes information and resources for properly planning your web site, transferring files from your computer to your Web space, the HTML structure of a Web page, formatting text, adding images, adding hyperlinks, and more. This class is not for Web designers, but for those new to HTML and Web design. Course fee: $60. Going Beyond the Basics (4-week class): $60.

For More Information…

Books

How to Start a Home-Based Web Design Business, by Jim Smith (Globe Pequot Press, 2001).

Pricing Guide for Web Services: How to Make Money on the Information Data Highway (Brenner Information Group, 1997).

The Ultimate Web Developer's Sourcebook, by Jessica Keyes (AMACOM, 2001).

Designing Web Usability: The Practice of Simplicity, by Jakob Nielson (Pearson Education, 1999).

Web Design Virtual Classroom, by Laurie Ann Ulrich (McGraw-Hill Professional, 2001).

Professional Web Design: Techniques & Templates, by Clint Eccher (Charles River Media, 2002).

E-books

Bizy's Guide To Creating Success in Web Design, by Jennifer Czawlytko, Webmaster for www.bizymoms.com ($16.95).

Bizy's Guide to Web Site Proofreading as a Business, by Bruce Noeske, www.bizymoms.com ($17.95).

Fabjob's Guide to Becoming a Web Developer, by Rachel Al Hetzel, www.fabjob.com ($14.95).

Organizations

The HTML Writer's Guild/International Webmaster's Association, 119 E. Union Street, Suite F, Pasadena, CA 91101, Web: www.hwg.org or www.iwanet.org.

International Association of Webmasters & Designers (IAWMD), 13833-E4 Wellington Terrace, PMB Suite 214, Wellington, FL 33414, Tel: 561-533-9008, Web: www.iawmd.com.

Web Design & Developers Association, 8515 Brower, Houston, TX 77017, Tel: 435-518-9784, Web: www.wdda.org, E-mail: wdda@wdda.org.

Web Sites

www.newhorizons.com—online classes in every Web design topic you could ask for

www.thunderlizard.com—a company that hosts large conferences on Web design and software

www.webdesign.thelist.com—Buyer's Guide to Web Designers

www.bignosebird.com—free CGI scripts, graphics, tutorials

http://javaboutique.internet.com—free Java applets, games, tutorials

www.certifiedwebmaster.net—self-paced online certification program from IAWMD (see above)

www.tlance.com—freelance opportunities

Wedding Planner

A wedding planner—sometimes called a bridal consultant or a wedding director—helps brides and grooms plan their special day. This is no small task. The schooling you need to become a bridal consultant covers many fields, from hospitality, event planning, decorating, and diplomacy, to name a few. Other abilities that come in handy are bookkeeping, marketing, and negotiating. The market for wedding planners is growing, as weddings are becoming more and more elaborate.

Out-of-town weddings, weekend weddings, and specialty weddings make help and support all the more necessary. Most wedding planners are self-employed.

Many of the programs listed offer beginning, intermediate, and advanced courses or certifications. Most of the intermediate and advanced options have experience requirements (a certain number of years in the profession). Topics cover the wedding itself (planning, budgeting, ceremony, bridal party, reception, and much more) as well as writing your business plan and marketing your business. Upon completion of some programs, you are eligible to use their certification logos on your materials.

At-Home Training Programs

Certified Wedding Specialist Program, Weddings Beautiful Worldwide, A Division of National Bridal Service, 5001 W. Broad Street, Suite 214, Richmond, VA 23230, Tel: 804-288-1220, Web: www.weddingsbeautiful.com or www. nationalbridalservice.com, E-mail: info@weddingsbeautiful.com

This self-paced course includes membership in Weddings Beautiful Worldwide for four months, which includes bi-monthly newsletter; authorization to use WBW logos on your promo materials; professional control forms for planning, budgeting, and coordinating weddings; a listing in their referral directory; and affiliation with World Bridal Destination Weddings. The course is comprised of 18 assignments: Developing Your Business Plan; Your Business Forms and Contracts; Wedding Invitations; Mental Power; Developing Wedding Expertise; Directing Protestant and Military Weddings; Directing Catholic and Jewish Weddings; Directing Afro-American, Hispanic, and Orthodox Weddings; Receptions; Philosophy of Success; All About Ethnic Traditions and the History of Wedding Traditions; Wedding Fashions; Tabletop and the Bridal Registry; Talk Less, Say More; Developing Management Techniques; The Ultimate You— Personal Public Relations; and a Final Exam. Course fee: $695.

Wedding Consultant Certification Program, June Wedding, Inc.®, An Association for Event Professionals, 584 Castro Street, #452, San Francisco, CA 94114-2594, Web: www.junewedding.com, E-mail: robbi@junewedding.com

June Wedding, Inc.® offers in-person wedding specialist seminars, as well as home study courses: The Beginner Wedding/Event Consultant; The Advanced Wedding/Event Consultant; and The Professional Wedding/Event Consultant. The courses are for people who want to develop and fine tune skills, techniques, and service. Students learn to be in control of their business at every juncture and to create efficient, manageable, and realistic business plans. Written work and three telephone consultations are required, and a student manual is included. Students must complete the course within three months. Course fee: $1,000.

> "After seven years of marriage, I'm sure of two things—
> first, never wallpaper together, and second, you'll
> need two bathrooms…both for her."—Dennis Miller

Wedding Consultant Course, Wedding Careers Institute, Inc., 16225 Park Ten Place, Suite 500, Houston, TX 77084, Tel: 281-994-4141, Web: www.weddingcareers.com, E-mail: info@weddingcareers.com

The Wedding Careers Institute distance education program is self-paced. Students are allocated 3 months to complete the 4 exams, and then another 3 months to complete certification. The program includes: three months membership in the Wedding Careers Institute, Inc. Worldwide Association; a comprehensive 30-chapter training manual; online or telephone tutoring; 3 session exams and 1 final exam; diploma; certification guidelines; preparation assistance for the certification portfolio; WCII Board reviews of your portfolio; and WCII Web site logo confirming graduation and certification. Course fee: $795.

Professional Wedding Consultant Program, Association of Certified Professional Wedding Consultants (ACPWC), 7791 Prestwick Circle, San Jose, CA 95135, Tel: 408-528-9000, Web: www.acpwc.com, E-mail: annnola1@earthlink.net

The program from ACPWC covers everything you need to know to set up a business as a Professional Wedding Consultant. Topics include: Setting Up Your Business; Marketing Your Business; Effective Networking; Selecting and Working with Wedding Professionals; Types of Wedding Consultants/Charging for Services; Planning the Wedding Budget; Contract Information; Wedding Planning Schedule; Ceremonial Sites Guidelines; Entertainment Types and Costs; The Wedding Gown and Attire for Bridal Party; Wedding Attendants' Special Duties; and much more. Worksheets, forms, guidelines, samples, diagrams, layouts, floor plans, and responsibilities are also included. Course fee: $795.

Professional Bridal Consultant™, Association of Bridal Consultants (ABC), 200 Chestnutland Road, New Milford, CT 06776-2521, Tel: 860-355-0464, Web: www.bridalassn.com, E-mail: office@bridalassn.com

Educational materials are available from the Association of Bridal Consultants to become a Professional Bridal Consultant™. Students must have novice, consultant, or consultant auxiliary membership to participate ($150-$225). Courses for the Professional Bridal Consultant program include: Etiquette; Sales and Marketing; Wedding Day; Related Services; and Planning and Consulting. ABC also has an Accredited Bridal Consultant™ program and a Master Bridal Consultant™ program, each with experience requirements. Each course: $60. Professional Development Program: $360.

> "When two people love each other, they don't look at each other, they look in the same direction."—Ginger Rogers

Professional Bridal Consultant Program, Education Direct, 925 Oak Street, Scranton, PA 18515, Tel: 800-275-4410, Web: www.educationdirect.com, E-mail: info@educationdirect.com

The Professional Bridal Consultant program from Education Direct is endorsed by the Association of Bridal Consultants (ABC®), see below. Trial membership in ABC is included in the program. Also included is the "Welcome to the World of Wedding Planning" video, *Bride's Guide to Wedding Music* CD, *Martha Stewart Weddings* book, and more. Topics covered include: The Many Parts of the Wedding; Basics of a Bridal Business; The Role of a Consultant; How to Participate in a Bridal Show; How to Organize a Bridal Show; Ethnic and Specialty Weddings; and The Business of Weddings. Course fee: $699.

Bridal Consultant Program, Professional Career Development Institute (PCDI), 430 Technology Parkway, Norcross, GA 30092-3406, Tel: 800-223-4542 or 770-729-8400, Web: www.pcdi-homestudy.com, E-mail: info@pcdi.com

The Bridal Consultant Program from PCDI consists of 14 lessons: Making Dreams Come True; You are Cordially Invited; Etiquette, Traditions; and Customs; Ceremonies; Time Management Guide; The Wedding Budget; Dressing the Part; All the Parties; Eat, Drink, and Be Married; Orchestrating and Decorating the Celebration; Capturing the Memories; The Honeymoon; Beating Wedding Stress; Starting a Business; and Marketing Your Business. Course fee: $589.

For More Information...

Books

Start Your Own Wedding Consulting Business: Your Step-by-Step Guide to Success, by Eileen Figure Sandlin (Entrepreneur Media, Inc., 2003).

The Portable Wedding Consultant: Invaluable Advice from the Industry's Experts for Saving Your Time, Money and Sanity, by Leah Ingram (McGraw-Hill/Contemporary Books, 1997).

The Perfect Wedding Reception: Stylish Ideas for Every Season, by Maria McBride Mellinger (HarperResource, 2000).

The Knot Ultimate Wedding Planner: Worksheets, Checklists, Etiquette, Calendars, & *Answers to Frequently Asked Questions*, by Carley Roney (Broadway Books, 1999).

Great Wedding Tips from the Experts: What Every Bride Can Learn from the Most Successful Wedding Planners, by Robbi Ernst III and Cele Goldsmith Lalli (McGraw-Hill/Contemporary Books, 2000).

Planning and Directing a Wedding: Guidelines for a Bride, Mother, and Director, by Dorothy Burdashaw Parrish (DOT Publishing, 1997).

<u>E-book</u>

Fabjob's Guide to Becoming a Wedding Planner, by Catherine Goulet and Jan Riddell, www.fabjob.com ($29.95).

<u>Organizations</u>

Association for Wedding Professionals International (AFWPI), 2740 Arden Way, Suite 100, Sacramento, CA 95825, Tel: 800-242-4461 or 916-482-3010, Web: www.afwpi.com, E-mail: richard@afwpi.com.

Association of Certified Professional Wedding Consultants (ACPWC), 7791 Prestwick Circle, San Jose, CA 95135, Tel: 408-528-9000, Web: www. acpwc.com, E-mail: annnola1@earthlink.net.

Weddings Beautiful Worldwide, A Division of National Bridal Service, 5001 W. Broad Street, Suite 214, Richmond, VA 23230, Tel: 804-288-1220, Web: www.weddingsbeautiful.com, E-mail: info@weddingsbeautiful.com.

June Wedding, Inc.®, An Association for Event Professionals, 1331 Burnham Ave., Las Vegas, NV 89104-3658, Tel: 702-474-9558, Web: www. junewedding.com, E-mail: robbi@junewedding.com.

WeddingCareers.com, The Worldwide Association for Wedding Professionals, 16225 Park Ten Place, Suite 500, Houston, TX 77084, Tel: 281-994-4141, Web: www.weddingcareers.com, E-mail: info@weddingcareers.com.

Association of Bridal Consultants (ABC), 200 Chestnutland Road, New Milford, CT 06776-2521, Tel: 860-355-0464, Web: www.bridalassn.com, E-mail: office@bridalassn.com.

<u>Web Sites</u>

http://messageboards.ivillage.com/iv-wfwfhwedding—iVillage.com Work-from-Home Wedding Pros message board

www.weddingchannel.com—wedding resources and information, bridal registries

www.theknot.com—large wedding site

www.RweddingSite.com—providing wedding Web sites

www.weddingsolutionssuperstore.com—wedding products

www.weddingclipart.com—wedding images for download for invitations and programs

Out-of-the-Box Work-at-Home Careers

Here are some more subjects you can learn at home and possibly parlay into a home career.

Art Therapy—Saint Mary-of-the-Woods College (Master degree), www.smwc.edu

Business Accounting—University of Phoenix Online Campus, www.uoponline.com

Certificate in Marriage Education—University of Bridgeport, (Undergraduate certificate) www.bridgeport.edu/scps/onlinel.htm

Cyber Security—Stevens Institute of Technology (Graduate certificate), www.webcampus.stevens.edu

Direct Marketing—Mercy College (Master degree), http://merlin.mercy.edu

Dog Obedience, Dog Trainer, or Pet Groomer—Education Direct, www.educationdirect.com

Dressmaking & Design—Education Direct, www.educationdirect.com

Landscape Design—Professional Career Development Institute, www.pcdi-homestudy.com

Music Therapy:

Open Learning Agency (Bachelor degree), www.ola.ca

Saint Mary of the Woods College (Master degree), www.smwc.edu

Nutrition and Dietetics:

American Academy of Nutrition, College of Nutrition (Associate degree), www.nutritioneducation.com

East Carolina University (Master degree), www.options.ecu.edu

Health and Nutrition Counseling—Thomas Edison College (Bachelor degree), www.tesc.edu

Occupational Therapy:

Florida International University (Master degree), www.fiu.edu

Texas Women's University (Master degree), www.twu.edu/dl

University of Florida (Master degree), www.fcd.ufl.edu

University of Southern Indiana (Master degree), www.usi.edu/distance

Small Business Marketing—Allied Business Schools, www.alliedschools.com

Earn an MBA Online

There a number of colleges and universities that offer MBAs via distance learning! But that is an entire other book. Check out *Peterson's Guide to MBA Distance Learning* (Peterson's, 2003), www.petersons.com.

MICHELLE'S BOOKSHELF AND BOOKMARKS: RECOMMENDED BOOKS AND WEB SITES

Bookshelf

Clicking: 16 Trends to Future Fit Your Life, Your Work, and Your Business, by Faith Popcorn and Lys Marigold (HarperCollins Publishers, 1996)

Finding Your Perfect Work: The New Career Guide to Making a Living, Creating a Life (revised edition), by Paul and Sarah Edwards (J.P. Tarcher, 2003)

The Work-at-Home Mom's Guide to Home Business: Stay at Home and Make Money with WAHM.com, by Cheryl Demas (Hazen Publishing, 2000)

It's a Jungle Out There, and a Zoo in Here: Run Your Home Business Without Letting it Overrun You, by Cheryl Demas (Warner Books, 2003)

EVEolution: The Eight Truths of Marketing to Women, by Faith Popcorn and Lys Marigold (Hyperion, 2000)

Turn Your Passion into Profits: How to Start the Business of Your Dreams, by Janet Allon and the editors of *Victoria* magazine (Hearst Books, 2001)

Do What You Are: Discover the Perfect Career for You Through the Secrets of Personality Type, by Paul D. Tieger and Barbara Barron-Tieger (Little, Brown & Co., 2001)

Guerilla Marketing: Secrets for Making Big Profits from Your Small Business, by Jay Conrad Levinson (Mariner Books, 1998)

Guerilla Marketing Online: The Entrepreneur's Guide to Earning Profits on the Internet, by Jay Conrad Levinson and Charles Rubin (Mariner Books, 1997)

The Guerilla Marketing Handbook, by Jay Conrad Levinson and Seth Godin (Mariner Books, 1994)

Home Office Know-How, by Jeffrey D. Zbar (Upstart Publishing Co., 1998)

The Stay-at-Home Mom's Guide to Making Money from Home: Choosing the Business That's Right for You Using the Skills and Interests You Already Have (2nd edition), by Liz Folger (Prima Publishing, 2000)

The Best Home Businesses for the 21st Century (3rd edition), by Paul and Sarah Edwards (Jeremy P. Tarcher/Putnam, 1999)

Making Money from Your Computer at Home (2nd edition), by Paul and Sarah Edwards (Putnam Pub. Group, 1997)

Cool Careers for Dummies, by Marty Nemko, and Paul and Sarah Edwards (IDG Books, 2001)

Mompreneurs: A Mother's Practical Step-by-Step Guide to Work-at-Home Success, by Ellen H. Parlapiano and Patricia Cobe (Berkeley Publishing Group, 1996)

Mompreneurs Online: Using the Internet to Build Work@Home Success, by Patricia Cobe and Ellen H. Parlapiano (Perigee, 2001)

How to Raise a Family and a Career Under One Roof, by Lisa Roberts (Bookhaven, 1997)

The Entrepreneurial Parent: How to Earn Your Living and Still Enjoy Your Family, Your Work and Your Life, by Lisa M. Roberts and Paul and Sarah Edwards (J.P. Tarcher, 2002)

Homemade Money: How to Select, Start, Manage, Market and Multiply the Profits of a Business at Home (Fifth edition), by Barbara Brabec (Betterway Publishers, 1997)

The Business Planning Guide: Creating a Plan for Success in Your Own Business, by David H. Bangs, Jr. (Upstart Books, 1993)

Easy Financials for Your Home-Based Business: The Friendly Guide to Successful Management Systems for Busy Home Entrepreneurs, by Norm Ray (Rayve Productions, Inc, 1993)

How to Write a Business Plan, by Mike McKeever (Nolo Press, 1993)

College Degrees by Mail & Internet: 100 Accredited Schools That Offer Bachelor's, Master's, Doctorates, and Law Degrees by Distance Learning (8th edition), by John Bear, Mariah P. Bear, and the editors of DegreeNet (Ten Speed Press, 2001)

The Work-at-Home Sourcebook (7th edition), by Lynie Arden (Live Oak Publications, 1999)

The Occupational Outlook Handbook 2002-2003, by U.S. Department of Labor (Jist Works, 2003)

Peterson's Guide to Distance Learning Programs (Petersons, 2002)

Bookmarks

www.faithpopcorn.com—the marketing goddess and all her products

www.wahm.com—Author Cheryl Demas' site for work-at-home moms (WAHMs)

www.bizymoms.com—Author Liz Folger's site, containing lots of info about home business for moms. She also publishes great start-up e-books.

www.powerhomebiz.com—Success stories, tools and solutions, and useful columns about home biz.

www.homeworkingmom.com—The Mother's Home Business Network

www.petersons.com—*Peterson's Guides* Web site with information on every major and school you could ever want to know about.

www.bls.gov.ocol—*The Occupational Outlook Handbook* online.

www.elearners.com—a great place to find other distance-learning courses.

www.aahbb.org—American Association of Home-Based Businesses

www.bluesuitmom.com—for all kinds of working moms

www.homejobstop.com—great home job listings for a one-time, lifetime membership fee

www.ivillage.com/work—iVillage's work site, with work-at-home info

www.mompreneurs.com—Authors Ellen Parlapiano and Pat Cobe's site

www.gohome.com—lists regional entrepreneur groups to join

www.en-parent.com—Author Lisa Roberts' site, The Entrepreneurial Parent

www.hbwm.com—Home-Based Working Moms

www.hoaa.com—Home Office Association of America

www.momsnetwork.com—Moms Network Exchange

www.m-oo.com—MOO: Mother Owned and Operated

www.parentpreneur.com—ParentPreneur Club

www.workingsolo.com—Working Solo

www.ezineuniversity.com—e-Zine University

www.athomedad.com—At-Home Dads

http://slowlane.com—Slowlane: The Online Resource for Stay-at-Home Dads

www.entrepreneur.com—*Entrepreneur* magazine

www.abwahq.org—e-learning business skills courses from the American Business Women's Association

www.ideamarketers.com—share articles and borrow articles for your ezine or Web site

www.wahmpreneur.com—*Wahmpreneur* magazine

www.presskits.com—great supplies and design ideas for your media kits

www.press-release-writing.com—press release writing tips, what else?

www.sba.gov—U.S. Small Business Administration (SBA)

www.fedlearn.com—Federal Training Network

www.freeskills.com—learn IT skills

www.brainbench.com—offers online certifications in a variety of skills

www.smartplanet.com—online IT courses

www.womens-onlineinstitute.com—Women's Online Institute "Fast Track Entrepreneurial Series"

www.takeaclass.com—look for courses in your local community

BIBLIOGRAPHY

Aalseth, Patricia. *Codebusters: A Quick Guide to Coding and Billing Compliance for Medical Practices.* Jones & Bartlett, 1999.

Ainsworth, Jim. *How to Become a Successful Financial Consultant.* John Wiley & Sons, 1997.

Alderman, Robert L., Esq. *How to Prosper as an Interior Designer: A Business and Legal Guide.* John Wiley & Sons, 1997.

Allon, Janet and the editors of *Victoria* magazine. *Turn Your Passion into Profits: How to Start the Business of Your Dreams.* Hearst Books, 2001.

American Institute of Graphic Arts. *AIGA Professional Practices in Graphic Design.* Allworth Press, 1997.

Anderson, Camille. *The Business of Gift Baskets: How to Make a Profit Working from Home.* Camille Anderson, 1993.

Andre, Joli. *Business Etiquette Mastery: The Power of Executive Leadership.* Polished Professionals, 1997.

Appelbaum, Judith. *How to Get Happily Published (5th edition).* HarperCollins, 1998.

Arden, Lynie. *The Work-at-Home Sourcebook (7th edition).* Live Oak Publications, 1999.

Aronson, Merry and Don Spetner. *The Public Relations Writers' Handbook.* Jossey-Bass, 1998.

Avila-Weil, Donna and Mary Glaccum. *The Independent Medical Transcriptionist: The Comprehensive Guidebook for Career Success in a Medical Transcription Business.* Rayve Productions, 2002.

Avila-Weil, Donna and Rhonda Regan. *Independent Medical Coding: The Comprehensive Guidebook for Career Success as a Medical Coder.* Rayve Productions, 1998.

Bangs, David H. Jr. *The Business Planning Guide: Creating a Plan for Success in Your Own Business.* Upstart Books, 1993.

Bear, John, Mariah P. Bear, and the editors of DegreeNet. *College Degrees by Mail & Internet: 100 Accredited Schools That Offer Bachelor's, Master's, Doctorates, and Law Degrees by Distance Learning (8th edition)*. Ten Speed Press, 2001.

Beauchemin, Cyndi. *The Daycare Provider's Workbook*. TCB Enterprises, 1999.

Bixler, Susan and Lisa Scherrer. *5 Steps to Professional Presence*. Adams Media Corp., 2000.

Bixler, Susan. *The New Professional Image: From Business Casual to the Ultimate Power Look*. Adams Media Corp., 1997.

Bowerman, Peter. *The Well-Fed Writer: Financial Self-Sufficiency as a Freelance Writer in Six Months or Less*. Fanove Publishing, 2000.

Brabec, Barbara. *Homemade Money: How to Select, Start, Manage, Market and Multiply the Profits of a Business at Home (Fifth edition)*. Betterway Publishers, 1997.

Bradley, Robert A. *Husband-Coached Childbirth: The Bradley Method of Natural Childbirth*. Bantam Doubleday Dell Publishing, 1996.

Brenner, Diane and Marilyn Rowland, eds. *Beyond Book Indexing: How to Get Started in Web Indexing, Embedded Indexing, and Other Computer-Based Media*. Information Today, 2000.

Brenner, Robert. *Pricing Guide for Web Services: How to Make Money on the Information Data Highway*. Brenner Information Group, 1997.

Brogan, Katie Struckel and Robert Brewer, eds. *The 2003 Writer's Market*. Writer's Digest Books, 2002.

Brooks, Douglas. *Program Design for Personal Trainers*. Human Kinetics Publishing, 1998.

Bruno, Michael H., ed. *Pocket Pal: A Graphic Arts Production Handbook, 18th ed.* GATFPress, 2000.

Buck, Carol J. *Step-by-Step Medical Coding*. W.B. Saunders, 2002.

Business Concepts. *Start Your Own Medical Claims Auditor/Transcriptions Business*. Prentice Hall Press, 1999.

Camp, Sue C. *Developing Proofreading and Editing Skills*. McGraw-Hill, 2000.

Cappon, Rene J. Word. *The Associated Press Guide to News Writing*. Arco Publishing, 2000.

Caywood, Clarke L. ed. *The Handbook of Strategic Public Relations and Integrated Communications*. McGraw-Hill Trade, 1997.

Chipkin, Dana and Wendy Mapstone. *Successful Freelance Court Reporting*. Delmar Learning, 2000.

Chisenhall, Frank. *Complete Typing Business Guide: Everything You Need to Know to Start and Successfully Operate a Home-Based Typing Business*. Supertest Publishing, 1990.

Cobe, Patricia and Ellen H. Parlapiano. *Mompreneurs Online: Using the Internet to Build Work@Home Success*. Perigee, 2001.

Collings, Darlene. *A Basic Guide to Starting Your Own Medical Billing Business*. Darlene Collings, 1999.

Copeland, Tom. *Family Child Care Contracts and Policies: How to Be Businesslike in a Caring Profession*. Redleaf Press, 1991.

Copeland, Tom. *Family Child Care Marketing Guide: How to Build Enrollment and Promote Your Business as a Child Professional*. Redleaf Press, 1999.

Corbett, Maryann, ed. *Directory of Indexing and Abstracting Courses and Seminars*. Information Today, 1998.

Coslick, Merlin. *Medical Billing Home-Based Business, Success in Management and Business Strategies*. Electronic Medical Billing Network of America, 1999.

Coslick, Merlin. *Setting Up Your Medical Billing Business*. Electronic Medical Billing Network of America, 1999.

Cox, John. *Professional Practices in Association Management, 2nd ed.*, American Society of Association Executives, 1998.

Cox, Mary. *2004 Artist's & Graphic Designer's Market*. F&W Publications, 2003.

Cozzi, Guy. *Home Inspection Business from A to Z*. Nemmar Real Estate Training, 2002.

Crawford, Tad and Eva Doman Bruck. *Business and Legal Forms for Interior Designers*. Allworth Press, 2001.

Davies, Mary E., Pat Hardy, Jo Ann M. Bell, and Susan Brown. *So…You Want to Be an Innkeeper: The Definitive Guide to Operating a Successful Bed-and-Breakfast or Country Inn*. Chronicle Books, 1996.

Demas, Cheryl. *It's a Jungle Out There, and a Zoo in Here: Run Your Home Business Without Letting it Overrun You*. Warner Books, 2003.

Demas, Cheryl. *The Work-at-Home Mom's Guide to Home Business: Stay at Home and Make Money with WAHM.com*. Hazen Publishing, 2000.

Deming, Kathleen. *Start Your Own Catering Business*. Prentice-Hall Trade, 1997.

DeVries, Mary. *The Professional Secretary's Handbook*. Houghton Mifflin, 1995.

DeWalt, Suzanne. *How to Start a Home-Based Interior Design Business*. Globe Pequot Press, 2003.

Drake, Keith. *Medical Transcription Career Handbook*. Prentice Hall, 1999.

Durst, Christine and Michael Haaren. *The Virtual Assistant's Building Your Client Base and Marketing 101 Manual and Workbook*. Entrepreneur Publishing, 2000.

Durst, Christine and Michael Haaren. *The Virtual Assistant's Pre-Launch Manual and Workbook*. Entrepreneur Publishing, 2000.

Eccher, Clint. *Professional Web Design: Techniques & Templates*. Charles River Media, 2002.

Edwards, Paul and Sarah Edwards. *Finding Your Perfect Work: The New Career Guide to Making a Living, Creating a Life (revised edition)*. J.P. Tarcher, 2003.

Edwards, Paul and Sarah Edwards. *Making Money from Your Computer at Home (2nd edition)*. Putnam Pub. Group, 1997.

Edwards, Paul and Sarah Edwards. *The Best Home Businesses for the 21st Century (3rd edition)*. Jeremy P. Tarcher/Putnam, 1999.

Ellis, Barbara Ross. *From Start to Finish…A Practical Guide for Your Labor Support Business*. Pennypress.

England, Pam. *Birthing from Within*. Partera Press, 1998.

Entrepreneur magazine. *How to Start a Medical Claims Billing Service: Your Step-by-Step Guide to Success*. Entrepreneur Media, Inc., 2003.

Ernst, Robbi III and Cele Goldsmith Lalli. *Great Wedding Tips from the Experts: What Every Bride Can Learn from the Most Successful Wedding Planners*. McGraw-Hill/Contemporary Books, 2000.

Ernstthal, Henry L. and Bob Jones. *Principles of Association Management*. American Society of Association Executives, 1996.

Estrin, Chere. *Paralegal Career Guide*. Prentice Hall, 2001.

Fetters, Linda K. *Handbook of Indexing Techniques: A Guide for Beginning Indexers*. Fetters Information Management, 2001.

Fleishman, Michael. *Starting Your Career as a Freelance Illustrator or Graphic Designer*. Allworth Press, 2001.

Folger, Liz. *The Stay-at-Home Mom's Guide to Making Money from Home: Choosing the Business That's Right for You Using the Skills and Interests You Already Have (2nd edition)*. Prima Publishing, 2000.

Foote, Cameron. *The Business Side of Creativity: The Complete Guide for Running a Graphic Design or Communications Business*. W.W. Norton & Co., 2002.

Fortgang, Laura Berman. *Take Yourself to the Top: The Secrets of American's #1 Career Coach*. Warner Books, 1998.

Foster-Walker, Mardi. *Start and Run a Gift Basket Business*. Self Counsel Press, 2000.

Fox, Jack. *Building a Profitable Online Accounting Practice*. John Wiley & Sons, 2001.

Fox, Jack. *Starting and Building Your Own Accounting Business, 3rd edition*. John Wiley & Sons, 2000.

Frazier, Shirley. *How to Start a Home-Based Gift Basket Business*. Globe Pequot Press, 1998.

Fujii, Donna. *Color with Style*. Graphic-Sha Publishing, 1992.

Gallagher, Patricia C. *So You Want to Open a Profitable Day Care Center?* Young Sparrow Press, 1995.

Gaut, Ed. *The Personal Trainer Business Handbook*. Pierpoint Martin, 1994.

Gibaldi, Joseph. *MLA Style Manual*. The Modern Language Association of America, 1998.

Gladstone, John and Edward Gillow. *How to Start Your Own P.R. Firm*. PRSA, 1998.

Goer, Henci. *The Thinking Woman's Guide to a Better Birth*. Perigee Books, 1999.

Graphic Artist's Guild. *Graphic Artist's Guild Handbook of Pricing and Ethical Guidelines*. Graphic Artists Guild, 2001.

Gunther, Claire and *Entrepreneur* magazine. *How to Start a Home Inspection Service: Your Step-by-Step Guide to Success*. Entrepreneur Media, Inc., 2003.

Hargrove, Robert. *Masterful Coaching*. Jossey-Bass/Pfeiffer, 2002.

Hayden, C.J. *Get Clients Now! A 28-Day Marketing Program for Professionals and Consultants*. AMACOM, 1999.

Health Professions Institute. *Medical Transcription: Fundamentals and Practice*. Prentice Hall, 1999.

Holtz, Herman. *How to Start and Run a Writing & Editing Business*. John Wiley & Sons, 1992.

Hunt, Kimberly. *Encyclopedia of Associations, 38th edition*. Gale Group, 2002.

Ingram, Leah. *The Portable Wedding Consultant: Invaluable Advice from the Industry's Experts for Saving Your Time, Money and Sanity*. McGraw-Hill/Contemporary Books, 1997.

Judd, Karen. *Copyediting: A Practical Guide (3rd edition)*. Crisp Pub., 2001.

Keyes, Jessica. *The Ultimate Web Developer's Sourcebook*. AMACOM, 2001.

Kinsel, Brenda. *40 Over 40: 40 Things Every Woman Over 40 Needs to Know About Getting Dressed.* Wildcat Canyon Press, 2000.

Kinsel, Brenda. *In the Dressing Room with Brenda.* Wildcat Canyon Press, 2001.

Klaus, Marshall M.D., Phyllis Klaus, and John Kennell. *The Doula Book: How a Trained Labor Companion Can Help You Have a Shorter, Easier, and Healthier Birth.* Perseus Publishing, 2002.

Kursmark, Louise. *How to Start a Home-Based Desktop Publishing Business.* Globe Pequot Press, 1996.

La Leche League International. *The Womanly Art of Breastfeeding.* Schaumburg, IL: 1997.

Larsen, Sonja and John Bourdean. *Legal Research for Beginners.* Barrons Educational Series, 1997.

Leach, Anne, Ed. *Marketing Your Indexing Services, 2nd Edition.* Information Today, 1998.

Leonard Thomas and Byron Larson. *The Portable Coach: 28 Surefire Strategies for Business and Personal Success.* Scribner, 1998.

Levinson, Jay Conrad and Charles Rubin. *Guerilla Marketing Online: The Entrepreneur's Guide to Earning Profits on the Internet.* Mariner Books, 1997.

Levinson, Jay Conrad and Seth Godin. *The Guerilla Marketing Handbook.* Mariner Books, 1994.

Levinson, Jay Conrad, Rick Frishman, and Jill Lublin. *Guerilla Publicity: Hundreds of Sure-Fire Tactics to Get Maximum Sales for Minimum Dollars.* Adams Media Corp., 2002.

Levinson, Jay Conrad. *Guerilla Marketing: Secrets for Making Big Profits from Your Small Business.* Mariner Books, 1998.

Lewis, Gordon P. *Bookkeeping & Tax Preparation: Start and Build a Prosperous Bookkeeping, Tax, & Financial Services Business.* Acton Circle Publishing Company, 1996.

Lumgair, Christopher. *Teach Yourself QuarkXPress.* McGraw-Hill, 1999.

Lynn, Jacquelyn and *Entrepreneur* magazine. *How to Start a Gift Basket Service: Your Step-by-Step Guide to Success.* Entrepreneur Media, Inc., 2003.

Mack, Charles. *The Executive's Handbook of Trade and Business Associations.* Greenwood Publishing Group, 1991.

Marks, Lynne Henderson and Dominique Isbecque. *The Perfect Fit: How to Start an Image Consulting Business.* FirstPublish LLC, 2001.

Mastrangelo, Craig and Kirk Galiani. *The Personal Trainer's Business Guide.* Exercise Science, 2001.

Mathis, Carla. *Triumph of Individual Style: A Guide to Dressing Your Body, Your Beauty, Yourself.* Fairchild, 2002.

McGarry, Michelle. *Train at Home to Become a Certified Personal/Life Coach.* Writer's Club Press, 2003.

McIntyre, Catherine V. *Writing Effective News Releases: How to Get Free Publicity for Yourself, Your Business, or Your Organization.* Piccadilly Books, 1992.

McKay, Cynthia and Carol Dorris. *The Business of Gift Baskets: A Guide for Survival.* 1601 S. Holdings Inc., 1998.

McKeever, Mike. *How to Write a Business Plan.* Nolo Press, 1993.

Mellinger, Maria McBride. *The Perfect Wedding Reception: Stylish Ideas for Every Season.* HarperResource, 2000.

Melnik, Jan. *How to Start a Home-Based Secretarial Services Business.* Globe Pequot Press, 1994.

Merriam-Webster. *Merriam-Webster's Secretarial Handbook.* Merriam-Webster, 1995.

Morgenstern, Steve. *No Sweat Desktop Publishing.* Amacom, 1995.

Morton, George. *How to Become a Medical Transcriptionist.* Medical Language Development, 1998.

Mulvany, Nancy. *Indexing Books.* University of Chicago Press, 1994.

Nemko, Marty and Paul and Sarah Edwards. *Cool Careers for Dummies.* IDG Books, 2001.

Nichols, Francine and Sharron Humenick. *Childbirth Education: Practice, Research and Theory.* W.B. Saunders, 2000.

Nielson, Jakob. *Designing Web Usability: The Practice of Simplicity.* Pearson Education, 1999.

O'Brien, Teri S. *The Personal Trainer's Handbook.* Human Kinetics Publishing, 2003.

Octogram Publishing. *By Design: The Graphic Designer's Essential Handbook—A Gallery of Professional Design, Popular Techniques, and Designer's Templates.* Hearst Books, 2001.

O'Neill, Mary Beth. *Executive Coaching with Backbone and Heart: A Systems Approach to Engaging Leaders with Their Challenges.* Jossey-Bass, 2000.

Parker, Lucy and Karen Ivory. *How to Start a Home-Based Writing Business*. Globe Pequot Press, 2000.

Parker, Roger C. *Looking Good in Print*. Paraglyph Press, 2003.

Parlapiano, Ellen H. and Patricia Cobe. *Mompreneurs: A Mother's Practical Step-by-Step Guide to Work-at-Home Success*. Berkeley Publishing Group, 1996.

Parrish, Dorothy Burdashaw. *Planning and Directing a Wedding: Guidelines for a Bride, Mother, and Director*. DOT Publishing, 1997.

Perez, Paulina and Cheryl Snedeker. *Special Women: The Role of the Professional Labor Assistant*. Cutting Edge Press, 1994.

Perlman, Janet, ed. *Running Your Indexing Business*. Information Today, 2001.

Petersons. *Peterson's Guide to Distance Learning Programs*. Petersons, 2002.

Phillips, Celeste. *Family Centered Maternity Care*. Mosby, 1996.

Pinson, Linda. *Keeping the Books: Basic Record Keeping and Accounting for the Small Business, 2nd edition*. Dearborn Trade Publishing, 2001.

Pompeii, Michael. *Become a Home Inspector!* Pompeii Publications, 2001.

Popcorn, Faith and Lys Marigold. *Clicking: 16 Trends to Future Fit Your Life, Your Work, and Your Business*. HarperCollins Publishers, 1996.

Popcorn, Faith and Lys Marigold. *EVEolution: The Eight Truths of Marketing to Women*. Hyperion, 2000.

Powell, Jo Ann. *Understanding Medical Insurance: A Guide to Professional Billing*. Delmar Learning, 1999.

Pruissen, Catherine. *Start and Run a Profitable Home Daycare*. Self Counsel Press, 2002.

Public Relations Society of America. *Successfully Managing Your Public Relations Practice*. Public Relations Society of America, 1998.

Rachmeler, Susan and National Business Library. *Start Your Own Information Broker Service*. Pfeiffer & Co., 1995.

Ramsay, Linda and Faren Maree Bachelis. *Start Your Own Interior Design Business and Keep it Growing: Your Guide to Business Success*. Touch of Design, 1994.

Ramsey, Dan. *Owning and Managing a Desktop Publishing Business*. Upstart Press, 1995.

Rattiner, Jeffrey. *Getting Started as a Financial Planner*. Bloomberg Press, 2000.

Ray, Norm. *Easy Financials for Your Home-Based Business: The Friendly Guide to Successful Management Systems for Busy Home Entrepreneurs.* Rayve Productions, Inc, 1993.

Richardson, Cheryl. *Take Time for Your Life: A Personal Coach's Seven-Step Program for Creating the Life You Want.* Broadway Books, 1999.

Roberts, Lisa M. and Paul and Sarah Edwards. *The Entrepreneurial Parent: How to Earn Your Living and Still Enjoy Your Family, Your Work and Your Life.* J.P. Tarcher, 2002.

Roberts, Lisa. *How to Raise a Family and a Career Under One Roof.* Bookhaven, 1997.

Roberts, Scott ed. *The Business of Personal Training.* Human Kinetics Publishing, 1996.

Robotti, Susan and Margaret Ann Inman. *Childbirth Instructor Magazine's Guide to Careers in Birth: How to Have a Fulfilling Job in Pregnancy, Labor, and Parenting Support without a Medical Degree.* John Wiley & Sons, 1998.

Robson, Gary. *Alternative Realtime Careers: A Guide to Closed Captioning and CART for Court Reporters.* National Court Reporters Association, 2000.

Roney, Carley. *The Knot Ultimate Wedding Planner: Worksheets, Checklists, Etiquette, Calendars, & Answers to Frequently Asked Questions.* Broadway Books, 1999.

Rugge, Sue and Alfred Glossbrenner. *The Information Broker's Handbook, 3rd edition.* McGraw-Hill, 1997.

Ryan, Ellen. *Innkeeping Unlimited: Practical Low-Cost Ways to Improve Your B&B and Win Repeat Business.* Can-Do Press, 1998.

Sandlin, Eileen Figure. *Start Your Own Wedding Consulting Business: Your Step-by-Step Guide to Success.* Entrepreneur Media, Inc., 2003.

Sawyer, Deborah. *Sawyer's Survival Guide for Information Brokers.* Burnell Enterprises, 1995.

Schuller, Catherine. *The Ultimate Plus-Size Modeling Guide.* Emerging Visions Enterprise, 1997.

Sears, William M.D. and Martha Sears, R.N. *The Birth Book.* Little, Brown & Co., 1994.

Secol, Dorothy. *Paralegal's Guide to Freelancing: How to Start and Manage Your Own Legal Services Business.,* John Wiley & Sons, 1996.

Simkin, Penny. *The Birth Partner: Everything You Need to Know to Help a Woman Through Childbirth, 2nd edition.* Harvard Common Press, 2001.

Smith Bucklin & Associates. *The Complete Guide to Nonprofit Management*. John Wiley & Sons, 2000.

Smith, Jim. *How to Start a Home-Based Web Design Business*. Globe Pequot Press, 2001.

Smucker, Bob. *The Nonprofit Lobbying Guide: Advocating Your Cause—and Getting Results*, Jossey-Bass Publishers, 1991.

Solomon, Lauren. *Image Matters! First Steps on the Journey to Your Best Self*. E-Squared Publications, 2002.

Splaver, Bernard, William N. Reynolds, and Michael Roman. *Successful Catering*. John Wiley & Sons, 1997.

Steelsmith, Shari. *How to Start a Home-Based Day Care Business*. Globe Pequot Press, 2000.

Stone, Edward. *Getting Started in Financial Consulting*. John Wiley & Sons, 2000.

Strunk, William Jr. and E.B. White. *The Elements of Style, 3rd edition*. Macmillan, 1979.

Tessier, Claudia. *The AAMT Book of Style for Medical Transcription*. American Association of Medical Transcriptionists, 1995.

Thompson, Brigette A. *The Home Daycare Complete Recordkeeping System*. Datamaster, 2003.

Tieger, Paul D. and Barbara Barron-Tieger. *Do What You Are: Discover the Perfect Career for You Through the Secrets of Personality Type*. Little, Brown & Co., 2001.

U.S. Department of Labor. *The Occupational Outlook Handbook 2002-2003*. Jist Works, 2002.

Ulrich, Laurie Ann. *Web Design Virtual Classroom*. McGraw-Hill Professional, 2001.

Vivaldo, Denise. *How to Start a Home-Based Catering Business, 4th edition*. Globe Pequot Press, 2002.

Wagner, Marsden. *Pursuing the Birth Machine: The Search for Appropriate Birth Technology*. ACE Graphics, 1994.

Warner, Ralph. *Independent Paralegal's Handbook: Everything You Need to Run a Business Preparing Legal Paperwork for the Public*. Nolo Press, 1999.

Weinberg, Bella Hass. *Can You Recommend a Good Book on Indexing?* Information Today, 1998.

Weitzen, H. Skip and Rick Parkhill. *Infopreneurs Online and Global: Taking the Hottest Business of the '90s into the 21st Century.* John Wiley & Sons, 1996.

Weitzen, H. Skip. *The Infopreneurs: Turning Data into Dollars.* John Wiley & Sons, 1991.

Whitworth. Laura, Henry House, Phil Sandahl, and Henry Kimsey-House. *Co-Active Coaching: New Skills for Coaching People Toward Success in Work and Life.* Davies-Black Publishers, 1998.

Williams, Patrick and Deborah C. Davis. *Therapist as Life Coach: Transforming Your Practice.* W.W. Norton & Co., 2002.

Williams, Robin. *The Non-Designer's Design Book.* Peachpit Press, 1994.

Williams, Thomas A. *Publish Your Own Magazine, Guidebook, or Weekly Newspaper: How to Manage and Profit from Your Own Homebased Publishing Company.* Sentient Publications, 2002.

Wooldridge, Mike and Michael Toot. *Teach Yourself Visually Illustrator 10.* John Wiley & Sons, 2002.

Wooldridge, Mike. *Teach Yourself Visually Photoshop 6.* John Wiley & Sons, 2001.

Wright, Susan. *How to Become a Caterer: Everything You Need to Know from Finding Clients to the Final Bill.* Citadel Press, 1996.

Yalden, Claudia. *Medical Billing: The Bottom Line.* CAY Medical Management, 1999.

Yale, David R. *Publicity and Media Relations Checklists.* McGraw-Hill Trade, 1995.

Zafran, Enid L., ed. *Starting an Indexing Business, 2nd Edition.* Information Today, 1998.

Zbar, Jeffrey D. *Home Office Know-How.* Upstart Publishing Co., 1998.

ABOUT THE AUTHOR

Michelle McGarry writes about work-at-home careers, education, and other topics that spark her interest. She has written two previous books, *The Internet Idea Book* and *Train at Home to Become a Certified Personal/Life Coach*. Michelle has a Master of Arts degree in writing and publishing and is a stay-at-home/work-at-home mom. In addition to writing books, raising two children, and taking the occasional distance-learning class, she also runs a home business with her husband Eddie (Green Line Music, www.eddiemcgarry.com). For more information about distance learning, work-at-home careers, or Michelle and her books, visit www.michellemedia.com.

INDEX

1-2-3 Guide to Medical Billing: Start and Market Your Own Medical Billing Business, 89

2004 Artist's & Graphic Designer's Market, 62, 145

40 Over 40, 70, 148

5 Steps to Professional Presence, 70, 144

A Basic Guide to Starting Your Own Medical Billing Business, 89, 145

A Guide to Making Money with Gift Baskets, 58

Aalseth, Patricia, 143

AAMT Book of Style for Medical Transcription, The, 97

Abundant Practice: A Program for Coaches, 105

Academy for Coach Training, 105

Academy of Art College, 61, 79

Accu-Spect Home Inspector Institute, 65

ADD Coaching Academy, 106

Advantage Coaching, 106

AIGA Professional Practices in Graphic Design, 62, 143

Ainsworth, Jim, 143

Alaska Pacific University, 20

Alderman, Robert L. Esq., 143

Allied Business Schools, 19, 36, 66, 88, 103, 123, 138

Alternative Realtime Careers, 120, 151

American Academy of Husband-Coached Childbirth, The, 27

American Academy of Professional Coders, 84, 90

American Association for Paralegal Education, 104

American Association of Medical Billers, 90

American Association of Medical Transcriptionists, 97-98, 152

American Bar Association, 104

American Bed & Breakfast Association, 12, 17

American College of Sports Medicine, 116

American Council on Exercise, 111, 116

American Health Information Management Association, 89-90, 98

American Institute of Certified Public Accountants, 21

American Institute of Graphic Arts, 62, 143

American Institute of Professional Bookkeepers, 18, 21

American Medical Billers Association, 85, 89
American Paralegal Institute, 102
American Society for Information Science, The, 77
American Society of Home Inspectors, 67
American Society of Indexers, 71, 74
American Society of Interior Designers, 79, 81
American Society of Journalists and Authors, 48
Anderson, Camille, 59, 143
Andre, Joli, 143
Andrews School, 86, 93
Appelbaum, Judith, 143
Arden, Lynie, 143
Aronson, Merry, 143
Art Institute International, The, 60, 78
Ashworth College, 20, 99
Associated Press Guide to News Writing, The, 118, 144
Association for Wedding Professionals International, 12, 135
Association for Wedding Professionals International, 12, 135
Association Management, 12-15, 145-146
Association of Bridal Consultants, 133-135
Association of Certified Professional Wedding Consultants, 133, 135
Association of Desktop Publishers, The, 38
Association of Image Consultants International, 69-70
Association of Independent Information Professionals, 77
Association of Labor Assistants and Childbirth Educators, 27, 40
Association of Registered Medical Professionals, 84
Athabasca University, 20
Avila-Weil, Donna, 143
Bailey, Maria T., vii
Bangs, David H. Jr., 143
Barnes & Noble University, 46, 130
Barron-Tieger, Barbara, 4, 139, 152
Basket Business, Newport Media, 56
Basket Connection, The, 55
Beauchemin, Cyndi, 144
Become a Home Inspector!, 67, 150
Bed and Breakfast, 15
Sage Blossom Consulting, 15
Bellevue Community College, 126
Best Home Businesses for the 21st Century, 12, 140, 146

BeST Scoping Techniques, 120
Beyond Book Indexing, 74, 144
Birth Book, The, 28, 151
Birthing from Within, 28, 146
Birth Partner, The, 42, 151
Bixler, Susan, 144
Bizy's Guide to Creating Success in Web Design, 131
Bizy's Guide to How to Start Your Own Virtual Assistant Biz, 123
Bizy's Guide to Starting a Profitable Home-Based Word Processing Business, 123
Bizy's Guide to Starting Your Own Successful Child Care Service, 32
Bizy's Guide to Web Site Editing and Proofreading as a Business, 47
Bizy's Guide to Web Site Editing and Proofreading as a Business, 47
Bookkeeping & Tax Preparation, 21, 148
Bookkeeping, 7, 18-19, 21-22, 88, 123, 131, 148
Bowerman, Peter, 144
Brabec, Barbara, 144
Bradley, Robert A. M.D., 27
Brandon, Jodi L., 48
Brenau University, 20
Brenner, Diane, 144
Broccoli Information Management, 73
Brogan, Katie Struckel, 144
Brooks, Douglas, 144
Bruno, Michael, 144
Buck, Carol J., 144
Building a Profitable Online Accounting Practice, 21, 147
Building Specs Inc. Inspection Systems, 65
Business and Legal Forms for an Interior Designer, 81, 145
Business Concepts, 89, 144
Business Etiquette Mastery, 70, 143
Business of Gift Baskets, The (Anderson*), 59, 143*
Business of Gift Baskets, The (McKay*), 58-59, 149*
Business of Personal Training, The, 115, 151
Business Planning Guide, The, 140, 143
Business Side of Creativity, The, 62, 146
By Design: The Graphic Designer's Essential Handbook, 62, 149
Caldwell College, 20
California College for Health Sciences, 91
Camp, Sue C., 144
Can You Recommend a Good Book on Indexing?, 74, 152

Cappon, Rene J. Word, 144

Career Coach Institute, 106

Career Step, 94

Carson Dunlop, 63

Catering, 22-25, 145, 152

Catering Magazine, 25

Caywood, Clarke L., 144

Certified Financial Planner Board of Standards, Inc., 49, 54

Champlain College, 20, 128

Chapman, Joyce, 108

Chicago Manual of Style, The, 47

Child Care Day Provider, 31

Childbirth and Postpartum Professional Association, 28, 41

    Childbirth Education, 25-29, 39-41, 149

    Doula Education, 27

Childbirth Education: Practice, Research and Theory, 28, 149

Childbirth Educator, 25-28, 38

Childbirth Instructor Magazine, 28-29, 151

Childbirth Instructor Magazine's Guide to Careers in Birth, 28, 151

Chipkin, Dana, 144

Chippewa Valley Technical College, 20

Chisenhall, Frank, 145

Christian Coaches Network, 110

Ciris Alliance, 106

City University, 20, 50

Claims Security of America, 88

Claims Transit, 87

Clicking, 139, 150

Coach for Life, 106

Coach University, 106-107

Coach, *see* Personal/Life Coach, 104

Coaches Training Institute, The, 106

Coaching from Spirit, 106

Coachville, 107, 110

Co-Active Coaching, 106, 109, 153

Coats, Beth, 89

Cobe, Patricia, 145

Codebusters: A Quick Guide to Coding and Billing Compliance for Medical Practices, 89, 143

College Degrees by Mail & Internet, 140, 144

College for Financial Planning, 51
College of Executive Coaching, 107
College of Southern Maryland, 20, 127
Collings, Darlene, 89, 145
Color with Style, 70-71, 147
Color Profiles Ltd., 69
Colour Designers International, 71
Communication Arts magazine, 62
Complete Guide to Nonprofit Management, The, 14, 152
Complete Typing Business Guide, 123, 145
Comprehensive Coaching U, 107
Cool Careers for Dummies, 140, 149
Copeland, Tom, 145
Copyediting: A Practical Guide, 47, 147
Corbett, Maryann, 145
Corporate Coach University International, 107
Coslick, Merlin, 145
Cox, John, 145
Cox, Mary, 145
Cozzi, Guy, 145
Crawford, Tad, 145
Czawlytko, Jennifer, 131
Davenport University Online, 20
Davies, Mary E., 145
Daycare Provider's Workbook, The, 32, 144
Demas, Cheryl, 145
Deming, Kathleen, 145
Designing Web Usability, 130, 149
Desktop Publisher, 33, 42, 60
Developing Proofreading and Editing Skills, 47, 144
DeVries, Mary, 145
DeWalt, Suzanne, 145
Dictionary of the Future, vii
Directory of Indexing and Abstracting Courses and Seminars, 74, 145
Distance learning, 2-3, 5-6, 15-16, 19, 29, 105, 112, 121, 138, 140, 144, 150, 155
Do What You Are, 4, 139, 152
Doula, 25-29, 38-39, 41-42, 148
Doula Book, The, 42, 148
Doulas of North America, 29, 39
Drake, Keith, 146

Durst, Christine, 146
East Carolina University, 129, 137
Easy Financials for Your Home-Based Business, 140, 150-151
Eccher, Clint, 146
Editorial Freelancers Association, 48
Editorial Services, 7, 42
Education Direct, 6, 24, 31, 35, 46, 66, 80, 103, 114, 130, 134, 137
EDUCOACH, 107
Edwards, Paul and Sarah, 146
Electronic Medical Billing Network of America, 86, 89-90, 145
Elements of Style, The, 47, 152
Ellis, Barbara Ross, 146
Encyclopedia of Associations, 14, 147
Encyclopedia of Journal Entries, The, 21
England, Pam, 146
Ennen, Diana, 123
Entertainment Publicists Professional Society, 119
Entrepreneur magazine, 55, 59, 67, 89, 141, 146-148
Entrepreneurial Parent, The, 140-141, 151
Ernst, Robbi III, 146
Ernstthal, Henry L., 146
Estrin, Claire, 104, 146
EVEolution: The Eight Truths of Marketing to Women, 139, 150
Excelsior College, 20
Executive Coach Academy, 107
Executive Coaching with Backbone and Heart, 109, 149
Executive's Handbook of Trade and Business Associations, The, 14, 148
Fabjob's Guide to Becoming a Book Editor, 48
Fabjob's Guide to Becoming a Doula, 42
Fabjob's Guide to Becoming a Personal Fitness Trainer, 115
Fabjob's Guide to Becoming a Web Designer, 131
Fabjob's Guide to Becoming a Wedding Planner, 135
Fabjob's Guide to Becoming an Interior Designer, 81
Family Centered Maternity Care, 42, 150
Family Child Care Contracts and Policies, 32, 145
Family Child Care Marketing Guide, 32, 145
Fetters, Linda, 146
Fill Your Coaching Practice, 107
Financial Planner, 48-49, 51, 54, 150
Financial Planning Association, The, 54

Finding Your Perfect Work, 4, 139, 146

Fleishman, Michael, 146

Florida State University, 52

Folger, Liz, 146

Foote, Cameron, 146

Fortgang, Laura Berman, 146

Foster-Walker, Mardi, 147

Fox, Jack, 147

Frazier, Shirley, 147

From Start to Finish: A Practical Guide for Your Labor Support Business, 42, 146

Fujii, Donna, 147

Gallagher, Patricia C., 147

Gaut, Ed, 147

George Mason University, 13

Get Clients Now!, 109, 147

Getting Started as a Financial Planner, 54, 150

Getting Started in Financial Consulting, 54, 152

Gibaldi, Joseph, 147

Gift Association of America, 59

Gift Basket Mentor, The, 56

Gift Basket Professionals Network, 59

Gift Basket Review magazine, 57, 59-60

Gift Baskets, 55-59, 143, 149

GiftBaskets 101, 56

Gladstone, John, 147

Global Medical Transcription Inc., 95-96

Goer, Henci, 147

Golden Gate University, 20, 49

Goulet, Catherine, 135

Graceland University, 20

Graphic Artist's Guild, 62, 147

Graphic Artist's Guild Handbook of Pricing and Ethical Guidelines, 62, 147

Graphic Designer, 33-34, 60-62, 125, 145-146, 149

Great Plains Interactive Distance Education Alliance, 52

Great Wedding Tips from the Experts, 135, 146

Guerilla Marketing Handbook, The, 139, 148

Guerilla Marketing Online: The Entrepreneur's Guide to Earning Profits on the Internet, 139, 148

Guerilla Marketing: Secrets for Making Big Profits from Your Small Business, 139, 148

Guerilla Publicity, 118, 148

Gunther, Claire, 147

Gurevich, Rachel, 42

Handbook of Indexing Techniques, 74, 146

Handbook of Strategic Public Relations and Integrated Communications, The, 118, 144

Hargrove, Robert, 147

Hayden, C.J., 147

HE School of Building Inspection, 64

Health Professions Institute, 93, 97, 147

Hetzel, Rachel, 131

Holbert, Susan, Indexing Services, 73

Holtz, Herman, 147

Home Daycare Complete Recordkeeping System, The, 32, 152

Home Inspection Business from A to Z, 67, 145

Home Inspector, 62, 64-67, 150

Home Office Know-How, 139, 153

Homemade Money, 140, 144

HomePro Systems, Inc., 64

Hotel & Catering International Management Association, 24

Housing Inspection Foundation, The, 67

How to Become a Caterer, 24, 153

How to Become a Medical Transcriptionist, 97, 149

How to Become a Successful Financial Consultant, 54, 143

How to Get Happily Published, 47-48, 143

How to Prosper as an Interior Designer, 81, 143

How to Raise a Family and a Career Under One Roof, 140, 151

How to Start a Gift Basket Service, 59, 148

How to Start a Home Inspection Service, 67, 147

How to Start a Home-Based Catering Business, 24, 152

How to Start a Home-Based Day Care Business, 32, 152

How to Start a Home-Based Desktop Publishing Business, 37, 148

How to Start a Home-Based Gift Basket Business, 58-59, 147

How to Start a Home-Based Interior Design Business, 81, 145

How to Start a Home-Based Secretarial Services Business, 123, 149

How to Start a Home-Based Web Design Business, 125, 130, 152

How to Start a Home-Based Writing Business, 47, 150

How to Start a Medical Claims Billing Service, 89, 146

How to Start and Run a Writing & Editing Business, 47, 147

How to Start Your Own P.R. Firm, 117-118, 147

How to Write a Business Plan, 140, 149

HTML Writer's Guild, The, 131

Hunt, Kimberly, 147

Husband-Coached Childbirth, 27-28, 144

Image Consultant, 68-69

Image Maker Inc., The, 68

Image Matters!, 70, 152

Image Resource Group, 70

In the Dressing Room with Brenda, 70, 148

Independent Medical Coding: The Comprehensive Guidebook for Career Success as a Medical Coder, 89, 143

Independent Medical Transcriptionist, The, 97, 143

Independent Paralegal's Handbook, 98, 104, 152

Indexing, 45, 71-75, 99, 144-146, 148-150, 152-153

Indexing and Abstracting Society of Canada, The, 75

Indexing Books, 71, 73-74, 149

Indiana Institute of Technology, 20

Infopreneurs: Turning Data into Dollars, The, 77, 153

Infopreneurs Online and Global, 77, 153

Information Broker, 75-77, 150-151

Information Broker's Handbook, The, 77, 151

Ingram, Leah, 147

Innkeeping Unlimited, 17, 151

Innkeeping, *see* bed and breakfast, 15

Inspection Training Associates, 64

Institute for Life Coach Training, 107

Interior Design Educator's Council, 81

Interior Design magazine, 81

Interior Designer/Decorator, 77

International Association of Administrative Professionals, 122, 124

International Association of Association Management Companies, 14-15

International Association of Culinary Professionals, 24

International Association of Mind-Body Professionals, 115

International Association of Personal and Professional Coaches, 109

International Association of Registered Financial Consultants, 54

International Association of Webmasters and Designers, 131

International Childbirth Education Association, 26, 40-41

International Coach Academy, 107

International Coach Federation, 109

International Fitness Professionals Association, 112, 116

International Interior Design Association, 79, 81

International Lactation Consultant Association, 29

International Public Relations Society, 119
International Sport Sciences Association, 113, 116
International Virtual Assistants, 124
International Virtual Assistants Association, 124
International Webmaster's Association, 131
Internet Scoping School, 120
It's a Jungle Out There, and a Zoo in Here, 139, 145
iVillage.com, 90, 98, 124, 135, 141
Ivy Tech State College-Wabash, 20
Judd, Karen, 147
June Wedding, Inc., 132, 135
Kadmon Academy of Human Potential, 108
Kaplan College, 52-53, 102
Keeping the Books, 21, 150
Keyes, Jessica, 147
Kinsel, Brenda, 148
Kit, Mom's Work-at-Home, vii
Kit, Claims Assistance Professional Business, 88
Klaus, Marshall M.D., 148
Knudson, Joyce, 68
Knot Ultimate Wedding Planner, The, 135, 151
Kursmark, Louise, 148
La Leche League International, 28-29, 42, 148
Laird's School of Medical Transcription, 96
Lakeland College, 20
Lamaze International, 25
Larsen, Sonja, 148
Le Gourmet Gift Basket, Inc., 57
Leach, Anne, 148
Legal Research for Beginners, 104, 148
Leonard, Thomas, 148
Levinson, Jay Conrad, 148
Life on Purpose Institute, 108
Life Purpose Institute, 108
Lindquist Associates, *see* Color Profiles Ltd., 69
Lindquist, Debra, 69
Lodge, The, 72
Looking Good in Print, 38, 150
Lumgair, Christopher, 148
Lynn, Jacquelyn, 148

Mack, Charles, 148

Madison Area Technical College, 122

Making Money from Your Computer at Home, 140, 146

Marketing Your Indexing Business, 74, 148

MarketingBase Mentor, 76

Marks, Lynne Henderson, 148

Masterful Coaching, 109, 147

Mastrangelo, Craig, 149

Mathis, Carla, 149

McKay, Cynthia, 149

McKeever, Mike, 149

Medical Association of Billers, 85, 88, 90

Medical Billing Home-Based Business, Success in Management and Business Strategies, 89, 145

Medical Billing/Claims and Medical Coding, 82, 88

Medical Billing: The Bottom Line, 89, 153

Medical Transcription, 90-98, 143, 146-147, 152

Medical Transcription Career Handbook, 97, 146

Medical Transcription Education Center, 94

Medical Transcription: Fundamentals and Practice, 97, 147

Meditec, 87, 95

MedTrans, 95

Melnik, Jan, 149

MentorCoach, 108

Merriam-Webster's Secretarial Handbook, 123, 149

Metropolitan Community College, 53

Minot State University, 35, 125

MLA Style Manual, 47, 147

Mompreneurs, 140-141, 145, 150

Mompreneurs Online, 140, 145

Morgenstern, Steve, 149

Morton, George, 149

Mulvany, Nancy, 149

National American University, 127

National Association for Family Child Care, 33

National Association for Fitness Certification, 112, 116

National Association for the Education of Young Children, 33

National Association of Catering Executives, 22, 24

National Association of Child Care Resource & Referral Agencies, 33

National Association of Claims Assistance Professionals, 122

National Association of Desktop Publishers, 38
National Association of Home Inspectors, 67
National Association of Legal Assistants, 104
National Association of Personal Financial Advisors, 54
National Association of Postpartum Care Services, 42
National Bed and Breakfast Association, 17
National Child Care Association, 32
National Child Care Information Center, 33
National Council for Interior Design Qualification, 79, 81
National Council for Marketing and Public Relations, 119
National Court Reporters Association, 120-121, 151
National Electronic Billers Alliance, 86, 90
National Endurance Sports Trainers Association, 113, 116
National Federation of Paralegal Associations, 104
National Institute of Building Inspectors, 65
National Paralegal Association, 104
National Resource Center for Health & Safety in Child Care, 33
National Specialty Gift Association, 59
National Strength & Conditioning Association, 116
National Writer's Union, 48
NDEITA, 114
New Horizons Computer Learning Centers, 36
New Professional Image, The, 70, 144
Nichols, Francine, 149
Nielson, Jakob, 149
No Sweat Desktop Publishing, 37, 149
Noeske, Bruce, 47, 131
Non-Designer's Design Book, The, 37, 153
Nonprofit Lobbying Guide, The, 14, 152
Northampton County Community College, 20, 30, 45
Northern Arizona University, 43-44
Northwest Missouri State University, 20
Northwest Technical College, 92
Northwestern Michigan College, 128
O'Brien, Teri S., 149
O'Neill, Mary Beth, 149
Oates & Bredfeldt, 16
Occupational Outlook Handbook 2002-2003, 140, 152
Optimal Functioning Institute, 108
Owning and Managing a Desktop Publishing Business, 37, 150

Pace University, 43
Paint and Decorating Retailers Association, 81
Paralegal's Guide to Freelancing, 98, 104, 151
Paralegal Career Guide, 104, 146
Paralegal Institute Inc., The, 100
Paralegal Service, 98
Parent as Coach Academy, 108
Parker, Lucy, 150
Parker, Roger C., 150
Parkland College, 20
Parlapiano, Ellen, 150
Parrish, Dorothy Burdashaw, 150
Patrick Henry Community College, 91
Pennsylvania State University, 126
Perez, Paulina, 150
Perfect Fit: How to Start an Image Consulting Business, The, 68, 70, 148
Perlman, Janet, 150
Personal Trainer, 110-115, 147, 149
Personal Trainer Business Handbook, The, 115, 147
Personal Trainer's Business Guide, The, 115, 149
Personal Trainer's Handbook, The, 115, 149
Personal/Life Coach, 7, 104-105, 109, 149, 155
Peterson's Guide to Culinary Schools 2003, 24
Peterson's Guide to Distance Learning Programs, 140, 150
Phillips, Celeste, 150
Piedmont Community College, 20, 101
Pinson, Linda, 150
Pitt Community College, 83
Planning and Directing a Wedding, 135, 150
Pocket Pal: A Graphic Arts Production Handbook, 62, 144
Pompeii, Michael, 150
Popcorn, Faith, 150
Portable Coach, The, 109, 148
Portable Wedding Consultant, The, 134, 147
Potter, Karen M., 32
Powell, Jo Ann, 150
Pricing Guide to Web Services, 130, 144
Principles of Association Management, 14, 146
Print-on-demand, 9
Professional Association of Innkeepers International, 15-17

Professional Career Development Institute, 19, 23, 31, 46, 53, 66, 80, 87, 97, 103, 115, 129, 134, 137

Professional Coach and Mentors Association, 110

Professional Practices in Association Management, 14, 145

Professional Secretary's Handbook, The, 123, 145

Professional Web Design: Techniques & Templates, 130, 146

Program Design for Personal Trainers, 114-115, 144

Pruissen, Catherine, 150

Public Relations Society of America, 117-119, 150

Public Relations Specialist, 116, 119

Public Relations Writers' Handbook, The, 118, 143

Publicity and Media Relations Checklists, 118, 153

Publish Your Own Magazine, Guidebook, or Weekly Newspaper, 47, 153

Publishing, self, *see* self-publishing, 9-10, 43, 48

Pursuing the Birth Machine, 28, 152

Rachmeler, Susan, 150

Ramsay, Linda, 150

Ramsey, Dan, 150

Rattiner, Jeffrey, 150

Ray, Norm, 150-151

Regis University, 126-127

Relationship Coaching Institute, 108

Reporter's Network, The, 48

Results Life Coaching, 109

Richardson, Cheryl, 151

Robert Morris University, 20

Roberts, Lisa, 151

Roberts, Scott, 151

Robotti, Suzanne, 28

Robson, Gary, 151

Rochester Community and Technical College, 34, 129

Rochester Institute of Technology, 35, 117

Roney, Carley, 151

Ross, Marilyn and Tom, vii

Rugge, Sue, 151

Running Your Indexing Business, 74, 150

Ryan, Ellen, 151

Sandlin, Eileen Figure, 151

Santa Barbara City College, 82

Sawyer's Survival Guide for Information Brokers, 77, 151

Schuller, Catherine, 151
Scopist, 119-121
Scopistry, 121
Sears, William M.D., 151
Secol, Dorothy, 151
Self-publishing, 9-10, 43, 48
*Setting Up Your Medical Billing Bu*siness, 86, 89, 145
Sheffield School of Interior Design, 79-80
Simkin, Penny, 151
Smith Bucklin & Associates, 14, 152
Smith, Jim, 152
Smucker, Bob, 152
So You Want to Open a Profitable Day Care Center?, 32, 147
So, You Want to be an Innkeeper, 17, 145
Society of Financial Consulting and Planning Education, 54
Society of Indexers, The, 74-75
Society of Publication Designers, 38
Solomon, Lauren, 152
Southern New Hampshire College, 20
Southwest Wisconsin Technical College, 83, 92
Special Libraries Association, 77
Special Women: The Role of the Professional Labor Assistant, 42, 150
Spencer, Lesley, vii
Splaver, Bernard, 152
St. Augustine School of Medical Assistants and Health Sciences, 114
St. Mary-of-the-Woods College, 20, 100, 118
Start and Run a Gift Basket Business, 59, 147
Start and Run a Profitable Home Day Care, 32, 150
Start Your Own Catering Business, 24, 145
Start Your Own Information Broker Service, 77, 150
Start Your Own Interior Design Business and Keep it Growing, 81, 150
Start Your Own Medical Claims Auditor/Transcriptions Business, 89, 144
Start Your Own Wedding Consultant Business, 134, 151
Starting an Indexing Business, 74, 153
Starting and Building Your Own Accounting Business, 21, 147
Starting Your Career as a Freelance Illustrator or Graphic Designer, 62, 146
Stay-at-Home Mom's Guide to Making Money from Home, The, 140, 146
Steelsmith, Shari, 152
Step-by-Step Medical Coding, 89, 144
Stone, Edward, 152

Strayer University, 21
Strunk, William, 152
Successful Catering, 24, 152
Successful Freelance Court Reporting, 120, 144
Successfully Managing Your Public Relations Practice, 118, 150
Sweet Florals, 57
Sweet Survival, 58
Take Time for Your Life, 109, 151
Take Yourself to the Top, 109, 146
Teach Yourself QuarkXPress, 38, 148
Teach Yourself Visually Illustrator 10, 38, 153
Teach Yourself Visually Photoshop 6, 38, 153
Tessier, Claudia, 152
The U.S. Court Reporters Association, 121
Therapist as Life Coach: Transforming Your Practice, 109, 153
Think Out of the Cubicle!, 10
Thinking Woman's Guide to Better Birth, The, 28, 147
Thomas Edison State College, 21
Tieger, Paul D., 152
Tompkins Cortland Community College, 100
Train at Home to Become a Certified Personal/Life Coach, 105, 109, 149, 155
Travis, Debbie, 81
Triumph of Individual Style, 70-71, 149
Turn Your Passion into Profits, 139, 143
Ulrich, Laurie Ann, 152
Ultimate Plus-Size Modeling Guide, The, 70, 151
Ultimate Web Developer's Sourcebook, The, 130, 147
Understanding Medical Insurance: A Guide to Professional Billing, 89, 150
Union Institute & University, 13-14
United States Sports Academy, 111
University Alliance, The, 21
University of Alabama, The, 51
University of California, Los Angeles, 21, 45, 50, 61, 79, 99, 111, 117
University of Central Florida, 44
University of Great Falls, 101
University of Houston Online, 23
University of Maine-Augusta, 75-76
University of Maryland University College, 21
University of Northwestern Ohio, 21, 122
University of Phoenix Online, 21, 137

Up Close and Virtual, 123

Upper Iowa University, 21

USDA Graduate School Correspondence Program, 45, 72

VA Certification, 13, 91

Victoria magazine, 139, 143

Video Professor, 36

Virtual Assistant, 121-124, 146

Virtual Assistant U, 122

Virtual Assistant's Building Your Client Base and Marketing 101 Manual and Workbook, The, 123, 146

Virtual Assistant's Pre-Launch Manual and Workbook, The, 123, 146

Vivaldo, Denise, 152

Wagner, Marsden, 152

Warner, Ralph, 152

Washington Online Learning Institute, The, 101

Washington State University, 44

Web Design & Developers Association, 131

Web Design Virtual Classroom, 130, 152

Web Site Designer/Webmaster, 124

Weber State University, 83

Webster University, 128

Wedding Careers Institute, 133

Wedding Planner, 131, 135, 151

WeddingCareers.com, 133, 135

Weddings Beautiful Worldwide, 132, 135

Wehner, Paige, 115

Weinberg, Bella Hass, 152

Weitzen, H. Skip, 153

Well-Fed Writer, The, 47, 144

Western Piedmont Community College, 101

Whitworth, Laura, 153

Williams, Patrick, 153

Williams, Robin, 153

Williams, Thomas A., 153

Winthrop University, 21

Womanly Art of Breastfeeding, The, 28, 148

Women's Home-Based Book of Answers, The, vii

Wooldridge, Mike, 153

Work-at-Home Mom's Guide to Home Business, The, 139, 145

Work-at-Home Sourcebook, The, 140, 143

Worldwide Association of Business Coaches, 109
Wright, Susan, 153
Writer's Market, The 2003, 47, 144
Writing Effective News Releases, 118, 149
Wytheville Community College, 126
Yalden, Claudia, 153
Yale, David R., 153
Zafran, Enid L., 153

FREE UPDATES: Subscribe to *Think Out of the Cubicle!*

Dear Reader,

The programs in this book are notorious for changing quickly. Class availability, tuition rates, and even program requirements sometimes change overnight. But I want to keep the information fresh and keep you up-to-date. After all, you spent your hard-earned money to buy the book—why be frustrated with a program that is no longer available, a book that's gone out of print, or a dead Web site link? On the other hand, distance-learning programs are also *growing* so quickly that new programs are popping up constantly too. I want to let you know about these as well. Why wait for a second edition?

To this end, I am offering a free newsletter—*Think Out of the Cubicle!* (get it?). But don't be afraid to subscribe to yet *another* e-mail newsletter, please. I know from experience how annoying it is to get a million newsletters in your e-mail box, only to have them filled with non-useful or repetitive information. This newsletter is aimed *solely* at giving you new information that will help you train at home to work at home.

By the way, I will never, never, never, never, *never* give your e-mail address to anyone. SPAM is my enemy number one, and giving me your e-mail address here will only be used for receiving this newsletter.

To subscribe, fill out the form below, copy or tear this sheet out of the book (don't worry, it's just the back page), and mail it to me at: Michelle McGarry, PO Box 67314, Chestnut Hill, MA 02467. Or, you can also send me an e-mail to cubicle@michellemedia.com. Thanks!

Sincerely,
Michelle McGarry
www.michellemedia.com
michelle@michellemedia.com

- -

❑ **Please send me a FREE monthly subscription to "Think Out of the Cubicle," Michelle McGarry's e-mail newsletter.**

My name: _____

E-mail: _____

Where did you buy *Train at Home to Work at Home*? (Just curious).

_____

Clip and mail to:
Michelle McGarry, P.O. Box 67314, Chestnut Hill, MA 02467
Or, simply send a blank e-mail to cubicle@michellemedia.com!

Add a Program to this Book, or Comments, Please!

Do you know of a program or class that fits into this book? Or, do you know a home career with home training that's missing? Is there a book or Web site you'd like added to a "For More Information" section? New program information will go out right away to readers with my e-mail newsletter, *Think Out of the Cubicle!*, as well as be included in the next edition of the book. *New editions are planned twice a year to keep the information fresh.*

Or perhaps you'd simply like to tell me if this book was helpful to you? Drop me a line—e-mail me at michelle@michellemedia.com, or you can send this form right to me: Michelle McGarry, P.O. Box 67314, Chestnut Hill, MA 02467. Thanks!

❐ **I know of a program, book, or Web site that should be in this book!**

Title of book/Web site/program: _____

Web address: _____

Email: _____

Description: _____

_____

_____

❐ **Or, I just have a comment...**

_____

_____

_____

_____

Your name & e-mail (optional): _____

_____

Clip and mail to: Michelle McGarry, P.O. Box 67314, Chestnut Hill, MA 02467 or e-mail michelle@michellemedia.com.

Give the Gift of Work-at-Home Education to a Friend

Check Your Local Bookstore, or Order Here!

□ *YES, I want ___ copies of* Train at Home to Work at Home *at $17.95 each (paperback). (Also available in hardcover.)*

Title: *Train at Home to Work at Home: How to Get Certified, Earn a Degree, or Take a Class from Home to Learn a Work-at-Home Career*

Author: Michelle McGarry

ISBN: 0-595-28450-7

Publisher: Writer's Club Press, an imprint of iUniverse, Inc.

Edition: 1

**To order directly from the publisher, visit
www.iuniverse.com/bookstore,
or call 877-823-9235 or 402-323-7800.**

**Visa, MasterCard, Discover, American Express
and Check/Money Order accepted.**

Also available at www.amazon.com,
www.barnesandnoble.com,
or at your local bookstore.

0-595-28450-7

Printed in the United States
55911LVS00004B/345